Rethinking College
Student Retention

Rethinking College Student Retention

John M. Braxton, William R. Doyle,
Harold V. Hartley III, Amy S. Hirschy,
Willis A. Jones, Michael K. McLendon

JOSSEY-BASS
A Wiley Imprint
www.josseybass.com

The Jossey-Bass Higher

and Adult Education Series

Contents

Preface

The problem of student departure requires both an understanding of the key forces that influence student persistence and the development of policies and practices designed to improve student retention rates based on our understanding of such key forces of student persistence. In this volume, we embrace the perspective that a framework for institutional policies and practices designed to improve institutional retention rates optimally emerges from empirical research guided by theory. The explanatory power of empirically tested theory provides institutional policymakers with a basis for action derived from the formulations of a theory. Such a rationale ensures fidelity in the enactment of a recommendation. Adjustments needed during the implementation of a lever of action also benefit from the understanding derived from the empirically tested theory.

As a consequence, we provide our findings from the empirical test of two theories of college student persistence—one theory for students in residential colleges and universities and another for students in commuter colleges and universities. We also offer a set of recommendations for institutional policy and practice that spring from these empirically tested theories of student persistence. We also used the findings of our process of "analytical cascading" to generate these recommendations. As we state in Chapter 1, analytical cascading implies discovering what factors shape the environment for improving student persistence decisions in the manner specified by theory. Such sources of influence constitute extensions of the concepts of each of the two theories empirically tested by us. In Chapters 5 and 6, we describe the theoretical extensions we used to identify possible sources of influence for our process of analytical cascading.

Organization of This Book

Because of the importance of policies and practices grounded in empirically tested theory to policymakers and institutional practitioners, we order this volume so that the chapters that offer such recommendations appear first. We then proceed to detail how we arrived at these various recommendations for policy and practice.

Beyond the first chapter, the arrangement of the chapters results in a book comprising three parts, as follows.

Part I: Recommendations for Policy and Practice

Part I consists of Chapters 2 and 3. In Chapter 2, "State Policy and Student Success," we assert that state and institutional policymakers are typically unaware of their respective efforts to improve college student retention. We use the literature to describe some of the possible reasons for the difficulty in creating lines of authority and responsibility in this area and suggest ways in which the current system could be redesigned to ensure that student success is seen as a joint responsibility among faculty, administrators, and state-level policymakers.

In Chapter 3, "Recommendations for Institutional Policy and Practice," we describe recommendations for policy and practice that rest on a foundation of empirical research guided by theory. We describe such recommendations for enactment by both residential and commuter colleges and universities as well as recommendations tailored specifically for residential and for commuter colleges and universities.

Part II: Theoretical and Research Context

Part II begins the discussion of how we arrived at the recommendations we advanced in Part I. This part consists of Chapters 4, 5, 6, and 7. In Chapter 4, "Explaining College Student Persistence," we begin with a brief review of the various conceptual perspectives that seek to explain college student persistence. We then turn our attention to Tinto's Interactionalist Theory of Student Departure and offer an empirical assessment of the validity of this theory. This assessment leads to a serious revision of Tinto's theory for residential colleges and universities and a different theory of student persistence in commuter colleges and universities.

In Chapter 5, "The Revision of Tinto's Theory for Residential Colleges and Universities," we describe the formulations of this serious revision of Tinto's theory. In Chapter 6, "A Theory of Student Persistence in Commuter Colleges and Universities," we present the formulations of the theory of student persistence in commuter colleges and universities. For our process of analytical cascading, we advance in Chapters 5 and 6 extensions of these two theories to identify possible sources of influence on the core concepts of these theories found to be statistically significant by our tests. From our empirical tests of these two theories and their extensions through analytical cascading, we derived the recommendations for institutional policy and practice we put forth in Chapter 3 of Part I.

We use two distinct studies in this volume. One study concentrates on understanding student persistence in residential colleges and universities, whereas the other study focuses on understanding student persistence in commuter colleges and universities. In Chapter 7, "Design of the Studies," we explain the design of these two studies by describing the instruments we used, the samples of the two studies, the variables used to test the respective theories, the variables used in analytical cascading, and the limitations of each of the two studies.

Part III: Key Factors in Student Persistence in Residential and Commuter Colleges and Universities

In Part III, we present the findings from our empirical tests of the two theories of student persistence as well as the findings of our process of analytical cascading that we used to generate the recommendations for institutional policy and practice presented in Chapter 3. This part consists of Chapters 8, 9, and 10. In Chapter 8, "Student Persistence in Residential Colleges and Universities," we provide details on the findings that emerged from our empirical test of the revised theory of student persistence in residential colleges and universities. A deepening of our knowledge and understanding of student persistence in residential colleges and universities also results from a delineation of factors that influence the key empirically supported concepts from this theory.

In Chapter 9, "Student Persistence in Commuter Colleges and Universities," we describe the findings of our test of theory of college student persistence in commuter colleges and universities that we described in Chapter 6. We also present the findings of our process of analytical cascading we used to identify factors that influence the key empirically supported concepts from this theory. These two sets of findings provide the basis for the recommendations for policy and practice we describe in Chapter 3.

In Chapter 10, "Conclusions and a Call for Further Research," we advance a set of six conclusions we derived from the pattern of findings we presented in Chapters 8 and 9. In this chapter, we also offer some implications for theory as well as some recommendations for further research.

Intended Audience for the Book

We view the contents of this volume as being of value to readers such as state policymakers, institutional policymakers, and scholars of higher education who study the college student experience in general and college student persistence in particular. In addition, presidents, chief academic affairs officers, chief student affairs officers, academic deans, chairpersons of academic departments, institutional researchers and planners, enrollment management officers, and student affairs professionals involved in programming for student growth and development, residence life, and student orientation will likewise find the contents valuable to their day-to-day professional work. Thus, both generalist and specialists constitute the audience for this book. We worked diligently to make the details of our empirical work accessible to this wide range of readers. Accordingly, we provide three appendices to this volume.

We developed Appendix A, "Design of the Study Tables," to serve as a companion to Chapter 7. This appendix includes eight tables that exhibit such details as our operational definitions of the variables used to test the two theories, the variables used in analytical cascading, the Cronbach reliability estimates of those variables measured as composite variables, and the means and standard deviations of these variables. Thus, the placement of such details of measurement in an appendix makes Chapter 7 more engaging and accessible to various readers.

We obtained the findings we report in Chapters 8 and 9 through the use of multivariate statistical procedures. To make these chapters more accessible and engaging to a wide range of readers, we describe the details of these multivariate statistical procedures in Appendix B, "Technical Appendix for Statistical Procedures."

In Appendix C, "Multivariate Analyses Results Tables," we place tables that report the results of the execution of the multivariate statistical procedures we used to derive the findings we present in Chapters 8 and 9. The placement of these tables in an appendix also renders Chapters 8 and 9 more reader-friendly. However, the inclusion of these tables allows readers to see our basis for the presentation of the findings we present in Chapters 8 and 9 and to make their own judgments regarding our findings. Appendix C includes nine tables.

Acknowledgments

M any individuals contributed to this book. Dawn Lyken-Segosebe, Michael Montgomery, Jeremy Tuchmayer, and Crystal Collins provided invaluable research support. Pat Callan reviewed much of the work described in Chapter 2 and provided helpful advice. The authors gratefully acknowledge Lumina Foundation for Education, which provided support for several of the research projects described in this book, and Holly Zanville, the program officer at Lumina who provided guidance and counsel as we were conducting our research. We are also grateful to anonymous reviewers of the first draft of this book for their invaluable suggestions for its improvement.

About the Authors

John M. Braxton is a professor of education in the Higher Education Leadership and Policy Program of the Department of Leadership, Policy, and Organizations at Peabody College of Vanderbilt University. His research interests center on the college student experience in general and college student persistence in particular, as well as the study of college and university faculty members. He has published over 95 publications in the form of articles in refereed journals, books, and book chapters. Of these 95 publications, 25 of them focus on college student persistence. These publications include the book *Understanding and Reducing College Student Departure* with Amy Hirschy and Shederick McClendon (ASHE-ERIC Higher Education Report, Jossey-Bass, 2004) and two edited books: *The Role of the Classroom in College Student Persistence* (New Directions for Teaching and Learning, Jossey-Bass, 2008) and *Reworking the Student Departure Puzzle* (Vanderbilt University Press, 1999). His other publications focused on college student persistence have appeared in *Higher Education: A Handbook of Theory and Research*, the *Journal of Higher Education*, *Research in Higher Education*, the *Review of Higher Education*, the *Journal of College Student Development*, and the *Journal of College Student Retention: Research, Theory, and Practice*.

Professor Braxton currently serves as the editor of the *Journal of College Student Development* and as associate editor for *Higher*

Education: A Handbook of Theory and Research. He also has served as a consulting editor for the *Journal of Higher Education and Research in Higher Education* and is a member of the editorial board of the *Journal of College Student Retention*. Braxton also is a past president of the Association for the Study of Higher Education.

William R. Doyle is an associate professor of higher education and coordinator of the Higher Education Leadership Program in the department of Leadership, Policy, and Organizations at Peabody College of Vanderbilt University. His research includes evaluating the impact, the antecedents, and outcomes of higher education policy at the state level and the study of political behavior as it affects higher education. Doyle's work has appeared in outlets such as the *Journal of Higher Education, Educational Evaluation and Policy Analysis* and *Economics of Education Review*. Prior to joining the faculty at Vanderbilt, he was senior policy analyst at the National Center for Public Policy and Higher Education. Doyle holds a master's degree in political science and a PhD in higher education administration from Stanford University.

Harold V. Hartley III has since 2008 served as senior vice president of the Council of Independent Colleges (CIC), an association of more than 700 independent colleges and universities and related organizations based in Washington, DC. He has lead responsibility for CIC's Presidents Institute, the largest annual gathering of college and university presidents in the country, and oversees CIC's vocation initiatives, including the Network for Vocation in Undergraduate Education (NetVUE) and the Presidential Vocation and Institutional Mission program. He joined CIC in 2005 as director of research and continues to provide oversight of CIC's research and assessment initiatives, which include the annual Key Indicators Tool (KIT) and Financial Indicators Tool (FIT) benchmarking reports, CIC's Making the Case website, the CIC Collegiate Learning Assessment (CLA) Consortium and its related Pathways Project, the CIC Degree Qualification Profile (DQP) Consortium, and the CIC

Engaging Evidence Consortium. Previously Hartley served for nearly ten years with the General Board of Higher Education & Ministry of The United Methodist Church in Nashville, Tennessee. He earlier served as chaplain at Ohio Northern University and at Emory & Henry College (VA). Hartley earned a BA at Westminster College (PA), an MDiv from Wesley Theological Seminary (Washington, DC), and an EdD in higher education leadership and policy at the Peabody College of Education of Vanderbilt University (TN). His research interests and publications have focused on such topics as the relationship between the undergraduate experience and persistence to degree, the impact of college attendance on students' religious faith, the advancement practices at smaller private colleges, and the characteristics and career patterns of college presidents and chief academic officers. He is the coauthor of several CIC reports, including *A Study of Presidents of Independent Colleges and Universities* (2012) and *A Study of Chief Academic Officers of Independent Colleges and Universities* (2010).

Amy S. Hirschy, PhD, is an assistant professor at the University of Louisville with a joint appointment in the Department of Educational and Counseling Psychology, Counseling, and College Student Personnel; and the Department of Educational Leadership, Foundations and Human Resource Education. Prior to doctoral study, Hirschy worked as a college administrator in Virginia, South Carolina, and Pennsylvania. Her work experience at private liberal arts colleges and medium and large state institutions informs both her research and teaching. Her research interests focus on examining theories of college student persistence, organizations, and college student development to identify what institutional factors promote and hinder student learning and success.

Willis A. Jones is an assistant professor of higher education at the University of Kentucky. Dr. Jones has a BA from the University of North Texas, a MEd in higher education administration from the University of Arkansas, and a PhD in higher education leadership and policy from Vanderbilt University

Michael K. McLendon is a professor of higher education policy and leadership and the associate dean at the Simmons School of Education and Human Development at Southern Methodist University. Prior to his appointment at SMU, Dr. McLendon served for thirteen years as a professor of public policy and higher education at Vanderbilt University, where he also held the role of executive associate dean of Peabody College of Education. His scholarship and teaching focus on governance, finance, and public policy of higher education. A primary strand of his research involves analysis of the factors shaping policy change and reform for higher education at both the state and campus levels.

Dr. McLendon's research has appeared in leading journals of the fields of both educational policy and higher-education studies, including the *Journal of Higher Education, Educational Evaluation and Policy Analysis, Research in Higher Education, Review of Higher Education, American Journal of Education, Teachers College Record,* and *Higher Education: Handbook of Theory of Research.* In addition, he serves or has served on the editorial boards of a number of these journals. Dr. McLendon earned his PhD in higher education policy from the University of Michigan. Prior to undertaking his doctoral studies, he served as a policy analyst in both the Florida House of Representatives and the United States Senate in Washington DC.

Rethinking College
Student Retention

1

Introduction: Rethinking College Student Retention

College student departure constitutes a long-standing, nettle-some problem that confronts individual colleges and universities as well as state and federal public policymakers. Tinto (1982) reports a constant rate of departure from 1880 to 1980 with a slight deviation in the rate occurring after the end of World War II. More recently, departure rates have varied little between 1983 and 2010 (American College Testing Program, 2012). In more specific terms, 45 percent of students enrolled in two-year colleges depart at the end of their first year, whereas approximately 28 percent of first-year students enrolled in four-year colleges or universities depart at the end of their first year (American College Testing Program, 2012). Given the enduring nature of these departure rates, a wan-ing of interest in this problem seems quite unlikely.

Although year-to-year retention and degree completion serve as markers of college student success, the attainment of other forms of success remain elusive without student retention. These other forms of student success resonate with the expectations for college attendance held by public policymakers, parents, and in-dividual colleges and universities. These additional markers of college student success include such domains as academic attain-ment through student learning, acquisition of general education, development of academic competence (e.g., writing and speaking in a clear manner), development of cognitive skills and intellectual dispositions, occupational attainment, preparation for adulthood and citizenship, personal accomplishments (e.g., work on the college newspaper, election to student office), and personal development (Braxton, 2008). In addition to the problematic attainment of these domains of student success, student departure negatively affects the stability of institutional enrollments, institutional budgets, and public perceptions of institutional quality (Braxton, Hirschy, and McClendon, 2004).

The importance of student persistence to the attainment of these other markers of student success, coupled with the negative impact of student departure on the stability of institutional enrollments, institutional budgets, and public perceptions of institutional quality, strongly suggest the need for actions by colleges and universities desiring to increase their rates of student retention. As a consequence, scholarly efforts should be directed toward the translation of theory and research into practice (Tinto, 2006–2007). Tinto more sharply defines this need by contending that, "Unfortunately, most institutions have not been able to translate what we know about student retention into forms of action that have led to substantial gains in student persistence and graduation" (p. 5). Tinto reinforces this perspective in his book *Completing College: Rethinking Institutional Action* (2012).

Two approaches to the translation of theory and research into practice take shape. One approach entails an identification of both the constraints and the supports that impact state-level efforts to formulate policy and design programs to increase institutional student rates of retention (Braxton, 2009–2010). Unfortunately, little or no empirical research has centered attention on this topic. In addition, and importantly, our work has identified an important gap—the lack of understanding of how state-level priorities are communicated to campus leaders. This book addresses this need.

The other approach involves the formulation of recommendations for levers of action to improve statewide and institutional retention rates. We assert herein that the development of levers of action must rest on a rock-bed of theoretically driven empirical research. Tinto (2012) emphasizes the need for a coherent framework for institutional action to reduce student departure. We concur; however, we assert that a coherent framework for institutional action optimally emerges from empirical research guided by theory. Such coherence stems from the explanatory power of empirically tested theory. A comprehension of the basis for an action, a basis derived from the formulations of a theory, ensures fidelity in the enactment of a recommendation. Adjustments needed during the implementation of a lever of action also benefit from the understanding derived from empirically tested theory.

Given our assertions about the need for policies and practices that rest on a rock-bed of findings of empirical research guided by theory, how might we depict the current status of theory focused on understanding college student persistence in higher education? We offer a brief assessment of the current status of theory in the following section and a more extensive discussion in Chapter 4.

Current Status of Theory on College Student Persistence

The problem of student departure has been the focus of research for more than 75 years (Braxton, 2000). The last three to four decades have produced the greatest understanding of this difficult problem. Tinto's Interactionalist Theory of Student Departure (1993) has contributed the most to this understanding. His theory enjoys paradigmatic stature, given that his work has received more than 775 citations (Braxton, Hirschy, and McClendon, 2004). Despite the paradigmatic stature of Tinto's theory, scholars question its validity. Braxton, Sullivan, and Johnson (1997) assessed the empirical internal consistency of Tinto's theory and found it in need of serious revision. In Chapter 4, we describe their assessments of empirical support for Tinto's theory, which found partial support in residential colleges and universities and little or no support in commuter colleges and universities.

A need for two separate theories emanates from key distinctions between residential and commuter colleges and universities. These distinctions entail the role of the external environment and the characteristics of social communities. In contrast to residential institutions, commuter colleges and universities lack well-defined and structured social communities for students to establish membership (Braxton, Hirschy, and McClendon, 2004). The external environment also plays an important role in commuter colleges and universities. Commuter students typically experience conflicts among their obligations to family, work, and college (Tinto, 1993). Their work and family obligations greatly determine their daily activities (Webb, 1990). In addition to these two key distinctions, commuter students make up more than 80 percent of today's college students (Horn and Nevill, 2006).

In "Understanding and Reducing College Student Departure," Braxton, Hirschy, and McClendon (2004) advance two theories: a serious revision of Tinto's theory to account for student persistence in residential colleges and universities and a new theory to account for student persistence in commuter colleges and universities. Additional progress in understanding student persistence requires an empirical testing of these two theories. We describe the formulations of these two theories in Chapters 5 and 6. Such testing constitutes one of the primary purposes of this book.

Questions Pursued by This Book

Given that further understanding of college student persistence requires an empirical testing of these two theories, we address the following two questions in this volume:

1. *What factors influence the first-year persistence of students enrolled in residential colleges and universities?* In addressing this question, we test the revised theory of student persistence in residential colleges and universities postulated by Braxton, Hirschy, and

McClendon (2004). We fully describe the formulations of this theory in Chapter 5.

2. *What factors influence the first-year persistence of students enrolled in commuter colleges and universities?* In pursuing this question, we test the theory of student persistence in commuter colleges and universities formulated by Braxton, Hirschy, and McClendon (2004). We describe the formulations of this theory in Chapter 6.

By focusing on these two questions, we contribute to the work of both the scholarly and practice communities concerned with college student persistence and retention. Moreover, little or no re-search has tested the formulations of the revision of Tinto's theory to account for student retention in residential colleges and universities (Braxton et al., 2004). The pursuit of question 1 provides such a test. Likewise, little or no research has tested the formulations of the theory of student retention in commuter colleges and universities advanced by Braxton, Hirschy, and McClendon (2004). The pursuit of question 2 presents such a test.

In addition, the findings of "analytical cascading" further our knowledge and understanding of college student persistence and provide a foundation for the development of institutional actions designed to improve institutional student retention rates. Analytical cascading entails empirically identifying influences on those theo-retically based factors found through our pursuit of questions 1 and 2 to shape student persistence decisions in both residential colleges and universities and commuter colleges and universities. Analytical cascading implies discovering what factors shape the environment for improving student persistence decisions in the manner specified by theory. Such sources of influence constitute extensions of the concepts of each of the two theories empirically tested by us.

In Chapters 5 and 6 we describe the theoretical extensions we used to identify possible sources of influence. We developed the process of analytical cascading for use in this book. We use the findings that emerge from analytical cascading to generate institutional levers of action designed to increase institutional rates of first-year student persistence. We used analytical cascading to address the following two questions that we pursue in this volume:

3. *What influences those factors that play a significant role in the first-year persistence of students enrolled in residential colleges and universities?* Put differently, we seek to delineate empirically those forces that influence the theoretically based factors found to shape student persistence decisions in residential colleges and universities.

4. *What influences those factors that play a significant role in the first-year persistence of students enrolled in commuter colleges and universities?* In addressing this question, we center attention on the empirical identification of those forces that influence the theoretically based factors found to influence student persistence decisions in commuter colleges and universities.

Our efforts to understand each of the four presented questions extended beyond the campus level to include state-level factors that could impact student persistence in a direct sense (through student grant funding or other means) and in an indirect sense (through campus funding or performance requirements). The results of this work help to set the stage for both the questions regarding direct impact on student persistence and the analytical cascading that occurs with regard to the second two questions. In Chapter 2, we report our review of extant research findings on state-level factors separately, because they differ in important ways from institutional-level findings and because they help to set the context for the institutional findings throughout the rest of this volume.

Retention and Persistence

In this volume, we abide by the clear distinction between persistence and retention made by Hagedorn (2005). She states that "institutions retain students and students persist" (p. 92). In addressing the research questions for this book, we focus on first- to second-year student persistence for several reasons. First, a large proportion of student departure occurs during the first year of college enrollment. The rates of departure we presented in the first paragraph of this chapter support this assertion. Second, Mortenson (2005) points to the vulnerability of students during the first year of college as a rationale for centering attention on the first- to second-year persistence of students. The formulations of the two theories tested in this volume attest to such student vulnerability. Mortenson (2005) offers the third reason, as he contends that colleges and universities can act more quickly with interventions to prevent departure during the first year of enrollment.

Part I

Recommendations for Policy and Practice

2

State Policy and Student Success

College completion is a key goal for many policymakers. There is a growing recognition that the long-standing goal of student access will not automatically result in higher levels of educational attainment in the broader population unless the commitment to access is tied to an equal, or even greater, commitment to student success in postsecondary education (Goldrick-Rab and Roksa, 2008; Turner, 2004).

Researchers have studied the impact of institutional-level characteristics and policies on student completion for decades (Braxton, Hirschy, and McLendon, 2004; Braxton, 2000). This research has amassed a large body of reliable findings. Less effort, however, has gone into understanding the impact of varying institutional contexts. These could include the regional labor market, the broader educational environment, or the political geography of the institution (Grogan, 1994; Barrileaux and Miller, 1988).

State leaders and policymakers play a key role in fostering student success. However, it is not clear to many what specific actions should be taken or how to coordinate those actions with institutional leaders. Our work—particularly our environmental scan of state policies—leads us to believe that on many campuses there is little to no awareness of state efforts to improve completion. Similarly, many state leaders may or may not know what campus-level efforts are being undertaken to improve completion. In this chapter, we will describe some of the possible reasons why it has been so difficult to create lines of authority and responsibility in this area and suggest ways in which the current system could be redesigned to ensure that student success is seen as a joint responsibility among faculty, administrators, and state-level policymakers.

To provide evidence for the assertions in this chapter, we utilize research findings from the broader literature and the results of our own research. We conducted several studies to attempt to understand the state-level factors that are associated with student success. The results of these are reported throughout the chapter. It should be noted that these studies focused on graduation as opposed to first-to-second-year persistence. This is a key difference between these studies and the campus-level studies reported in the rest of this volume. At the institutional level, first-to-second-year persistence is highly correlated with eventual completion, making the two concepts closely related (Strauss and Volkwein, 2004).

We begin by emphasizing the role of structural constraints that form the environment for state policymakers. State leaders cannot undertake any action they want to improve college completion. Instead, they face multiple slow-changing constraints that limit their range of options. It is crucial to consider these constraints before considering policy options for change. These constraints include the state's economy and budget, political culture and public opinion within the state, and the given set of institutions that are available to enroll students—or the "enrollment ecology" of the state. We then turn to the set of policy levers that we think are most viable for policymakers, including changing the mix of faculty, the use of performance funding, changes to remediation and gateway courses, funding effective campus-based innovations, utilizing more effective governance arrangements, and creating more effective pathways for communication between policymakers and campus leaders.

actual knowledge of policy makers

conversations generally not w/ boots on the ground

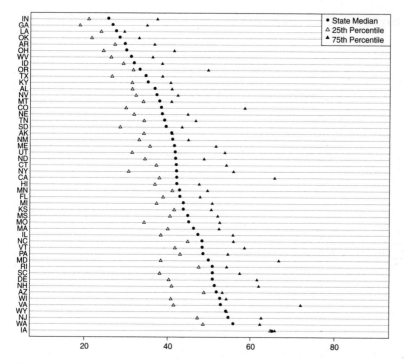

Figure 2.1   State-to-state variation in graduation rates across states.

At the outset of this chapter we note that variation in graduation rates should be considered amenable to state policy. Figure 2.1
shows the state-to-state variation in graduation rates across states.
We consider this variation to be the result of *both* structural constraints and states' utilization of available policy levers. In addition, as the figure shows, even in states with relatively high *average*
graduation rates, there are many institutions with low graduation
rates, indicating a need for active policy-making to ensure success
for all students. Our primary assertion in this chapter is that with
appropriate use of policy levers, state leaders can overcome many
of the structural constraints, described next.

We conclude by considering the kinds of questions that we
think policymakers should be considering when moving toward
action on improving student completion.

Structural Constraints

In every state, a set of structural constraints exist that set limits on the actions policymakers can take (Majone, 1989). These constraints allow for some actions, while making others much more difficult. It is not always easy to determine which of these constraints are self-imposed, as opposed to being the result of factors truly outside of human control. From one perspective, the only true constraints for leaders in a given state are based on geography and weather. From another, all but the smallest policy innovations will be nearly impossible because of the enormous difficulty in making change. We take a middle position in this chapter. We focus on policy levers that can be acted upon in the short term—within a two- or three-year window. Some changes to a state, such as rewriting the tax code or comprehensively reforming the educational system, may result in positive changes. However, these alterations cannot be accomplished in a time period within which most politicians would be willing to work. Areas of state policy that are unlikely to be changed within two or three years are referred to as "structural constraints" in our work.

We begin by discussing the state's economy and budget. All states have recently struggled as a result of the Great Recession, and state budgets show continued weakness (National Governors Association and National Association of State Budget Officers, 2012). The bottom line for higher education is that there will be no new money for state efforts to improve completion rates. We then turn to the preparation of high school graduates. Every state system of higher education has a given "pool" of young people to work with. In states with a struggling K–12 system, students may not be as well prepared for college-level work as they would be in states with strong schools (National Center for Public Policy and Higher Education, 2000). We then turn to the area of state political culture and public opinion. One particular difficulty of creating policy for increased college completion is that there is generally little public demand for such changes (Immerwahr and Foleno, 2000). Last, we turn to the "enrollment ecology" of a state (Doyle, McLendon, and Hearn, 2010).

State Economy and Budget

Beginning in 2008, state funding for higher education declined precipitously (Palmer, 2012). In many states, the worst effects of this decline were not felt immediately, due to the availability of funds from the American Recovery and Reinvestment Act of 2009 (State Higher Education Executive Officers Association, 2012). As stimulus funding has run out, states have been forced to turn to cuts in higher education. As of this writing, per-student inflation-adjusted funding for colleges and universities had declined and is projected to continue to decline (State Higher Education Executive Officers, 2012; Palmer, 2012).

Delaney and Doyle (2011) discuss the role of higher education in state finance. As higher education is a discretionary budget item, it is not subject to mandatory minimum spending. This stands in stark contrast to other areas such as K–12 education or spending on health care, both of which have specific guidelines for funding in many states (National Governors Association and National Association of State Budget Officers, 2012). In addition, higher education has a viable alternative source of revenue in the form of tuition. Other areas of state expenditure such as corrections or transportation do not have similarly large sources of alternative revenues. In financial hard times, higher education funding can and will be cut more than other budget categories, with the expectation that the cuts will be made up by increases in tuition. This is essentially a transfer of responsibility for funding higher education from the state to students and their families. In good times, higher education funding will expand—in fact, it will expand more than spending in other state budget categories. For this reason, Hal

Hovey, a longtime state budget analyst, called higher education the "balance wheel" of state finance (1999). Hovey's assertion is borne out by Delaney and Doyle's (2011) analysis of state spending patterns over time.

Our own research suggests that college completion is tied to institutional revenues. In a study we conducted using data from the Integrated Postsecondary Education Data System, we investigated the impact of various state- and institutional-level characteristics on the six-year graduation rate.[1] We found that institutions with higher levels of revenues tend to have higher graduation rates.

Given this reality, campus leaders should not expect large increases in state funding at any time in the near future. In addition, any increases that do come during the next economic upswing will likely be short-lived. Any proposed policy efforts to improve retention or completion that involve the expenditure of large amounts of new state money are unrealistic and cannot be expected to occur.

Preparation of High School Graduates

Although calls for P-16 reform have been heard from many quarters for the last 25 years, the fact remains that K–12 and higher education are quite separate systems, divided by different funding modes, different governance, different traditions, and starkly different workforces (Kirst and Venezia, 2004). In each state, higher education bears responsibility for the level of educational achievement of high school graduates through its teacher preparation efforts and through its communication of standards and expectations to high schools (Callan et al., 2006, 2009). However, school reform is a "bridge too far" for many higher education leaders, and it is unlikely that a major change in the preparation of high school graduates can be effected in a short period of time. For this reason, we consider the preparation of high school graduates to be a constraint for policy-making in this area.

Campus leaders must expect to work with the students that they have, not a hypothetical set of students they would like to have. If students are inadequately prepared for college, this will be an important constraint for action for leaders.

State Political Culture and Public Opinion

Elazar (1966) states that three parts of a state's political culture are most important in terms of changing state politics:

> (1) The set of perceptions of what politics is and what can be expected from government . . . (2) the kinds of people who become active in government and politics and (3) the actual way in which the art of government is practiced (p. 90).

Elazar's formulation of political culture has been influential in the political science literature, but one need not adopt his particular schema of political culture to agree that the shared set of assumptions about the role of government and the interaction between state government and higher education will form an important and slow-changing constraint on policy-making for higher education. For instance, in New Hampshire, public colleges and universities receive very little state funding but have considerably more autonomy than their peer institutions in other states. This is most likely a reflection of that state's political culture of autonomy for local institutions, including local schools, which also have a high level of autonomy.

In every state, a shared set of assumptions about what should and can be done regarding higher education policy exists (Marshall et al., 1989; Mitchell et al., 1991). Policymakers and campus leaders must consider these as constraints on their range of action and work on appropriate policy solutions within these constraints. For example, in some states it may not be considered the role of state government to closely oversee the operations of institutions of higher education. This is the case in Michigan, where constitutional autonomy grants campuses considerable latitude in their actions (Richardson et al., 1999). In these states, the use of cooperative agreements or incentive programs may be more appropriate than attempting regulatory interventions. More generally, the particular political culture of a given state must be considered before attempting to enact a policy reform in this (or any other) arena.

Another important consideration is whether public opinion supports interventions on behalf of students. In most areas, policy efforts broadly follow public opinion (Erikson et al., 1993). Unfortunately, public opinion in general does not support the idea of providing large amounts of help to students who are struggling in college (Immerwahr and Johnson, 2007, 2009, 2010; Immerwahr and Foleno, 2000). As Immerwahr (1999) notes,

> Once a student reaches college age, people seem to feel that it is up to the student to take responsibility for his or her own life. If a student drops out of college, the assumption is that the student was not sufficiently motivated (p. 5).

Both policymakers and campus leaders must consider that there is little public appetite for efforts and resources to be spent on increasing college completion. From the perspective of the public, most believe that this is properly the responsibility of students, not the state or institutions.

Enrollment Ecology of the System of Higher Education

The mix of institutions in a given state is an important constraint for policymakers to consider (Doyle et al., 2010). In some states, a large number of students enroll in community colleges, while in other states, most students are enrolled in private four-year colleges. The mix of institutional options available to students will change only slowly through time, with community colleges being the most notable example of rapid growth in the last 50 years (Doyle and Gorbunov, 2011). It's unlikely in the next 25 years that we will see such rapid growth in a particular institutional type. Given this constraint, our research examined whether some states are constrained from success by virtue of having more open-access institutions (those admitting at least 80 percent of applicants). It could be the case that having more of these types of institutions limits the ability of a given state to be successful in graduating more students.

In searching for the factors that might be associated with increasing college graduation rates, we focused on the ways in which some states have managed to improve their college graduation rates over time. We began by looking at which states have improved the most in terms of college completion rates at their public four-year institutions. We found that Nebraska, Georgia, Missouri, Minnesota, and Louisiana were the top five states in terms of improving college completion at public four-year institutions (Doyle, 2010). Figure 2.2 shows the distribution of gains in graduation rates across states.

As the figure shows, increases in these states are much larger than the nationwide increase of only 4 percent. According to Doyle (2010), in a handful of states, including Hawaii, Idaho, Alaska, and Florida, graduation rates at public four-year institutions have been declining since 1999.

One possible reason why these states showed improvement might be funding changes. To investigate this, we looked at per-student funding in all 50 states and sought to determine any possible correlation with improvements in college graduation rates. We did not find that states with increased funding were the same states that had increased graduation rates (Doyle, 2010).

We next sought to understand which institutions in these states were most responsible for increasing the levels of college completion in the fastest improving states. What we found surprised us.

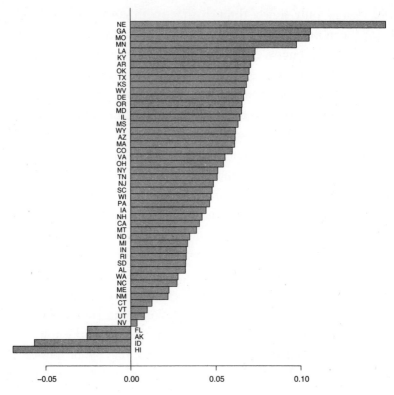

Figure 2.2   Distribution of gains in graduation rates across states.

In six of the top ten states, open-access or nearly open-access institutions were responsible for the largest portion of the increase in college graduation. In four of the states, these institutions accounted for more than 80 percent of the observed improvement in college graduation rates. To further verify this result, we conducted a statistical test, which revealed a negative relationship between selectivity and improving college completion (Doyle, 2010).

Our research reveals that mostly open-access institutions are crucial contributors to college access and completion. In conducting this same analysis on all 50 states, we found that in 37 of 50 states, open-access institutions accounted for the majority of the increase in college graduation rates. In 19 states, these institutions accounted for more than 75 percent of the increase in college graduation (Doyle, 2010).

Some have suggested that the only way to increase college graduation rates is to make colleges more selective. Our research does not support this assertion, however. Instead, we find that colleges and universities that are not particularly selective have nevertheless been able to improve their college graduation rates substantially (Doyle, 2010). Previous research has shown that students rarely leave higher education because they are flunking out—purely academic reasons for departure are rare. Instead, students' level of engagement on campus is a key factor in determining whether they will stay (Braxton, 2000).

Our results suggest that states wanting to improve college completion must begin with open-access or mostly open-access institutions. These institutions are the most vulnerable to economic difficulty, since they are primarily funded by state appropriations and tuition. Therefore, if states want to weather this downturn without decreasing college graduation rates, we recommend that they focus their policy efforts on open-access institutions. These are the places where the greatest improvements can be found for the lowest cost.

The enrollment ecology of a given state therefore serves as an important precondition within which policymakers must work, but it does not necessarily leave any state at a serious disadvantage, because states with many open-access institutions have seen rapid growth in college completion.

Policy Levers

In this section we detail the policy levers available to state policymakers that have been discussed in the available literature and our understanding of the best practices for making use of these tools. We begin by discussing the role of faculty, including the use of more tenure-line faculty. We then discuss the role of performance funding, which many have suggested may dramatically improve completion rates. We then turn our thoughts to a different kind of performance funding, one in which promising avenues of reform are funded and brought to scale across institutions. Another policy level available for state policymakers is changing the structure of remediation. Last, we reflect on our findings regarding communication between institutional leaders and state policymakers. Much progress could be made in improving completion rates if state policymakers and campus leaders were made aware of each other's priorities and current activities.

Faculty

A large and growing body of evidence suggests that students who are engaged with full-time, tenure-track faculty are more likely to persist and succeed in higher education (Ehrenberg and Zhang, 2005a). Researchers have confirmed this finding in a variety of settings, making this one of the clearest campus-level policy levers available to change (Ehrenberg and Zhang, 2005a; Umbach and Wawrzynski, 2005; Bettinger and Long, 2004; Hoffmann and Oreopoulos, 2009).

Our work finds much the same results as the work of other researchers. After controlling for a host of other characteristics, we find that the presence of more tenure-line faculty on a given campus is associated with higher levels of completion. This holds even after controlling for other factors, such as levels of funding and selectivity for an institution (Doyle, Braxton, and Jones, 2008).

State policymakers have not utilized this finding, nor do they seem to be aware of it. Few state plans for improving completion involve explicit calls for relying on more tenure-line faculty. The reason is obvious—tenure-line faculty are more expensive than adjunct or contingent faculty, and economic resources are constrained and are likely to continue to be constrained. The long-term trend

 # doesn't matter, how they are evaluated

in higher education during the last 50 years has been to rely increasingly on adjunct and contingent faculty, while tenure-line faculty form an increasingly small part of the professoriate (Ehrenberg and Zhang, 2005b). This has generally been perceived as an "outcome-neutral" policy change—one that does not affect students. This is not so, however, because one of the effects of the shift has likely been to decrease completion rates.

There is no easy solution to this problem. It is unlikely that we will see a resurgence in the proportion of full-time faculty. The findings in the literature, however, suggest that students should be guaranteed at least some exposure to full-time faculty during the course of their higher education careers, particularly in the first two years. Campus leaders and state policymakers should consider ways in which full-time, tenure-line faculty can be a part of first-year instruction in general education courses on all campuses. In addition, tenure-line faculty can and should be engaged in the delivery of larger technology-aided classes such as those created through the work of the National Center for Academic Transformation. Although it may not be possible for every student to be enrolled in a small classroom with a full-time faculty member, it should be possible to expose more students to core faculty on campus.

Performance Funding

Performance funding has been heralded as the key innovation that will ensure that more students will leave college having achieved their educational goals. The idea is simple. Leaders in colleges and universities respond to the way funding is provided. Currently, funding is provided on the basis of enrollment in the vast majority of public colleges and universities. Campus leaders pursue enrollments (subject to constraints) to maximize the amount of funding directed at their campus. Since colleges and universities do not receive more money if more students graduate, there is no incentive to ensure that students graduate. If a student fails to re-enroll, another student can be found to take his or her place, ensuring a steady stream of funding (Burke, 2002, 2005).

If we changed to a system based on funding outcomes, then college and university leaders would have the correct incentives. Instead of simply focusing on enrollments, they would focus on graduates. This would result in higher graduation rates—or so the theory suggests (Burke, 2005; McLendon et al., 2006).

A system very much like the one described above (albeit more complex) has been created in Tennessee (Tennessee Higher Education Commission, 2011). It's too soon to know whether it will actually accomplish its objectives. In general, the results on performance funding more broadly are not clear. Dougherty has undertaken the most extensive review to date of performance funding systems and has found little to no evidence one way or another on their effectiveness (Dougherty et al., 2012; Dougherty and Reddy, 2011). Despite the fact that many states have tried some variant of a performance funding system, no strong evidence suggests that these systems have done anything to improve student success.

Recent developments in the literature on the effect of incentives in educational policy should give advocates of performance funding pause. In one of the most famous experiments on the use of incentives to improve student performance in schools, randomly selected teachers in a school district were given substantial bonuses if their students' scores improved on the state standards test. As it turned out, test scores of students who were taught by teachers that could receive bonuses improved no more than those of students who were taught by teachers on a normal salary schedule (Springer et al., 2011).

In another experiment, randomly selected students in New York and Chicago were offered cash rewards for higher grades or test scores. These students did not perform better than their peers. In other experiments in Washington, D.C., and Dallas, students were offered cash incentives for inputs to education such as attendance and behavior. These students did complete more of these inputs more often than their peers. Lastly, in a study in Houston, students were rewarded for mastering specific math objectives. This study was unusual in that parents and teachers also had aligned objectives. Treated students in this study achieved gains in the specific math objectives rewarded, but they achieved only very small gains in the state mathematics exam (Fryer, 2010).

A possible emerging finding from the literature on incentives is provided by Fryer (2010): "incentives increase achievement when the rewards are given for inputs to the educational production function, but incentives tied to output are not effective" (p. 1). Although much work remains to be done, it is hard to ignore the findings of several of the best-designed and largest scale experiments to date regarding the impact of incentives.

The implications of this literature for performance funding suggest that policymakers seeking to improve completion should not focus their incentives on completion itself, but on steps campuses can take that are known to increase completion. Many of the interventions suggested in this book, such as increasing institutional commitment to student welfare or maximizing opportunities for engaged learning, could be incentivized by state performance funding systems.

Remediation and Gateway Courses

There has been an active and important debate about the role of remediation (or developmental education) in student departure. The facts are clear: very few remedial students go on to complete their educational objectives. Adelman (1999, 2006) was one of the first to demonstrate that students who enroll in remedial courses are much less likely to graduate than other students.

This finding has sparked a debate. On one side of the debate are those who argue that developmental education provides a necessary intervention to ensure that underprepared students are ready to succeed in higher education. This group states that many students would simply fail their introductory courses without first enrolling in some form of education designed to prepare them for the rigors of college-level coursework (Boylan and Goudas, 2012). On the other side of the debate are those who argue that remedial education is a "path to nowhere." They contend that students who are placed in remedial education can never succeed, as they are spending time and effort in college without building up actual college-level skills (Complete College America, 2012).

The policy interventions suggested by either side are accordingly different. Those who say that remediation is necessary suggest better funding and better staffing for remedial courses. Those who say that remediation is failing suggest providing support and interventions to students while they are taking their introductory courses, as opposed to before they take these courses. This is sometimes described as the co-requisite approach, as opposed to the prerequisite approach (Boylan and Goudas, 2012; Complete College America, 2012).

The key problem with the vast majority of studies done on remediation is one of selection bias. Students who enter into remedial coursework are likely to be academically underprepared. Many of these students might depart from higher education whether or not they enrolled in remedial coursework. The question is whether remedial coursework by itself caused these students to depart from college.

Some of the most compelling evidence on the impact of remedial education comes from work done by Eric Bettinger and Bridget Terry Long (2009). The authors take advantage of a quirk in the way that students in Ohio public colleges are assigned to remedial coursework. If all public colleges in Ohio used the same basic framework for assigning students to remedial education, then ACT scores and GPA should predict assignment to remediation in a similar fashion across colleges—as students with a given ACT score and GPA should expect to be assigned to remedial education or not at about the same rate regardless of which institution they

attend. This is not the case, however. Instead, the rate of assignment to remedial education is quite different, even among students
with very similar GPAs and ACT scores.

Bettinger and Long (2009) use this variation in assignment to
compare outcomes among students with similar ACT scores and
GPAs, some of whom were assigned to remedial coursework and
others of whom were not. Their findings are summarized as follows:

> In summary, we estimate that students in remedia-
> tion have better educational outcomes in comparison
> to students with similar backgrounds and preparation
> [who] were not required to take the courses. While OLS
> estimates suggest remediation has a negative effect,
> once controlling for selection issues the results become
> positive, thereby emphasizing how inappropriate it is to
> simply compare the outcomes of remediated and non-
> remediated students (p. 760).

The authors' work demonstrates somewhat counterintuitively
that remediation improves persistence and graduation, particularly
among marginal students. This work, which is among the most rigorous studies completed to date, suggests that outright elimination
of remediation would be dangerous and counterproductive.

One promising reform comes from California, where high school
students are asked to complete several questions from the California
State University's placement exam as part of their high school exit
exam. In the state's Early Assessment Program (EAP), students
are given information about their performance and told whether
or not they would be placed in remediation on a CSU campus.
An early study of the effects of this program (Howell et al., 2010)
found that the EAP reduced the need for remediation among
students attending a CSU campus. As more and more states utilize
high school exit exams, they should incorporate information about
college placement as part of their standards.

We take a middle path in the debate on remedial education. When employed carefully for marginal students, remedial education does appear to be an effective tool for increasing student persistence and success. Eliminating remedial education or denying admission to students based on their remedial status would be an ineffective policy direction. However, one viable path for reducing the need for remediation altogether is to communicate to high school students how their current academic performance would result in placement in the colleges. Even better, aligning high school assessments with college-level placement exams could give students clear and consistent messages about what will be expected of them once they move on to postsecondary education.

Governance of Higher Education

Although the literature on higher education governance is still under development, one of the key emerging findings appears to be that more centralized systems are more adept at accomplishing state goals. As most states have at least articulated increased student success as a goal, such an outcome seems likely to be accomplished through these more centralized systems. In our own research, we expected to find that the governance structure of a state would affect college completion, and our results bear this out. If a single entity is responsible only for public four-year institutions, completion rates are predicted to be substantially higher at the institutional level (Doyle, Braxton, and Jones, 2008). Our finding here connects with the growing literature on the importance of state-level governance (Richardson and Martinez, 2009).

Funding Cost-Effective, Campus-Based Interventions

As an alternative to performance funding, state policymakers should consider funding and bringing to scale small campus-based interventions that have been shown to be cost-effective. A basic methodology for this approach is laid out by Harris and

Goldrick-Rab (2010). In their work on assessing the effectiveness of various interventions designed to improve graduation rates, they begin by defining an effectiveness cost ratio. As they describe it, an effectiveness cost ratio is a multiplier-adjusted effect divided by a multiplier-adjusted cost. In their work, they standardize on an effect of one additional graduate for every $1,000 spent.

Harris and Goldrick-Rab (2010) found that the intervention with the highest effectiveness cost ratio was using call centers. These call centers operate by "literally making phone calls to students who apply but do not register, register but do not show up for class, show up for class initially but then stop attending, and so on" (p. 18). These call centers follow up on these calls by providing recommendations or directing services to the student. The call centers were found to produce 0.6 additional graduates for every $1,000 spent, a considerably larger effectiveness cost ratio than other interventions studied, including the use of more full-time faculty, remediation, and financial aid.

Although the results of the Harris and Goldrick-Rab study are still somewhat speculative and based out of necessity on a relatively small amount of research, this method could be used productively on campuses and across states. Campuses should routinely calculate the effectiveness cost ratio of various interventions designed to improve graduation rates. Interventions found to be highly cost effective should receive additional "venture funding" from state funds in order to grow and be implemented across campuses. State leaders operating in this role should think of themselves less as directing specific policy interventions and more as venture capitalists, funding a variety of initiatives that are likely to fail, but some of which may prove to be sufficiently powerful to make the overall effort worthwhile.

Communication

How do state policymakers make campus leaders aware of their goals? Do states with lower levels of completion have different

policy goals that are communicated to their campuses? Can we observe different levels of communication in states with differential
completion rates? To answer these questions, our research took up
the problem of state policy environments for higher education.

This strand of the research we conducted had to do with how
state policies and institutional polices can work together to improve graduation rates. The first stage of this research involved
collecting data from eight states, four of which were rated as high
performing by the National Center for Public Policy and Higher
Education report card, *Measuring Up 2000*. The remaining four
states were rated as low performing by the *Measuring Up* methodology. In this research, we looked for differences in the policy environment between high-performing and low-performing states. Our
work reviewed all of the relevant policy documents and statements
regarding college completion from high-level policymakers and
state officials, including state-of-the-state addresses, master planning documents, budgeting performance funding, and budgeting
practices (McLendon, Tuchmayer, and Park, 2009).

We found that state policymakers in the eight study states paid
an increasing amount of attention to this issue over the period
of time studied (2001–2007). For example, we found three times
more coverage of the issues in state-of-the-state addresses delivered
in the four-year period from 2004 to 2007 than in the previous
four-year period, 2000 to 2003. Our research found that governors
in low-performing states showed a great deal of awareness and concern about their college graduation rates. In all four low-performing
states, we found a great deal of high-level policy attention given
to the problem of low levels of student success and observed that
the amount of attention paid to the problem in recent years seems
to have risen quite notably. In addition, governors in these low-
performing states addressed this problem in their state-of-the-state
addresses, and the issue of college completion was quite likely to be
taken up by the master planning process in the states (McLendon,
Tuchmayer, and Park, 2009).

However, our research also found that governors in high-performing states (many of which had very poor performance at individual institutions) paid substantially less attention to the issue of college graduation rates. In addition, master planning documents in high-performing states showed limited attention to the issue of college completion (McLendon, Tuchmayer, and Park, 2009).

We also reviewed the funding and budgeting process in each of the eight study states to understand what incentives, if any, were in place to encourage higher graduation rates. We found that only one state had explicitly tied institutional funding to higher graduation rates. In all four low-performing states, no connection could be found between institutional funding and college completion rates (McLendon, Tuchmayer, and Park, 2009).

We next sought to understand the actions that individual institutions were taking in these eight states (four high-performing, four low-performing). To accomplish this, we conducted a survey, asking institutions in these states to detail their efforts at studying and improving retention and graduation rates (Jones and Braxton, 2009).[2] We then analyzed the extent to which these institutions were conducting methodologically complex studies of college completion rates. We found that only a third were conducting the kinds of studies that help to accurately assess the campus-level factors associated with reduced student departure. The remaining campuses, while concerned about college completion rates, were conducting analyses that were not consistent with established practices in the field (Jones and Braxton, 2009).

We also found that campuses in the lower performing states were more likely to be conducting fairly straightforward analyses, while campuses in higher performing states conducted more complex analyses of the student departure problem (Jones and Braxton, 2009).

We recommend that campuses utilize methodologically rigorous studies of college student retention. To achieve this, institutional administrators and state policymakers must provide departments of institutional research, student affairs, and enrollment management with the funding and personnel necessary to conduct this level of research. This recommendation is especially salient for those institutions with lower student retention rates, such as commuter and public institutions. In addition, institutional funding for campus-based research into student retention should be supported by state funding in those states that are low performing in the area of college graduation. Institutional leaders should be provided incentives to better understand what policies and practices are associated with greater retention rates.

Much of our research highlights the continuing disconnect between campus-level efforts to improve completion and state-level policy attention to the problem. Much could be accomplished if state policymakers sought to leverage and improve existing efforts on campuses and if campus leaders were better informed regarding state-level efforts to improve completion.

Conclusions and Questions for Policymakers

Our research has led us to conclude that, although effective policy levers exist to improve student completion, little progress will be made without more explicit connections between state-level actions and campus-level initiatives. We begin by posing some questions for policymakers in all states:

1. What are the current college completion rates at institutions in your state? Is this data collected from student unit record data or on an institution-by-institution basis? How have these rates changed over time?
2. Who is responsible at the state level for improving college completion rates? If this responsibility is shared, how do the various parties coordinate their efforts?
3. What kind of policies are currently in place at the institutional, system, and state levels to encourage higher completion rates? Are these aligned throughout the system?

4. What resources are available for institutions to conduct their own studies of college departure?

5. How are state priorities for college completion communicated to campuses?

6. Do state policies emphasize the importance of ensuring that students are connected to their campuses?

7. What incentives exist for faculty and institutional leaders to improve performance in the area of college completion?

8. What mechanism exists for rewarding and bringing to scale campus-level initiatives that have been shown to be cost effective?

Too much of the current effort to improve completion rates at the state level has taken on a top-down approach. Although state policymakers should assume responsibility for this important policy goal and seek to leverage effective policies, they should also be prepared to understand and learn from existing campus initiatives. At the same time, campus leaders should seek out and understand state priorities. Campus leaders must also conduct and utilize methodologically rigorous studies of college departure. With a continued dialogue and improved understanding, we expect that both an improved policy environment and improved college completion rates will result.

Endnotes

1. The dependent variable for the study in this chapter is the graduation rate as defined by the National Center for Education Statistics: the percentage of full-time, first-time students who graduate from the same institution in six years.

2. We received responses from 54 of the 304 institutions in these states.

3

Recommendations for Institutional Policy and Practice

Although there is wide agreement on the consequences of attrition for students and institutions, the vast array of recommendations to improve persistence rates can be overwhelming and confusing for educational leaders. Reason (2009) offers that "practitioners will do well to focus on characteristics and experiences over which they have more control" (p. 666) and should direct their efforts toward those policies and programs that have the best chance of making a difference for improving student success. Recommendations that are based on empirical evidence offer practitioners the most stable ground on which to design and build programs and policies. Further, recommendations tailored to the type of institution can help retention coordinators discern what interventions may be most salient for their campuses.

This chapter presents recommendations for empirically based institutional policy and practices, based on research findings that are described in detail in later chapters of this volume. We present overarching recommendations as well as more specific recommendations for commuter colleges and universities and for residential colleges and universities. Recommendations pertaining to state-level policy and practice are presented in Chapter 2. We assert that the recommendations advanced in this chapter constitute levers of action. Their power stems from their theoretical and empirical grounding. Put differently, the findings of this volume provide a robust foundation for the generation of recommendations for action.

Recommendations for Institutional Policy and Action

In advancing the recommendations for institutional policy and action, we concur with Tinto's (2012) call for a coherent framework for institutional action to reduce student departure. As stated in Chapter 1, we assert that a coherent framework for institutional action optimally emerges from empirical research guided by theories such as those tested in this volume. This coherence emanates from the explanatory power of empirically tested theory. The set of recommendations we put forth in this chapter forms such a coherent framework for actions in the form of policy levers.

We also assert that institutional policymakers must make use of the vast majority of the recommendations we put forth in this chapter. We make this assertion because the problem of college student persistence requires institutional action that employs multiple levers of action. Our contention resonates with the assertion of Pascarella and Terenzini (1991, p. 655) that many small policy levers may be more effective in achieving an institutional goal than a single large-scale policy lever. The ill-structured nature of the problem of student departure requires institutional action that makes use of multiple policy levers (Braxton, Hirschy, and McClendon, 2004; Braxton and Mundy, 2001–2002). Ill-structured problems defy a single solution and require a range of possible solutions that may not solve the problem (Kitchener, 1986; Wood, 1983). The problem of student persistence defies a single solution, because most forces of influence wield an indirect rather than a direct influence on student persistence. The empirical findings of this book as well as those reviewed by Braxton, Sullivan, and Johnson (1997) and Braxton, Hirschy, and McClendon (2004) suggest indirect rather than direct sources of influence on student persistence.

Overarching Levers of Action

We present four overarching recommendations, or levers of action, for enactment by both commuter and residential colleges and universities.

Use an Integrated Design Approach

In "Understanding and Reducing College Student Departure," Braxton, Hirschy, and McClendon (2004) called for an integrated design approach to institutional efforts to increase their rates of student retention. We reiterate their call in this particular overarching recommendation. Braxton et al. (2004) also state the following:

- An integrated design approach involves the intentional and coordinated enactment of all policies and practices adopted by the institution to increase student retention.

- An integrated design approach also stresses the importance of the commitment and support for the selected policies and practices by such officers of the central administration as the president and chief academic affairs officer as well as by other members of the administration, faculty, and staff of the institution.

- An integrated design approach also acknowledges that some student departure may be in the best interest of both the student and the institution and that the reduction of unnecessary student departure stands as the primary objective of institutional policies and practices.

- An integrated design approach embraces the importance of institutional assessment of the efficacy of policies and practices enacted to increase institutional rates of student retention.

We strongly recommend institutional adherence to an integrated design approach.

Follow Nine Imperatives

The findings of Chapters 8 and 9 (see the summary sections of these two chapters) together indicate that commitment of the institution to student welfare and institutional integrity play an important, indirect role in influencing student persistence in both residential and commuter colleges and universities. In residential colleges and universities, commitment of the institution to student welfare positively influences both social integration and subsequent institutional commitment. This commitment to student welfare exerts a positive influence on academic and intellectual development in commuter colleges and universities as well. In commuter colleges and universities, institutional integrity wields a positive influence on both academic and intellectual development and subsequent institutional commitment as well as a positive influence on social integration in residential colleges and universities. Social integration plays an important, but indirect, role in student persistence in residential colleges and universities, while academic and intellectual development plays a similar role in commuter colleges and universities as well. Subsequent institutional commitment plays a direct and important part in student persistence in both residential and commuter colleges and universities. The findings described in Chapters 8 and 9 support these assertions.

As discussed later in this volume (Chapters 5 and 6), commitment of the institution to student welfare and institutional integrity reflect the culture of a given college or university. Because these two organizational attributes embody the cultural values of a college or university, their day-to-day enactment requires little or no direct financial costs. We put forth nine imperatives for the administrators, staff members, and clerical workers of both residential and commuter colleges and universities to follow in the performance of their organizational roles. These imperatives arise from and reinforce an institution's commitment to the welfare of its students and its institutional integrity. Consequently, college and university administrators, staff members, and clerical workers who follow these imperatives contribute to their college or university's efforts to increase student retention. The imperatives are as follows:

1. *Administrators, staff members, and clerical workers should embrace a commitment to safeguarding the welfare of students as clients of the institution.* Such a commitment entails the communication to students that they are highly valued members of the campus community. Communicating threats to campus safety in a timely manner with sufficient detail so that community members can evaluate the level of risk is an example of safeguarding the welfare of students as clients.

2. *In the day-to-day administration of institutional policies and procedures, administrators, staff members, and clerical workers should treat students equitably and fairly.* Favoritism toward some students and not others should not occur. Student appeal processes should be communicated clearly, and institutional leaders should consider designating an ombudsperson to investigate student claims of unfair treatment by academic or administrative processes.

3. *A respect for each student as an individual should manifest itself in the day-to-day interactions college and university administrators, staff members, and clerical workers have with students.* In particular, staff members and clerical workers in the registrar's office, financial aid, student counseling, student accounts, residential life, and other offices that have frequent contact with students should display such respect. To gather more information about interactions between students and campus community members, retention coordinators can conduct exit interviews with departing students, faculty, and staff members with significant student contact.

4. *College and university administrators should ensure that institutional policies and procedures coincide with the mission, goals, and*

values espoused by their college or university. Policies and practices incongruent with the mission, goals, and values of the institution must be either discontinued or modified in a way that supports the mission, goals, or values of the institution. New policies and procedures must also support the mission, goals, and values of the college or university. New and existing policies and practices should be routinely assessed to ensure that they align with the mission, goals, and values of the institution.

5. *The day-to-day actions of college and university administrators, staff members, and clerical workers should support the mission, goals, and values of the institution.* Those actions observed by students should, in particular, support the institutional mission, goals, and values. Performance appraisal forms for administrators, staff members, and clerical workers should include items that assess the congruence of their actions with the mission, goals, and values of the institution.

6. *The reward structure for administrators, staff members, and clerical workers should recognize those individuals who highly value students, treat students equitably, and demonstrate respect for students as individuals in their day-to-day work.* Individuals whose actions are congruent with the mission and goals of the institution should also be recognized. Such behaviors should receive appropriate weight in the allocation of such institutional rewards as annual reappointment, promotion, and annual salary increases. However, individuals who do not demonstrate a commitment to student welfare, by treating students disrespectfully and unequally, and who act in ways that undermine the mission, goals, and values of the institution should be counseled and expected to show significant improvement. Clerical staff members with frequent student contact should be provided opportunities to develop strategies of assisting others with difficult personalities. Similarly, they can be offered training on how to manage difficult situations that affect students adversely.

7. *Institutional publications and documents should communicate, when appropriate, the college or university's abiding concern*

for the growth and development of its students. The contents of the institutional publications and documents should also support the mission, goals, and values espoused by the college or university. In particular, view books, catalogues, and other materials used in the recruitment of students should receive careful scrutiny to ensure that the college or university portrays itself accurately to prospective students.

8. *Public speeches made by the president, chief academic officer, chief student affairs officer, academic deans, and admissions officers should communicate the high value their college or university places on students as members of the academic community.* Such speeches should also resonate with the mission, goals, and values of the college or university.

9. *Ongoing assessments of the student experience should inform improvements in college and university policies and practice to communicate the commitment of the institution to the welfare of students.* Administrative offices and academic departments should conduct periodic reviews to determine what information or procedures are in place that confuses students. Once identified, student consultants can recommend changes and improvements.

College and university administrators, staff members, and clerical workers who follow these nine imperatives in their day-to-day work provide students with opportunities to observe the reinforcement of the organizational values of commitment of the institution to the welfare of its students and institutional integrity. Consequently, adherence to the nine imperatives by college and university administrators, staff members, and clerical workers contributes to institutional efforts to increase college student retention. Steadfast adherence to these imperatives also fosters the success of programs and activities designed by the institution to increase student retention.

Moreover, observance of the imperatives requires little or no direct institutional cost. Enactment of the imperatives, however, requires considerable expenditure of effort on a daily basis by individual college and university administrators, staff members, and clerical workers. To ensure the expenditure of such daily individual effort, the president, chief academic officer, chief student affairs officer, and chief admissions officer should also embrace and follow these nine imperatives.

Enact the Strategic Retention Initiative

Brier, Hirschy, and Braxton (2008) describe a "strategic retention initiative" that embodies the two organizational attributes of commitment of the institution to student welfare and institutional integrity. Accordingly, we recommend the strategic retention initiative for implementation by both commuter and residential universities. Brier (1999) developed this initiative, which entails contacting each first-year student during the fourth and fifth week of the fall term with a follow-up call made during the spring semester. The purpose of the call is to inquire about the student's academic and social experiences up to this point in their first semester of enrollment (Brier, Hirschy, and Braxton, 2008). If a student indicates some difficulties adjusting either academically or socially, the caller makes referrals to appropriate campus support services. The caller can also make follow-up calls to determine the outcome of the referrals made. The caller takes notes on student comments during the call and uses these as prompts during the spring semester phone call. These calls should be short, focused, and personalized (Brier, Hirschy, and Braxton, 2008). Clearly, these calls communicate to the student the high value the institution places on their growth and development. This approach can be extended to the suggestion by Habley, Bloom, and Robbins (2012) that institutions identify students who are at risk of persisting and systematically contact those individuals to connect them with services linked to their needs.

Fully Recognize the Role of Faculty Members in Student Persistence

A configuration of findings suggest recommendations for policy and practice regarding the role of faculty members at both residential and commuter institutions of higher education. As stated, both institutional integrity and commitment of the institution to student welfare play an important, indirect part in student persistence in both commuter and residential colleges and universities. In Chapters 8 and 9 we also discuss how student perceptions that faculty at their institution display a genuine interest in their welfare affects their perceptions of the commitment of their institution to students and to institutional integrity in a positive way in both commuter and residential colleges and universities. This configuration of findings leads to the delineation recommendations for policy and practice pertaining to faculty members in both residential and commuter institutions. These recommendations pertain to the faculty selection process, new faculty orientation, and the faculty reward system.

Faculty Selection Process

During on-campus interviews with faculty candidates, individuals involved in the election process should clearly communicate the high value placed on student welfare by the institution in general and the importance of demonstrating regard and respect for students as individuals in particular as palpable expressions of the commitment of the institution to the welfare of its students. Faculty search committees at both residential and commuter institutions should also work to gather indices of whether faculty candidates place a high value on students, respect them as individuals, evince concern for their growth and development, and hold a genuine interest in students. Interview questions should probe for such expressions of such student-centered values. Further, involving students in the search process in meaningful ways (e.g., as search committee members or as interviewers) symbolically signals that students and their opinions are valued.

Teaching demonstrations, or pedagogical colloquiums, during the campus visit phase of the faculty selection process offer another approach to ascertaining whether a faculty candidate holds these student-centered values. Shulman (1995) describes two models for a pedagogical colloquium that search committees could use. The first approach entails the use of a syllabus by the faculty candidate to explain how they would teach a course, the topics to be covered, and the nature of the experience for both students and faculty (Shulman, 1995). Through this model, faculty candidates show their philosophy about teaching and learning (Shulman, 1995). The second approach entails the selection by the faculty candidate of a difficult disciplinary concept for students to learn (Shulman, 1995). The candidate describes the approaches they would use to help students learn the concept (Shulman, 1995).

New Faculty Orientation

Orientation programs for faculty members new to the institution should stress the importance of the role that faculty members play in carrying out the institution's commitment to the welfare of its students by treating students equitably and with respect and by making choices in their teaching that contribute to students' growth and development. Such programs should also discuss the role of such behaviors as well as displaying a genuine interest in students in the faculty reward system.

Faculty Reward System

Commuter and residential colleges and universities should reward those faculty members who consistently treat students equitably and with respect, who make choices in their teaching that contribute to student growth and development, and who display a genuine interest in students. Items included on student course rating instruments provide a method for gathering such evidence. The scores on such items could be used as a criterion for decisions important to the retention of individual faculty members as annual increments in salary, reappointment of untenured faculty members, the awarding of tenure and promotion, as well as for discretionary rewards such as travel and funding for research and teaching initiatives.

Residential Colleges and Universities: Multiple Levers for Institutional Action

In this section, we present general recommendations for increasing student retention at residential colleges and universities. We refer to these recommendations as general because they apply to all groups of college students. We arrange these recommendations according to the institutional domains of practice most likely to implement a given recommendation to show that responsibility for increasing an institution's rate of student retention depends on the actions of many organizational units and individual members of the campus community. Put differently, all members of the campus community of a residential institution of higher education must embrace a commitment to the successful implementation of those institutional policies and practices that enact the recommendations put forth in this section of this chapter.

Administration and Governance

The central administration—president, chief academic affairs officer, and chief student affairs officer—of a college or university plays a key role in the formulation of institutional policies and practices that contribute to the realization of the institution's mission and goals. We present the following levers of institutional action for implementation by the central administration of residential colleges and universities.

- Keep students well-informed of institutional policies, rules, and regulations and provide adequate explanation of their intent and application.

- Provide opportunities for students to participate in the development, assessment, and recommendations for changes of campus policies, rules, and regulations.

These two recommendations spring from our identification of fairness in the administration of rules and regulations as a positive source of influence on student perceptions of their institution's commitment to student welfare. We report this finding in Chapter 8.

The following three recommendations emanate from the negative influence of student perceptions of prejudice and racial discrimination at their college or university on both commitment of the institution to student welfare and institutional integrity (see Chapter 8 for these findings):

- Establish campus policies and procedures that promote racial equality and understanding and the equitable treatment of all members of the campus community and that make prejudicial behaviors and racial discrimination unacceptable.

- Uniformly enforce campus policies and procedures that make prejudicial behaviors and racial discrimination unacceptable.

- Clearly communicate in speeches by campus leaders and in printed and electronic materials that the institution is committed to racial equality and understanding and the equitable treatment of all members of the campus community. This message should be clearly articulated by the president and other senior campus leaders,

including the chief academic officer and the chief
student affairs officer.

Enrollment Management

As an organizational function, enrollment management seeks to
control the size and characteristics of a college or university's student body proactively according to Hossler and Bean (1990). As
such, enrollment management focuses both on the recruitment
and retention of students (Hossler and Bean, 1990). We present
levers of institutional action for enactment as instruments of enrollment management that we derived from our delineation of the
fulfillment of academic expectations for college as a positive influence on student perceptions of the institutional integrity of their
residential college or university (see Chapter 8). Because student
expectations for college develop from the images that they hold of
the colleges and universities to which they make application, we
offer the following recommendations:

- Provide marketing materials in print and online that accurately depict the academic program of the institution.

- Develop marketing materials that accurately reflect current student perceptions of the academic program.

- Develop marketing materials that accurately reflect
  faculty expectations of student academic performance.

- Develop marketing materials that accurately reflect
  the institutional code of conduct regarding academic
  matters.

As we learned from the testing of the revised theory of student
departure from residential colleges and universities, as described
in Chapter 8, students who enroll with a positive affinity for the

college or university of matriculation are more likely to stay enrolled. A student's initial commitment to the institution not only positively affects their persistence, but has a pervasive impact on the student's subsequent commitment to the institution at the end of the first year. Furthermore, a student who has a strong commitment to the institution upon enrolling is more likely to perceive that the college or university is committed to the welfare of its students and that the institution acts with integrity.

Given this durable influence, we encourage residential colleges and universities to do the following:

- Focus their recruitment efforts on students who are more likely to be committed to the institution upon enrollment.

  - Encourage prospective student visits to campus and participation in campus events.

  - Encourage prospective student interaction with alumni, faculty, and current students.

- Develop strategies to reinforce student commitment after being accepted.

  - Maintain frequent, positive communication with the student.

  - Continue to encourage student visits to campus and participation in campus events.

  - Encourage student participation in summer orientation programs.

  - Encourage prospective student visits to campus and participation in campus events.

  - Encourage prospective student interaction with alumni, faculty, and current students.

- Communicate upcoming campus events to prospective students.

- Communicate current student success stories.

Faculty Teaching Role

Research and teaching constitute the core functions of the academic profession (Parsons and Platt, 1973). However, teaching role performance stands as the primary interest and activity of most college and university faculty members (Boyer, 1990). As a consequence, we present some levers of institutional action centered on the undergraduate teaching role of faculty members in residential colleges and universities.

In Chapter 8, we identify student reports of good teaching by faculty members as a positive influence on student perceptions of the commitment of the institution to student welfare. This particular finding, derived from our process of analytical cascading, gives rise to five recommendations for institutional action pertaining to faculty. These recommendations are as follows:

- Provide faculty development opportunities to promote good teaching practices. Tinto (2012) also urges the use of faculty development as a form of institutional action to improve institutional student retention. Contingent faculty, such as graduate assistants, adjunct faculty, postdoctoral researchers, full-time term faculty, and other types of faculty who are not on the tenure track, should be included in those development opportunities, as they may influence student persistence decisions (Eagan and Jaeger, 2008).

- Provide a faculty teaching and learning center to support good teaching practices.

- Carefully monitor student perceptions of good teaching by faculty members through student course evaluations and other means.

- Include good teaching by faculty members as part of faculty rewards and incentives such as annual salary adjustments, reappointment of untenured faculty members, and promotion and tenure decisions. Items on student course ratings instruments could plumb for student perceptions of good teaching.

- Recognize in visible ways, such as through annual teaching excellence awards, faculty members who are exemplary in their teaching and advising. Solicit student nominations of faculty excellence for such recognition awards.

The finding that student observations of faculty violations of the teaching norm of condescending negativism negatively influences their perception of the commitment of the institution to student welfare yields the following levers of institutional action (see Chapter 8 for this finding):

- Institutions should create teaching integrity committees (Braxton and Bayer, 1999) to handle allegations of faculty violations of the norm of condescending negativism as well as the other norms of teaching described in Chapter 8. Such committees should ensure the protection and confidentiality of both the accuser and the accused. Reporting processes should make it easy for students to report incidents of teaching misconduct.

- Sanctions for violating the norm of condescending negativism should be clearly communicated to members of the faculty and specified in the faculty handbook.

- Sanctions for violating the norm of condescending negativism should be uniformly enforced and carried out in a consistent and equitable manner.

The negative influence of student perceptions of prejudice and racial discrimination at their college or university on their perceptions of both institutional integrity and commitment of the institution to student welfare (see Chapter 8) generates two recommendations of institutional action:

- Communicate campus norms and policies regarding racial discrimination in orientation programs for new faculty. Such institutional norms and policies reinforce an institution's commitment to the welfare of its students by stressing the importance of treating students equitably and with respect as individuals.

- Provide sensitivity training for all faculty.

Institutional Research

Institutional research stands as a critical aspect of enrollment management (Hossler and Bean, 1990). Offices of institutional research conduct analytical studies to inform institutional decision- and policy-making as well as to improve institutional functioning (Hossler and Bean, 1990). Accordingly, we urge the execution of such analytical studies as assessments of the campus environment focused on student perceptions of institutional integrity, commitment of the institution to student welfare, and prejudice and racial discrimination. The importance of these foci of assessment to student persistence in residential colleges and universities indicates a need for their assessment.

Residence Life

Residence life stands as a functional area of student affairs (Dungy, 2003). The responsibilities of residence life include educational programming, facilities management and roommate assignments, as well as the selection, training, and direction of student residential advisors (Dungy, 2003).

Through our testing of the theory of student persistence in residential colleges and universities, discussed in Chapter 8, we delineated living on campus as a positive influence on the social integration of first-year students in residential colleges and universities. This finding gives rise to our recommendation that *residential colleges and universities require that first-year students live on campus in the residence halls of the institution.* We make this recommendation with much fervor. This recommendation echoes that of Braxton and McClendon (2001–2002).

Our process of analytical cascading yields other findings that provide the basis for institutional action focused on residence life and housing. First, we recommend that *residence hall staff offer programs and workshops that teach strategies for coping with stress, such as the strategy of positive reinterpretation and growth.* This recommendation is based on the finding that proactive social adjustment (through the use of positive growth and interpretation as a strategy for coping with stress) exerts a positive influence on communal potential (see Chapter 8 for this finding).

The positive influence of the dimensions of a sense of community—identity, interaction, and solidarity—in residence halls on either psychosocial engagement or communal potential generates levers of action at the level of the residence hall and at the level of the floor of a residence hall. More specifically, we delineated identity and interaction as positive influences on psychosocial engagement of first-year students, whereas we found that both of these dimensions as well as solidarity influence communal potential in a positive manner. At the level of the residence hall, we recommend the following:

- Provide training to residence hall staff to orient them to the importance of residence hall living and equip them with activities that foster identity, solidarity, and interaction.

- Provide adequate funding and support for residence hall staff to develop programs and activities that foster identity, solidarity, and interaction on each residence hall floor.

At the level of the floor, residence hall staff members are encouraged to offer programs and activities that foster identity, solidarity, and interaction, such as the following:

- Programs that foster a sense of community among students living on the same residence hall floor, such as programs that encourage students to socialize with other students on their floor.

- Activities that foster a sense of identity among students in a given residence hall floor, such as sports teams that compete within halls or between halls.

- Programs and activities that encourage students on the floor to work together to solve problems.

  - Participatory residence hall government.

  - Working together to address hall concerns (e.g., establishing and maintaining quiet hours for studying).

  - Team-building activities based on problem-solving techniques.

- Programs and activities that encourage students on the floor to work together to achieve common goals.

  - Activities that raise funds for charitable goals.

  - Participating together in a common community service project.

- Programs and activities that provide frequent face-to-face interactions among residents of the floor.

- Weekly social activities such as pizza night or game night.

Student Affairs Programming

The division of student affairs at many colleges and universities develop workshops and other types of programs on selected topics of importance to the academic and social success of college students (Braxton and McClendon, 2001–2002). The process of analytical cascading identified findings that hold relevance to the development of programs and workshops. The positive influence of proactive social adjustment on communal potential (Chapter 8) and the negative influence of student perceptions of prejudice and racial discrimination on campus on both student perceptions of the commitment of the institution to student welfare and institutional integrity (Chapter 8) indicate a need for the following types of workshops and programs:

- Provide sensitivity training for leaders of student clubs and organizations to ensure that all student activities promote racial equality and understanding.

- Offer campus programs that teach strategies for coping with stress. In particular, teach strategy of positive reinterpretation and growth.

Student Orientation

Typically, the student affairs division of a college or university assumes responsibility for new student orientation programs (Dungy, 2003). Orientation programs for incoming first-year students strive to familiarize students with the academic and social life at the institution by informing students of administrative and academic regulations, giving them a knowledge of the various student organizations and activities, making them aware of the availability of various student services, communicating degree requirements, and providing students with an opportunity to select courses for their first semester (Pascarella, Terenzini, and Wolfe, 1986). Put differently, the preparation of students for success in the academic and social environments of their institution forms the underlying intent of first-year orientation programs.

The recommendations we advance for student orientation emerged from a pattern of findings described in Chapter 8. First, our process of analytical cascading found that the more students view their college or university's first-year orientation program as adequate preparation for success in their institution's social environment, the greater their perceived level of communal potential. As we also learned from the analytical cascading described in Chapter 8 that communal potential functions as a positive source of influence on psychosocial engagement of first-year students in residential colleges and universities. Other findings such as the positive influence of proactive social adjustment on communal potential (Chapter 8) and the negative influence of student perceptions of prejudice and racial discrimination on both commitment of the institution to student welfare and to institutional integrity (Chapter 8) indicate a need to incorporate these factors into the fabric of first-year orientation programs. We also identified the fulfillment of academic expectations for college as a positive influence on student perceptions of institutional integrity (Chapter 8). As a consequence, first-year orientation programs should attend to these factors in the development of orientation programs for first-year students. As a consequence, we offer the following recommendations regarding first-year orientation programs in residential college and universities:

- Establish policies that require first-year students to participate in fall orientation programs.

- Provide programming in first-year orientation programs that will help students anticipate and respond constructively to the social challenges, demands, pressures, and stressors that they may face in their first year.

- Ensure that summer and fall orientation programs for first-year students reinforce the depiction of the academic program of the institution and faculty expectations of student academic performance.

- Communicate campus norms and policies in orientation programs for new students regarding the institution's commitment to multiculturalism to reduce on-campus prejudice and racial discrimination.

- Offer orientation programs that provide multiple opportunities for first-year students to meet and interact socially with other first-year students. This recommendation follows the recommendation of Braxton and McClendon (2001–2002).

Commuter Colleges and Universities: Multiple Levers for Institutional Action

In this section of the chapter, we offer recommendations for increasing student retention at commuter colleges and universities that apply to all groups of students. We assert these recommendations, or levers of action, according to the institutional domain of practice most likely to implement a given recommendation. Such an assortment conveys efforts to increase student retention as an institution-wide responsibility.

Academic Advising

Academic advising is "a decision-making process during which students realize their maximum educational potential through communication and information exchanges with an advisor" (Grites, 1979, p. 1). As such, academic advising deals with the personal, intellectual, social, vocational, and psychological needs of students (Voorhees, 1990). More specifically, Braxton and Mundy (2001–2002) posit that academic advisors—faculty members or professional staff members—inform students of the institutional degree requirements and the academic requirements of different majors. Academic advisors typically meet periodically during the academic year to counsel students and give advice about their academic experiences and goals (Braxton and Mundy, 2001–2002).

Our process of analytical cascading revealed that academic advising positively influences commuting students' perceptions of their academic and intellectual development (Chapter 9) as well as their institution's commitment to the welfare of its students (Chapter 9). We also learned that student perceptions that university offices that serve students (e.g., financial aid, counseling, registrar) are open at convenient times for working students also positively influences both commitment of the institution to student welfare and institutional integrity.

This arrangement of findings generates the following recommendation for institutional action for academic advising in commuter colleges and universities:

- Design an academic advising program that serves the needs of commuter students and provides access to academic advisors at times convenient to students, particularly in the evenings and on weekends to accommodate the needs of working students and those with family demands.

In addition to this lever, we present an additional lever that springs from our pervasive set of findings regarding full-time attendance. From our test of the theory of student persistence in commuter colleges and universities (Chapter 9), we found that full-time attendance influences academic and intellectual development, subsequent institutional commitment, and student persistence in a positive manner. Conversely, attending part-time adversely affects these three key factors of student persistence in commuter colleges and universities. As a consequence of this important set of findings, we strongly recommend the following levers of institutional action pertaining to academic advising:

- Upon matriculation to the institution, all part-time students must be assigned an academic advisor.

- All part-time students must meet periodically with their assigned academic advisor, at times convenient for the student, during the course of a semester and academic year to discuss their academic progress and future academic plans.

Academic Programs

Academic programs attend to the intellectual growth and development of college students through a focus on the classroom (Braxton and Mundy, 2001–2002). The rubric of academic programs includes such curricular arrangements as the development and offering of learning communities, which we describe in Chapter 9, as well as the scheduling of courses offered by the various academic departments of a college or university.

Through theory testing and analytical cascading, we derived a set of findings that provide the basis for levers of action pertaining to academic programs. More specifically, through our process of analytical cascading (Chapter 9), we identified participation in a learning community as a source of positive influence on the academic and intellectual development of commuting students. We also found that student reports of having classes offered at times convenient for them positively influences both their perceptions of institutional integrity (Chapter 9) and the level of support they receive from their significant others for their college attendance (Chapter 9). Moreover, we learned from our test of the theory of student persistence in commuter colleges and universities that support from significant others (Chapter 9) wields a positive influence on the subsequent institutional commitment of students in commuter colleges and universities.

For this institutional domain of practice, we present the following levers of institutional action that spring from these findings:

- Provide opportunities for students to participate in learning communities, including the block-scheduling of courses that are organized around a particular theme.

- Offer classes at times convenient to students, particularly in the evenings and on weekends to accommodate the needs of working students and those with family demands.

Administration and Governance

As previously stated in this chapter, the central administration—president, chief academic affairs officer, chief student affairs officer—of a college or university develops institutional policies and practices that contribute to the realization of an institution's mission and goals. A confluence of various findings derived both from theory testing (Chapter 9) and analytical cascading (Chapter 9) give rise to the following levers of institutional action:

- Commuter colleges and universities should require first-time, first-year students to enroll on a full-time basis for their first semester of enrollment. This bold recommendation stems from our all-encompassing set of findings, derived from theory testing, regarding the positive influence of full-time attendance on such factors important to student persistence in commuter colleges and universities as their perceptions of their academic and intellectual development, their subsequent level of commitment to the institution, and persistence.

- Commuter colleges and universities should establish an office of family services. This particular recommendation emanates from our finding derived from theory testing (Chapter 9) that support from significant others positively influences subsequent commitment to the institution.

Four roles and responsibilities for an office of family services spring from our findings, derived from analytical cascading (Chapter 9), that the impression that significant others feel welcomed at university events positively influences student support from significant others. Moreover, we learned that the perception that significant others feel welcomed at university events is positively shaped by creating a website containing information for significant others and by encouragement by the university for significant others to attend the orientation for new students. These four roles and responsibilities for an office of family services are as follows:

- An office of family services should develop programs to ensure that family members and significant others are welcomed at the college.

- An office of family services should design campus events so that family members and significant others feel welcomed to attend by providing special invitations to campus events, by providing special seating or other logistical arrangements for family members and significant others, and by including words of welcome and special recognition for family members and significant others.

- An office of family services should also develop a website offering information for significant others that includes a special message of welcome, provides pertinent information about campus programs and events, and provides pertinent information about services and support for family members and significant others.

- An office of family services should work with the office that conducts the first-year student orientation to offer a specifically designated first-year orientation for family members and significant others. Accordingly, the office of family services should encourage family members and significant others to attend the orientation for new students by providing special invitations to orientation and by designing special sessions for family members and significant others.

An assortment of findings derived from analytical cascading suggests some further recommendations for action by the institutional domain of administration and governance. Having ample parking on campus for commuting students and having university offices that serve students (e.g., financial aid, counseling, registrar) being open at convenient times for working students positively influences both student perceptions of institutional integrity and commitment of the institution to student welfare (Chapter 9). In addition, having general-use computers with Internet access available throughout the campus positively influences student perceptions of the commitment of the institution to student welfare (Chapter 9), whereas having reliable transportation to and from campus leads to support from significant others for college attendance (Chapter 9). This array of findings gives rise to the following levers of action by the central administration of commuter colleges and universities:

- Ensure that administrative offices that serve students, such as financial aid, counseling, and the registrar, are open and adequately staffed at times convenient to students, particularly in the evenings and on weekends, to accommodate the needs of working students and those with family demands.

- Provide comprehensive information to prospective and current students regarding transportation options to and from campus, including public transportation and campus shuttle services.

- Work with local authorities to develop reliable public transportation options throughout the surrounding community to and from the campus, particularly at times when students need to attend classes.

- Consider providing campus-based transportation and shuttle services to and from areas or at times not served by existing public transportation.

- Ensure adequate facilities in the library, student center, and academic buildings for students to study, type papers, and make copies of course materials while on campus.

- Ensure that facilities with study space are open around times that classes are scheduled, including in the evenings and on weekends.

- Ensure that ample space for parking in close proximity to classroom locations is available to commuter students.

- Ensure that there is adequate availability of computers with Internet access in the library, student center, and academic buildings.

- Ensure that computers are available around times that classes are scheduled, including in the evenings and on weekends.

- Provide dedicated information technology (IT) support staff, including computer help desk staff, to troubleshoot computer problems when computer labs are open.

Enrollment Management

As previously indicated in this chapter, the enrollment and retention of students constitute the primary functions of enrollment management (Hossler and Bean, 1990). The proactive control of the size and characteristics of the student body of a college or university underlies these two functions of enrollment management (Hossler and Bean, 1990). Recruitment activities and financial aid play key roles in enrollment management (Braxton and McClendon, 2001–2002).

Our pervasive finding that full-time attendance positively influences such key factors of student persistence in commuter colleges and universities such as academic and intellectual development, subsequent institutional commitment, and persistence (Chapter 9), coupled with our finding that being satisfied with the costs of attending their college or university positively affects subsequent institutional commitments (Chapter 9) provide an empirical foundation for the delineation of levers of institutional action pertaining to enrollment management. These levers of action for enrollment management are as follows:

- Develop programs and policies that make it financially viable for students to attend full time.

- Make students aware of financial aid options including scholarships, grants, and loans to finance their education.

- Provide financial counseling that helps students see the long-term value of investing in their education to complete their degrees more quickly and begin to reap the benefits of credentialed employment or further study at a four-year institution.

- Develop programs and services that help students understand the costs of attending and benefits that accrue from investing in higher education.

- Provide financial counseling that helps students see the long-term value of investing in their education.

- Make students aware of financial aid options including scholarships, grants, and loans to finance their education so that they feel better satisfied with their ability to afford the costs.

Faculty Teaching Role

The word "complex" accurately describes the professorial task of undergraduate college teaching (Braxton, 2008). Faculty teaching role performance includes such tasks as course design, teaching preparations, pedagogical practices, and course assessment activities. Professional preferences and choices determine the way faculty perform these tasks (Braxton, 2008). Pedagogical practices include faculty teaching skills as well as such approaches or methods of teaching as active learning (Braxton 2008).

Our process of analytical cascading yields findings regarding faculty use of active learning in class and the teaching skills of instructional clarity and organization and preparation. Specifically, faculty use of active learning positively influences student perceptions of their academic and intellectual development (Chapter 9), whereas both the teaching skills of instructional clarity and organization and preparation positively influence academic and intellectual development, and student perceptions of the commitment of the institution to student welfare and of institutional integrity (Chapter 9).

This array of findings concerning faculty pedagogical practices generates the following levers of institutional action involving the faculty role of teaching:

- Clearly communicate to members of the faculty that competency in teaching skills, especially instructional clarity, instructional organization and preparation, and active learning is highly valued by the institution and serve to promote student success.

  - At faculty hiring through position announcements, application materials, and search committee questions

  - In orientation for new faculty members

- Provide faculty development opportunities to promote good teaching practices.

- Provide a faculty teaching and learning center to support good teaching practices.

- Include competency in teaching skills as part of faculty rewards and incentives.

  - Promotion and tenure decisions

  - Compensation decisions

  - Discretionary rewards such as travel and funding for research and teaching initiatives

- Recognize in visible ways faculty members who are exemplary in their teaching and advising skills.

Institutional Research

As stated previously, offices of institutional research conduct analytical studies to inform institutional decision and policy-making as well as to improve institutional functioning (Hossler and Bean, 1990). Thus, we recommend institutional assessments of the campus environment of commuter colleges and universities that concentrate on student perceptions of institutional integrity and the commitment of the institution to student welfare. After assessing the student experience, we recommend involving students in reviewing the results, as they may generate innovative suggestions. Concerted efforts to communicate the results to the campus community should outline the resultant actions for improvement. This iterative, inclusive process demonstrates a high value placed on student experiences. We also recommend that the roles and responsibilities of an office of family services, such as we have outlined here, should also be the focus of assessments by institutional research offices of commuter colleges and universities.

Student Orientation

As stated previously in this chapter, orientation programs for incoming first-year students inform students of administrative and academic regulations, give them a knowledge of the various student organizations and activities, make them aware of the availability of various student services, communicate degree requirements, and provide them with an opportunity to select courses for their first semester (Pascarella, Terenzini, and Wolfe, 1986).

For students in commuter colleges and universities, preparation for success in the academic environment of their institution looms particularly important as a focus of first-year student orientation. This assertion receives empirical support through our process of analytical cascading. We learned through this process that student perceptions that first-year student orientation provides them with adequate preparation for academic success at their college or university positively affects their perceptions of their academic and intellectual development (Chapter 9) as well as their perceptions of institutional integrity and commitment of the institution to student welfare (Chapter 9). This pattern of findings yields the following levers of action for the design of first-year student orientation programs at commuter colleges and universities:

- Establish policies that require first-year students to participate in orientation programs. Both full- and part-time students should be required to attend.

- Provide an orientation program for first-year students at the start of each academic term.

The office of student orientation should also cooperate with the office of family services by encouraging family members and significant others to attend the orientation for new students and by designing special sessions for family members and significant others. We provided the empirical basis for this particular recommendation under our recommendation for the creation of an office of family services.

In Summary

In this chapter, we put forth a multitude of levers for institutional action. The ill-structured nature of the problem of student retention dictates the need for such a collection of levers. These levers rest on a robust foundation of theory-driven empirical research. As we asserted in Chapter 1, levers of action derived from theoretically based research ensures reliability in the enactment of a given lever of action. Modifications needed during the implementation of a lever of action also benefit from the understanding derived from empirically tested theory.

Part II

Theoretical and Research Context

4

Explaining College Student Persistence

We begin this chapter with a brief review of the various conceptual perspectives that seek to explain college student persistence: economic, organizational, psychological, and sociological. (For a thorough review of these theoretical perspectives, readers may refer to Habley, Bloom, and Robbins, 2012.) We then turn our attention to Tinto's Interactionalist Theory of Student Departure, a sociological perspective on student persistence, and offer an empirical assessment of the validity of Tinto's theory. This empirical assessment leads to a serious revision of Tinto's theory for residential colleges and universities and a different theory of student persistence in commuter colleges and universities. We close this chapter by presenting a rationale for needing these two theories as well as the common attributes of these two theories. In Chapters 5 (the revision of Tinto's theory for residential colleges and universities) and 6 (the theory of student persistence in commuter colleges and universities) we describe the formulations of these two theories, and subsequent chapters in this volume explore the findings of empirical tests of these two theories.

Economic Perspective

The weighing of costs and benefits of attending a given college or university by the individual student constitutes the crux of an economic perspective on college student persistence (Tinto, 1986).

Accordingly, student persistence likely results if a student perceives that the benefits of attending a particular college or university exceed the costs of attendance (Braxton, 2003).

Studies of college student departure using an economic perspective concentrate on the costs of attending a particular college or university and an individual's ability to pay. A student's ability to pay and the student's perceptions of the costs of their education influence persistence (Cabrera, Nora, and Castaneda, 1993; Cabrera, Stampen, and Hansen, 1990; St. John, 1994; St. John, Paulson, and Starkey, 1996; Stampen and Cabrera, 1988). St. John, Cabrera, Nora, and Asker (2000) offer a broad discussion of economic factors related to the college student departure puzzle.

Organizational Perspective

The role of organizational structure and organizational behavior in the college student persistence process constitutes the organizational perspective on student persistence (Berger and Braxton, 1998; Tinto, 1986). The actions of administrators, faculty, and staff represent forms of organizational behavior that may influence student persistence decisions (Tinto, 1986).

Psychological Perspective

The psychological orientation emphasizes the role of psychological characteristics and psychological processes in seeking an understanding of the phenomenon of college student persistence (Tinto, 1986, 1993). Psychological characteristics and processes that distinguish between students who persist and those who depart are at the level of the individual student and at the level of the environment of a college or university. Such environments may be at the level of the college or university as an organization (Baird, 2000) or at the suborganizational level (Braxton, 2000). Psychological characteristics and processes that may affect student departure include academic aptitude and skills, motivational states, personality traits, and student development theories.

Sociological Perspective

The sociological perspective stresses the influence of social structure and social forces on college student persistence (Braxton, 2000; Tinto, 1986). College student peers, family socioeconomic status, mechanisms of anticipatory socialization, and the support of significant others constitute important social forces that influence college student persistence. Given that Tinto's Interactionalist Theory (1975, 1993) puts emphasis on the student's interpretation of their interactions with the academic and social communities of a given college or university, his theory may be viewed as embracing a sociological orientation to student persistence.

Of the various perspectives on college student persistence, only Tinto's Interactionalist Theory enjoys paradigmatic stature. One dimension of paradigmatic development centers on consensus on a particular theory to explain a focal phenomenon (Kuhn, 1962, 1970). The extent of consensus on the relevance of Tinto's Interactionalist Theory in accounting for college student persistence manifests itself in the number of citations to this theory. For example, Braxton, Sullivan, and Johnson (1997) noted that more than 400 citations and 170 dissertations make reference to this theory. In 2004, Braxton, Hirschy, and McClendon (2008) reported more than 775 citations to this theory. Given the paradigmatic stature of Tinto's theory, we review its formulations in the next section of this chapter.

Tinto's Interactionalist Theory

Tinto views student departure, or student persistence, as a longitudinal process that involves the meanings the individual student places on their interactions with the formal and informal dimensions of a given college or university (Braxton, Sullivan, and Johnson, 1997; Tinto, 1986, 1993). Such interactions occur between the individual student and the academic and social systems of a college or university. These interactions resonate with the sociological perspective on student persistence. Tinto (1975) clearly states that his theory explains voluntary student departure.

To elaborate, Tinto (1975) asserts that various individual characteristics (for example, family background, individual attributes, and pre-college schooling experiences) that students possess as they enter college directly influence their persistence decisions as well as their initial commitments to the institution and to the goal of college graduation. Initial commitment to the institution and initial commitment to the goal of graduation influence the level of a student's integration into the academic and social systems of the college or university.

According to Tinto (1975, p. 104), academic integration consists of structural and normative dimensions. Structural integration entails the meeting of explicit standards of the college or university, whereas normative integration pertains to an individual's identification with the normative structure of the academic system. Social integration pertains to the extent of congruency between the individual student and the social system of a college or university. Tinto holds that social integration occurs both at the level of the college or university and at the level of subcultures of an institution (Tinto, 1975, p. 107).

Tinto further postulates that academic and social integration influence a student's subsequent commitments to the institution and to the goal of college graduation. The greater the student's level of academic integration, the greater the level of subsequent commitment to the goal of college graduation. Also, the greater the student's level of social integration, the greater the level of subsequent commitment to the focal college or university (Tinto, 1975, p. 110). The student's initial level of commitments—to the institution and to the goal of college graduation goal—also influences their level of subsequent commitments. In turn, the greater the levels of both subsequent institutional commitment and commitment to the goal of college graduation, the greater the likelihood the individual will persist in college.

Tinto (1982, 1986) clarifies and refines his foundational theory on student attrition and further develops the theory in his book, *Leaving College: Rethinking the Causes and Cures of Student Attrition* (1993). The revisions in the 1975 model acknowledge the influences of financial resources, connection with an external community (such as family and/or work), and classroom experiences on a student's decision to persist.

From the above formulations of the 1975 statement of Tinto's Interactionalist Theory, 13 testable propositions emerge (Braxton, Sullivan, and Johnson, 1997). Tinto does not specify a direction (positive or negative) for propositions 1 to 7, whereas he states a positive direction for propositions 8 to 13 (Braxton et al., 1997). The 13 propositions are as follows:

1. Student entry characteristics affect the level of initial commitment to the institution.
2. Student entry characteristics affect the level of initial commitment to the goal of graduation from college.
3. Student entry characteristics directly affect the student's likelihood of persistence in college.
4. Initial commitment to the goal of graduation from college affects the level of academic integration.
5. Initial commitment to the goal of graduation from college affects the level of social integration.
6. Initial commitment to the institution affects the level of social integration.
7. Initial commitment to the institution affects the level of academic integration.
8. The greater the degree of academic integration, the greater the level of subsequent commitment to the goal of graduation from college.

9. The greater the degree of social integration, the greater the level of subsequent commitment to the institution.

10. The initial level of institutional commitment affects the subsequent level of institutional commitment.

11. The initial level of commitment to the goal of graduation from college affects the subsequent level of commitment to the goal of college graduation.

12. The greater the level of subsequent commitment to the goal of graduation from college, the greater the likelihood of student persistence in college.

13. The greater the level of subsequent commitment to the institution, the greater the likelihood of student persistence in college.

Because propositions 12 and 13 hypothesize a positive influence on student persistence, these propositions loom important to the explanatory power of Tinto's theory (Braxton, Sullivan, and Johnson, 1997). However, Braxton, Hirschy, and McClendon (2004) contend that the validity of Tinto's Interactionalist Theory also requires strong empirical backing of propositions 8 and 9. Lacking sturdy empirical affirmation for the role of either academic or social integration in student persistence, serious questions surface about the influence of the outcomes of the interactions a student makes with the academic or social communities of a college or university on student persistence decisions (Braxton et al., 2004).

The 13 testable propositions are logically interrelated and, as a set, seek to account for individual student persistence. Although these 13 propositions possess internal consistency, a key question springs forth: Does Tinto's theory also possess empirical internal consistency (Braxton et al., 2004)? The validity of this theory depends on empirical internal consistency (Braxton et al., 2004).

Tinto's Theory Empirically Appraised

Braxton, Sullivan, and Johnson (1997) contend that the extent to which each of the 13 propositions acquires empirical backing provides the basis for determining the empirical internal consistency of Tinto's theory. As a consequence, they conducted such an assessment, using the 1975 version of Tinto's theory rather than the 1987 and 1993 revised versions for two reasons. First, as of 1997, only two studies tested constructs unique to these two later versions (Allen and Nelson, 1989; Pavel, 1991). Second, those formulations that characterize Tinto's theory as interactionalist exist in the 1975 formulations (Braxton, Hirschy, and McClendon, 2004).

The "box score" method provided the basis for determining the magnitude of support for each of the 13 propositions. Braxton, Sullivan, and Johnson (1997) computed the box score for a given proposition as the percentage of tests of that proposition that statistically affirm that proposition. Based on the derived box scores, they labeled support for a given proposition as strong, moderate, weak, or indeterminate. They ascribed strong empirical support to a proposition if 66 percent or more of three or more tests of that proposition yielded statistically significant affirmation of it. Moderate support was accorded to a given proposition if between 34 and 65 percent of three or more tests of that proposition produced statistically significant backing. Weak empirical support was assigned to those propositions for which 33 percent or less of three or more tests of that proposition produced statistically significant and confirming results. Braxton, Sullivan, and Johnson classified those propositions that were tested one or two times as having indeterminate support, because subsequent tests might confirm or fail to confirm the focal proposition.

Moreover, they used in their derivation of box scores only those tests of the 13 propositions that included face valid measures of Tinto's constructs and were tested using such robust multivariate statistical techniques as path analysis, multiple linear regression,

LISREL (linear structural relationships), and/or logistic regression (Braxton et al., 1997, p. 113).

Support by Institutional Type for Tinto's Theory

Braxton, Sullivan, and Johnson (1997) considered the extent of empirical support for the 13 propositions of Tinto's theory by institutional type: residential universities, commuter universities, liberal arts colleges, and two-year colleges. Based on the box scores obtained, they concluded that the validity of Tinto's theory remains an open empirical question in both liberal arts and two-year colleges given that they found that no tests of the 13 propositions were conducted in liberal arts colleges and only one proposition received strong empirical support in two-year colleges. In addition, they ascertained that for two-year colleges, the remaining 12 propositions either received indeterminate support or were not the object of empirical testing (Braxton et al., 1997).

Furthermore, the empirical validity of Tinto's theory also surfaces as problematic with important differences between residential and commuter colleges and universities. Empirical tests conducted in residential colleges and universities afford strong support for 5 of the 13 propositions derived from Tinto's formulations (Braxton, Sullivan, and Johnson, 1997): propositions 5, 9, 10, 11, and 13. In contrast, only two of the 13 propositions receive strong empirical backing from tests conducted in commuter colleges and universities (Braxton et al., 1997): propositions 1 and 10. Accordingly, they concluded that Tinto's theory receives partial support in residential universities but lacks explanatory power in commuter institutional settings.

Partial support for Tinto's theory in residential institutions stems from two factors. First, two of the previously delineated core propositions to Tinto's theory received robust empirical backing: propositions 9 and 13. However, the core propositions 8 and 12 failed to receive strong empirical affirmation. Thus, the role

of academic integration looms questionable in residential institutions of higher education based on the lack of strong empirical support for proposition 8.

In the case of commuter institutions, none of the four core
propositions to Tinto's theory (propositions 8, 9, 12, and 13) received strong empirical support (Braxton, Sullivan, and Johnson,
1997). As a consequence, their conclusion that Tinto's theory lacks
explanatory power in commuter institutions appears warranted.

Because of this mixed pattern of support for Tinto's theory,
Braxton, Hirschy, and McClendon (2004) elected to revise Tinto's
theory to explain student persistence in residential colleges and
universities and to construct a different theory to account for student persistence in commuter colleges and universities. In addition
to questions concerning the validity of Tinto's theory in these two
types of institutional settings, the need for different theories to account for student persistence in residential colleges and universities
and in commuter colleges and universities stems from fundamental
differences between these two types of institutions of higher education. Social communities and the external environment stand
as differentiating dimensions between these two types of colleges
and universities. In contrast to residential institutions, commuter
colleges and universities lack well-defined and structured social
communities for students to establish membership (Braxton et
al., 2004). Moreover, a wide variety of students attend commuter
colleges and universities. Commuter students include traditionally aged students who live at home with their parents, older
students, students with family obligations, working students, and
part-time and full-time students (Bean and Metzner, 1985; Stewart and Rue, 1983). Whereas many traditionally aged students in
residential institutions choose to attend college "instead" of doing
something else, most adult students attend college "in addition" to
their other day-to-day involvements and obligations, such as family and work (Tinto, 1993, p. 126). Commuter students typically
experience conflicts among their obligations to family, work and

college (Tinto, 1993). Such obligations shape the daily activities of commuter students (Webb, 1990). Accordingly, the external environments in commuter colleges and universities play a defining role the college experience for students in commuter colleges and universities that substantially differ from residential institutions (Braxton and Hirschy, 2005).

In this volume, we present the findings of empirical tests of these two theories: the revised theory of student persistence in residential colleges and universities (Chapter 8) the theory of student persistence in commuter colleges and universities (Chapter 9). Although basically different, these two theoretical statements share some common attributes (Braxton and Hirschy, 2005). Before describing each of these theories in Chapters 5 and 6, we delineate these commonalities in the next section of this chapter.

Common Attributes of the Two Theories

The theories of student persistence in residential and commuter institutions share three attributes previously delineated by Braxton and Hirschy (2005). These commonalities are as follows:

1. The two theoretical formulations spring from the process of inductive theory construction. Inductive theory construction uses the findings of empirical research to derive new concepts, patterns of understanding, and generalizations (Wallace, 1971). Put differently, new concepts, patterns of understanding, and empirical generalizations emerge from a "conceptual factor analysis" of the results of empirical research.

2. These two theoretical statements are theories of the middle range (Braxton, Hirschy, and McClendon, 2004). Merton (1968) offers distinctions between grand and middle range theory. Grand theory seeks to explain a wide range of phenomena, whereas middle range theories endeavor to explain a limited range of phenomena (Merton, 1968). In the case

of these two theories, one accounts for student persistence in residential colleges and universities, whereas the other aims to explain student persistence in commuter colleges and universities.

3. Both of these theories match three criteria for a good theory (Braxton, Hirschy, and McClendon, 2004). First, both theories account for extant research findings (Chafetz, 1978). Both theories derive their formulations and propositions from research on the college student departure process. Second, the empirical measurement of the propositions of both theories is possible. As a consequence, both theories are amenable to empirical testing (Chafetz, 1978). Third, both of the theories described in this chapter are relatively parsimonious. Parsimony is a desirable trait of theories (Chafetz, 1978). Put in different words, a theory should be explained with the fewest number of constructs and propositions possible. Nevertheless, the propositions included in each theory are needed to account for relevant findings from research.

In Chapter 5, we describe the formulations of the revision of Tinto's theory for residential colleges and universities. We describe the formulations of the theory of student persistence in commuter colleges and universities in Chapter 6.

5

The Revision of Tinto's Theory for Residential Colleges and Universities

As we stated in Chapter 4, propositions 5, 9, 10, 11, and 13 of Tinto's theory garnered strong empirical confirmation in residential institutions of higher education (Braxton, Sullivan, and Johnson, 1997). Of the five propositions, proposition 11 fails to relate logically to any of the other four propositions. However, the other four propositions are logically related to one another. In narrative form, these four propositions read as follows: The initial commitment to the goal of graduation from college affects the level of social integration (proposition 5). Social integration, in turn, positively affects subsequent institutional commitment (proposition 9). Initial commitment to the institution also influences subsequent institutional commitment (proposition 10). The greater the level of subsequent commitment to the institution, the greater the likelihood of student persistence in college (proposition 13).

Moreover, two of these five propositions also hold explanatory power because of their status as core concepts of Tinto's Interactionalist Theory (propositions 9 and 13). These two propositions read as follows: The greater the level of social integration, the greater the level of subsequent institutional commitment (proposition 9) and the greater the level of subsequent institutional commitment, the greater the likelihood of student persistence in college (proposition 13) (Braxton, Sullivan, and Johnson, 1997, p. 135). In addition, the relationship between social integration and subsequent institutional commitment enjoys a high level of reliability, as 16 out of 19 tests of this relationship yield empirical support (Braxton and Lee, 2005). Likewise, the relationship between subsequent institutional commitment and student persistence is highly reliable given that 11 of 13 empirical tests provide support (Braxton and Lee, 2005).

The Revised Theory

Propositions 9 and 13 provide the foundation for the revised theory of college student persistence for residential college and universities posited by Braxton, Hirschy, and McClendon (2004). Social integration plays a pivotal role in the formulations of this revised theory. Social integration reflects the student's perception of their degree of social affiliation with others and their degree of congruency with the attitudes, beliefs, norms, and values of the social communities of a college or university (Durkheim, 1951; Tinto, 1975). Social integration occurs at the level of the college or university or at the level of a subculture of an institution (Tinto, 1975, p. 107). Because of its centrality to the explanatory power of Tinto's 1975 theoretical formulations and to this revision of it, the primary thrust of this revised theory concentrates on the delineation of six factors that influence social integration—factors that function as antecedents of social integration.

Of the six factors that function as antecedents of social integration in the revised theory of student persistence in residential colleges and universities, five spring from the process of inductive theory construction or "conceptual factor analysis" previously discussed: commitment of the institution to student welfare, communal potential, institutional integrity, proactive social adjustment, and psychosocial engagement. Ability to pay, the sixth antecedent of social integration, was derived directly from research findings.

Through the process of inductive theory construction, Braxton and Hirschy (2004) report that they derived commitment of the institution to student welfare, communal potential, and institutional integrity from the findings of 62 empirical tests of factors influencing social integration in a statistically significant way. These tests were conducted using traditional-aged college students in residential colleges and universities. Moreover, Braxton, Hirschy, and McClendon (2004) also derived the antecedents of social integration of proactive social adjustment and psychosocial engagement though the process of inductive theory construction. Next, we delineate the specific findings used by Braxton and Hirschy (2004) and Braxton, Hirschy, and McClendon (2004) to conceptualize these five antecedents of social integration.

These six factors form the core of this revised theory for residential colleges and universities given their hypothesized role as antecedents of social integration. Moreover, these six antecedents are not arrayed in any hierarchy or conditional relationships with respect to one another, nor are they arrayed in any temporal sequence. We describe these six factors in the paragraphs that follow.

Ability to Pay

This factor springs from the research of Cabrera, Stampen, and Hansen (1990), who found that students who feel satisfied with the cost of attending their college or university are more likely to persist than unsatisfied students. Although ability to pay stands as an antecedent of social integration, it also functions as a student entry characteristic. Its posited influence on social integration springs from the contention of Cabrera et al. (1990) that the ability to pay tends to reduce barriers to student participation in the social communities of their college or university because of the lower salience of their financial concerns about paying for college. Ability to pay finds expression in the degree of satisfaction students express about the costs of attending their chosen college or university. Braxton, Hirschy, and McClendon (2004) advance the following proposition concerning the influence of the ability to pay on social integration: the greater the student's satisfaction with the cost of attending their chosen college or university, the greater the student's degree of social integration.

Commitment of the Institution to Student Welfare

An abiding concern for the growth and development of its students expressed by a given college or university constitutes the core defining attribute of this factor (Braxton and Hirschy, 2004; Braxton, Hirschy, and McClendon, 2004). Other salient dimensions of this factor include the high value the institution places on its students, treating each student with respect as an individual, and the equitable treatment of students (Braxton and Hirschy, 2004; Braxton, Hirschy, and McClendon, 2004). These dimension flow from the culture of a given college or university. Tierney (1988) asserts that the culture of a college or university reveals itself in "what is done, how it is done, and who is involved in doing it." Put differently, institutional actions, decisions, and communications flow from institutional culture.

Braxton and Hirschy (2004) generated the dimensions of commitment of the institution to student welfare from various research findings. Berger and Braxton (1998) report a set of three findings that student perceptions of fair administration of rules and policies, communicating institutional polices and requirements to students, and giving students an opportunity to participate in decision-making regarding institutional rules and policies positively influences social integration. From these three findings, dimensions of commitment of the institution to student welfare, such as the valuing of students, respect for students as individuals, and the equitable treatment of students, emerged (Braxton and Hirschy, 2004). Braxton and Hirschy also derived the dimension of an abiding concern for the growth and development of students from three additional research findings: the positive influence of participation in a two-day first-year-student orientation program (Pascarella, Terenzini, and Wolfe, 1986), positive effects of such faculty teaching practices as active learning (Braxton, Milem, and Sullivan, 2000), and teaching skills of organization and preparation and clarity (Braxton, Bray, and Berger, 2000).

Commitment of the institution to student welfare parallels Joseph Hermanowicz's (2003) concept of "enforced success." He derived this concept from case studies of four highly selective research universities that vary in their retention rates. The university with the highest retention rate has what Hermanowicz terms a "culture of enforced success." In such a culture, all students are treated as if they are at-risk. Key people in this university believe in the promise of each student in a fervently held way. These formulations generate the following proposition: the more a student perceives that the institution is committed to the welfare of its students, the greater the student's level of social integration.

Communal Potential

This factor involves the extent to which a student perceives that a subgroup of students exits within the various communities of their college or university that hold values, beliefs, and goals similar to their own (Braxton and Hirschy, 2004; Braxton, Hirschy, and McClendon, 2004). Put differently, an anticipation of community membership connotes communal potential. Student perceptions about their communal potential stem from experiences with student peers in residences halls (Berger, 1997), in classrooms (Tinto, 1997, 2000), and in student peer groups (Newcomb, 1966). The more a student perceives the potential for community on campus, the greater the student's level of social integration.

Braxton and Hirschy (2004) derived the construct of communal potential from three sets of research findings. First, Berger

(1997) reports that three aspects of community in residence halls—identity, solidarity, and interaction—wield a positive effect on student social integration. Second, the social approach and social avoidance behaviors students employ to cope with stress also affect social integration (Eaton and Bean, 1995). Specifically, formal and informal social approach behaviors foster social integration, while social avoidance behaviors impede the social integration of students who engage in such behaviors. Third, students who receive social support from their college student peers also experience a sense of social integration (Berger and Milem, 1999; Milem and Berger, 1997).

Institutional Integrity

This posited antecedent of social integration pertains to the degree of congruency between the espoused mission and goals of a college or university and the actions of its administrators, faculty, and staff (Braxton and Hirschy, 2004; Braxton, Hirschy, and McClendon, 2004). Put differently, institutional integrity manifests itself when a college or university remains true to its espoused mission and goals. The more a student perceives that the institution exhibits institutional integrity, the greater the student's level of social integration. Like commitment of the institution to student welfare, institutional integrity also reflects the culture of a college or university given that institutional integrity pertains to the actions, decisions, and communications of organizational members.

Two research findings provided the basis for the generation of this construct by Braxton and Hirschy (2004). They assert that institutional integrity manifests itself in policies and rules that are administered in a fair manner (Braxton and Hirschy, 2004). Specifically, Berger and Braxton (1998) found that fairness in the administration of institutional policies and rules positively influences student social integration. Institutional integrity also reveals itself in the extent to which student expectations for college get fulfilled. Students who experience the fulfillment of their expectations for college also experience a positive degree of social integration (Helland, Stallings, and Braxton, 2001–2002). Admissions publications and information that accurately portrays the institution to prospective students, for example, contribute to their sense of fulfillment of expectations for college.

Proactive Social Adjustment

The first year of college presents many social challenges to students. Social interactions place demands and pressures on students (Braxton, Hirschy, and McClendon, 2004). Proactive social adjustment entails the recognition by students that they need to adjust to such social interactions in a proactive manner. Proactive student actions include participating in orientation programs for first-year students. Orientation programs give students opportunities to learn the norms, attitudes, values, and behaviors needed to gain membership in the social communities of the focal college or university (Braxton, Hirschy, and McClendon, 2004). Proactive social adjustment also involves the strategies students use to cope with stress they experience. Students who view stress in a positive way by using a coping strategy termed "positive reinterpretation and growth" demonstrate proactive social adjustment (Carver, Scheier, and Weintraub, 1989). Bray, Braxton, and Sullivan (1999) found that first-year student use of this coping strategy positively influenced their degree of social integration in a residential university. The greater the student's use of proactive adjustment strategies, the greater the student's level of social integration.

Braxton, Hirschy, and McClendon (2004) formed this construct from several research findings. Specifically, psychological maturity wields a positive influence on student social integration (Miller, 1994). Heath (1980) asserts that maturity enables individuals to adapt by "creating an optimal relation between adjusting to the demands of one's environment and fulfilling one's own needs and exercising one's fullest ranges of talents" (p. 396). As levels of psychological maturity increase, first-year students are better equipped to meet the social challenges they typically encounter. Proactive social adjustment also emerges from the finding that the need for social affiliation promotes the social integration of students (Pascarella and Chapman, 1983).

Anticipatory socialization is the process by which nonmembers seek to emulate the attitudes, values, and behaviors of the group to which they seek membership (Merton, 1968). Braxton and Hirschy (2004) point to the finding that attending a two-day orientation program for first-year students positively affects the social integration of students (Pascarella, Terenzini, and Wolfe, 1986) and provides some support for the role of anticipatory socialization as a proactive social adjustment strategy. Orientation programs enable students to learn the behaviors, values, and attitudes needed to establish membership in the campus community.

The strategies students use to cope with stress also provided Braxton and Hirschy (2004) with a basis for the conceptualization of the construct of proactive social adjustment. More specifically, the coping strategy of positive reinterpretation and growth wields a positive influence on student social integration in a residential university (Bray, Braxton, and Sullivan, 1999). Positive reinterpretation and growth refers to individual efforts to see the source of stress in a positive way (Carver, Scheier, and Weintraub, 1989).

Psychosocial Engagement

This antecedent of social integration refers to the amount of psychological energy students invest in their social interactions with peers and in their participation in extracurricular activities (Braxton, Hirschy, and McClendon, 2004). Engagement recognizes that aspects of collegiate social life require a considerable amount of time and a considerable investment of psychological energy by college students. Varying degrees of psychosocial engagement in campus social life equip students with experiences to gauge their own level of social integration (Braxton et al., 2004). Thus, the greater the level of psychological energy that a student invests in various social interactions at their college or university, the greater the student's degree of social integration.

Braxton, Hirschy, and McClendon (2004) induced this construct from a pattern of several research findings. First, students in their first year who participate in college social activities such as dating and participating in fraternity and sorority social activities during the spring tend to experience greater levels of social integration (Milem and Berger, 1997). Second, students who exhibit no academic involvement (e.g., miss classes, fail to complete course work on time) during the spring semester experience lower degrees of social integration (Berger and Milem, 1999; Milem and Berger, 1997). Third, participation in extracurricular activities facilitates student social integration in a residential university, because students view extracurricular activities as a means to link themselves with the college environment and to provide themselves with opportunities to meet peers and develop friendships (Christie and Dinham, 1991).

In addition to these three research findings, Braxton, Hirschy, and McClendon (2004) point to the finding that approach behaviors used by individuals to cope with stress also influence student social integration since social approach behaviors require the investment of psychological energy. To elaborate, informal and formal social approach behaviors positively affect social integration (Eaton and Bean, 1995). Informal social approach behaviors involve student social choices and interactions (e.g., attending informal parties with friends), whereas formal social approach behaviors refer to a student's level of participation in campus leadership and formal social structures (e.g., holding office in a campus organization).

Psychosocial engagement parallels Astin's (1984) notion of involvement as it pertains to the amount of physical and psychological energy students invest in the academic experience. Like Braxton, Hirschy, and McClendon (2004), we chose to label the factor psychosocial engagement, as Astin viewed involvement, as taking the form of academic involvement, athletic involvement, involvement with faculty, involvement with student government, and involvement in research (Astin, 1977). In contrast, psychosocial engagement constitutes a more specific form of involvement rather than the more global form posited by Astin (1977).

Narrative Form of the Revised Theory

Like Tinto (1975), we view the process of student persistence at residential colleges and universities as a longitudinal process, as Figure 5.1 indicates. Also like Tinto (1993, p. 112), we view this theory as explaining the process of student persistence in a given college or university rather than as a systems model. Figure 5.1 graphically depicts this theory. We express the theory in narrative form in the paragraphs that follow.

Student entry characteristics shape the student's initial commitment to the goal of attaining a degree (GC-1) and the student's initial commitment to the institution (IC-1) (Braxton and Hirschy, 2005; Braxton, Hirschy, and McClendon, 2004). Entry characteristics include the student's gender, racial or ethnic background, socioeconomic status, academic ability, high school academic preparation, parental education, and the ability to pay for college. The student's initial commitment to the institution (IC-1), in turn, influences the student's perceptions of the institution's commitment to the welfare of students, the integrity of the institution, and the potential for social community with peers (communal potential). The level of the student's initial commitment to the institution also wields an influence on the level of the student's proactive social adjustment and degree of psychosocial engagement. The greater the student's level of initial commitment to the institution (IC-1), the more favorable their perceptions of commitment of the institution to the welfare of its

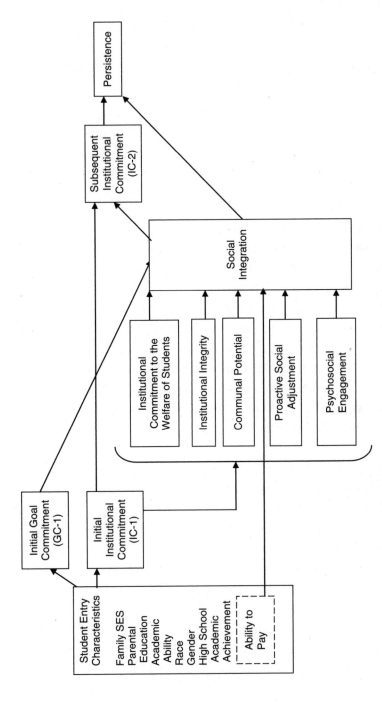

Figure 5.1 Revised theory for student persistence in residential colleges and universities.

Source: Adapted from Braxton, Hirschy, and McClendon, 2004.

students, institutional integrity, and communal potential. Likewise, the greater the student's level of initial commitment to the institution (IC-1), the greater the student's levels of proactive social adjustment and psychosocial engagement (Braxton and Hirschy, 2005).

Initial institutional commitment (IC-1) and initial goal commitment (GC-1) also positively influence social integration. Students at residential institutions who display high levels of commitment to earn a college degree are more likely to immerse themselves in the social realm of the institution with other students. Thus, the higher the student's initial commitment to attain a degree (GC-1), the greater the student's level of social integration (Braxton and Hirschy, 2005).

Both social integration and a student's initial commitment to the institution affect the student's subsequent institutional commitment (IC-2). The greater the student's level of initial commitment to the college or university, the greater the level of subsequent commitment to the institution. Likewise, the greater the student's degree of social integration, the greater the student's level of subsequent commitment to the college or university. In turn, the greater the level of subsequent commitment to the institution, the more likely the student will persist in college. Because of its central role in residential colleges and universities, social integration has a direct effect on student persistence.

Because of the centrality of social integration and subsequent institutional commitment to this revised theory, we focus our attention in this volume on the empirical testing of propositions that pertain to these two core aspects posited to influence student persistence in residential college and universities. The formulations of this theory yield eight pertinent propositions amenable to empirical treatment. These eight propositions are as follows:

1. The greater the student's belief that they have the ability to pay for the cost of attending the chosen college or university, the greater the student's degree of social integration.

2. The more a student perceives that the institution is committed to the welfare of its students, the greater the student's level of social integration.

3. The more a student perceives the potential for community on campus, the greater the student's level of social integration.

4. The more a student perceives that the institution exhibits institutional integrity, the greater the student's level of social integration.

5. The greater the student's use of proactive adjustment strategies, the greater the student's level of social integration.

6. The greater the level of psychological energy that a student invests in various social interactions at their college or university, the greater the student's degree of social integration.

7. The greater the student's degree of social integration, the greater their level of subsequent commitment to the college or university.

8. The greater the level of subsequent commitment to the institution, the more likely the student persists in college.

In the next section of this chapter, we describe how we use analytical cascading to extend Tinto's theory in residential institutions. In Chapter 1, we described the process of analytical cascading that we developed for use in this book.

Analytical Cascading: Extensions of the Theory of Student Persistence in Residential Colleges and Universities

Analytical cascading entails the empirical identification of influences on theoretically based factors found to shape student persistence decisions both in residential colleges and universities and in commuter colleges. As we stated in Chapter 1, the findings that emerge from analytical cascading serve two purposes. The generation of recommendations for institutional practice constitutes one purpose. We contend that recommendations for levers of institutional action or recommendations for institutional policy and practice designed for residential colleges and universities to improve their rates of student retention should rest on a rock-bed of findings derived from empirical research. The possible revision or refinement of the revised theory of student persistence in residential colleges and universities constitutes the second reason for our use of the process of analytical cascading. We assert that research findings should provide the foundation for any revision or refinement of the theory of student persistence in residential colleges and universities that we tested for this book.

As specified in Chapters 3 and 8, our test of the revised theory of residential colleges and universities resulted in the demarcation of three antecedents of social integration that positively influence social integration in a statistically significant manner. Psychosocial engagement, commitment of the institution to student welfare, and institutional integrity constitute these three antecedents of social integration. In this section, we present possible sources of influence on each of these antecedents of social integration, rationales for their possible influence, and their measurement. In Chapter 7, we present the operational definitions of these possible sources of influence.

Possible Sources of Influence on Psychosocial Engagement

Through an extension of the theory of student persistence in residential colleges and universities and previous research, we identify six possible forces that influence varying degrees of student psychosocial engagement: ability to pay, cultural capital, fall orientation programs, proactive social adjustment, communal potential, and sense of community in residence halls. We describe these six possible forces in the following paragraphs.

Ability to Pay

The revised theory of student persistence in residential colleges and universities viewed ability to pay as an antecedent of social integration. Our subsequent test of this theory failed to support this contention (see Chapter 8). However, ability to pay may instead function as a source of influence on psychosocial engagement. As stated previously in this chapter, Cabrera, Stampen, and Hansen (1990) assert that ability to pay tends to reduce barriers to student participation in the social communities of their college or university because of the lower salience of their financial concerns about paying for college. As a consequence, students with less concern about their ability to finance their college education may expend the necessary psychological energy to become psychosocially engaged.

Cultural Capital

French sociologist Pierre Bourdieu's (1973, 1977, 1986, 1990, 1994) theoretical formulations regarding the process of social reproduction advanced the concept of capital, including cultural capital, to describe the reproduction of existing social class structure. His formulations seek to explain the unequal social opportunities and educational achievement of children from differing social strata (1977). Like forms of material wealth (i.e., economic capital), children inherit, or receive, cultural as well as social capital from their parents in the form of credentials, cultural knowledge, mannerisms, attitudes, and preferences that differentiate one class from another, which can in turn be invested, or exchanged, for social gain. Bourdieu (1977) defines cultural capital as the educational attainment of one's parents (and grandparents), and as involvement in cultural activities, such as reading books, and attending concerts, plays, and museums (Bourdieu and Boltanski, 1981).

Berger (2000) extends Bourdieu's (1973, 1977) concept of cultural capital to college student departure, as Berger asserts that college student persistence is a part of the larger social reproduction process. He contends that college students hold varying levels of cultural capital and that "students with higher levels of cultural capital are more likely to persist, across all types of institution, than are students with less access to cultural capital" (Berger, p. 114). Berger further postulates that "students with higher levels of cultural capital are more likely to become integrated into the social systems of institutions with correspondingly high levels of organizational cultural capital" (p. 116).

We concur with Berger's proposition that cultural capital plays in role in the social integration of college students. However, cultural capital may also play a direct role in influencing the psychosocial engagement of first-year full-time students in residential colleges and universities (Hartley, Hirschy, and Braxton, 2006). To elaborate, the possession of cultural capital provides students with self-esteem and social self-confidence that enables them to participate fully in a wide range of extracurricular activities and social interactions with peers. Their levels of cultural capital equip them with cultural knowledge, mannerisms, and attitudes that create a high level of social comfort in such social exchanges. Such social exchanges require the investment of psychological energy. Thus, students with higher levels of cultural capital will more likely expend greater degrees of psychological energy than their peers with lower levels of cultural capital.

Fall First-Year Student Orientation

Orientation programs for incoming first-year students strive to familiarize students with the academic and social life at the institution. Put differently, the preparation of students for success in the academic and social environments of their institution forms the underlying intent of first-year orientation programs. Topics include administrative and academic regulations, student organizations and activities, student services, and academic program design (Pascarella, Terenzini, and Wolfe, 1986). Research suggests that student attendance at a college orientation plays an indirect role in student persistence at a residential college (Pascarella et al.,

1986). Students who feel that the first-year orientation program adequately prepared them for success in their institution's social environment may feel more inclined to invest the psychological energy necessary to make friends and participate in various extracurricular activities (Braxton, Hirschy, and McClendon, 2004).

Proactive Social Adjustment

We previously described the role of proactive social adjustment as an antecedent of social integration for students in residential colleges and universities. However, our test of the revised theory of student persistence in residential colleges and universities failed to confirm the contention by Braxton, Hirschy, and McClendon (2004) that the use of proactive adjustment strategies by students wields a positive influence on their degree of social integration (see Chapter 8).

Whereas proactive social adjustment may not directly influence social integration, it may positively affect the psychosocial engagement of college students. As previously stated, students face many social challenges during their first year of college that may place demands and pressures on them (Braxton, Hirschy, and McClendon, 2004). Students who acknowledge the need to respond to social interactions in a proactive manner may employ strategies to cope with the stress they experience. Students who view stress in a positive way by using a coping strategy of positive reinterpretation and growth (Carver, Scheier, and Weintraub, 1989) demonstrate proactive social adjustment. Similarly, students who cope with stress through the coping strategy of positive reinterpretation and growth may possess the necessary psychological energy to engage in a wide range of extracurricular activities and social interactions with peers.

Communal Potential

As described, communal potential pertains to the extent to which students perceive that a subgroup of students exits within the various communities of their college or university that holds values, be-liefs, and goals similar to their own (Braxton and Hirschy, 2004; Braxton, Hirschy, and McClendon, 2004). Thus, communal po-tential connotes student anticipation of community membership.

Braxton, Hirschy, and McClendon (2004) posit that communal potential works as an antecedent of social integration. More specifically, they hypothesize that the more a student perceives the potential for community on campus, the greater the student's level of social integration. Our test of the revised theory of student per-sistence in residential colleges and universities failed to yield affir-mation of this proposition (see Chapter 8). However, we contend that communal potential may instead directly and positively in-fluence the level of psychosocial engagement of first-year college students in residential colleges and universities.

To elaborate, experiences with student peers in residences halls (Berger, 1997), the classroom (Tinto, 1997, 2000), and student peer groups (Newcomb, 1966) shape the perceptions that students form regarding their potential for community. The more students perceive that a subgroup of students exists within the various communi-ties of their college or university that holds values, beliefs, and goals similar to their own, the greater their level of psychosocial engagement. A willingness to expend the needed psychological energy to participate in a wide range of extracurricular activities and social interactions with peers stems from the likelihood of communal potential.

Sense of Community in Residence Halls

College and university residence halls constitute one of the primary social communities of a residential college or university (Berger, 1997). Tinto (1993) asserts that residence halls help "newcomers to find an early physical, social, and academic anchor during the transi-tion to college life" (p. 125). As a consequence, a sense of commu-nity in residence halls looms important for first-time students.

Berger (1997) empirically derived three dimensions of a sense of community in residence halls: identity, solidarity, and interaction. Identity pertains to the degree to which students view themselves as members of a community in their residence hall. They "identify with and attach importance to the community in their living unit" (p. 445). Berger also asserts that the extent to which students in residence halls share similar beliefs, goals, and an eagerness to work together to solve problems denotes the dimension of solidarity in residence halls. Interaction concerns the frequency and intensity of face-to-face interactions among the residents of a residence hall. (Berger, 1997). Each of these three dimensions pertains to a sense of community at the level of the floor of a residence hall.

All three of these dimensions of community in residence halls positively affect the relationships first-year students have with their peers in a highly selective private residential research oriented university (Berger, 1997). By extension, we assert herein that each of these three dimensions of community—identity, solidarity, and interaction—in residence halls will exert a positive influence on the psychosocial engagement of first-year, full-time students in residential colleges and universities.

Possible Sources of Influence on Commitment of the Institution to Student Welfare

The revised theory of student persistence in residential colleges and universities along with supporting research point to 13 forces that may influence student perceptions of the commitment of their college or university to the welfare of its students. These possible forces involve value patterns and behaviors of organizational agents such as administrators, faculty, staff, and clerical workers of individual colleges and universities. These possible forces include academic advising (Voorhees, 1990); first-year student orientation (Pascarella, Terenzini, and Wolfe,1986; Dunphy, Miller, Woodruff, and Nelson, 1987; Fidler and Hunter, 1989); organizational behaviors involving communication, justice, and participation in decision making (Bean, 1980, 1983; Braxton and Brier, 1989; Berger and Braxton, 1998; Braxton, Hirschy, and McClendon, 2004); student perceptions of prejudice and racial discrimination at their institution (Cabrera et al., 1999); faculty interest in students, good teaching, and faculty active learning practices (Braxton, Milem, and Sullivan, 2000; Braxton, Jones, Hirschy, and Hartley, 2008); and student observations of faculty violations of teaching norms (Braxton and Bayer, 1999). With the exception of faculty active learning practices (Braxton, Jones, Hirschy, and Hartley, 2008), little or no empirical research exists that addresses the influence of these forces directly on the commitment of the institution to student welfare.

Academic Advising

At its best, academic advising addresses the personal, intellectual, social, vocational, and psychological needs of students (Voorhees, 1990). Thus, academic advising performed well communicates to students that their college or university values them and has an abiding concern for their growth and development. Accordingly, satisfaction with academic advising may positively affect student perceptions of the commitment of their college or university to the welfare of its students.

Fall First-Year Student Orientation

Orientation programs for incoming first-year students aim to familiarize students with the academic and social life at the institution. As noted, topics include administrative and academic regulations, student organizations and activities, student services, and academic program design. Research by Pascarella, Terenzini, and Wolfe (1986) suggests that student attendance at a college orientation plays an indirect role in student persistence at a residential college.

Favorable student opinions about the success of orientation pro-grams preparing them for the academic environment may likewise shape positive perceptions of students regarding the commitment of their college or university to student welfare. Such positive per-ceptions emanate from student views that their college or univer-sity values them and wants them to grow and develop.

Organizational Behavior

Organizational behavior pertains to the actions of faculty, admin-istrators, staff, and clerical workers at a given college or university (Berger, 2001–2002). Communication, fairness, and participation in decision making constitute forms of organizational behavior empirically linked to student persistence (Bean, 1980, 1983; Braxton and Brier, 1989; Berger and Braxton, 1998). Students ob-serve actions involving communication of rules and requirements, fairness in the administration of rules and requirements, and the provision of opportunities to participate in making decisions re-garding matters of importance to students. If students feel well informed about rules and requirements pertinent to student life, then they perceive that their institution places a high value on students. If students feel that rules and regulations pertinent to them are fairly administered, then they come to perceive that their institution treats students in an equitable way. Students also feel highly valued if given the opportunity to participate in decisions regarding matters pertinent to them. Given these formulations, we might expect that communication, fairness, and participation in decision making stand as forces of influence on student perceptions of the commitment of their college or university to the welfare of its students.

Student Perceptions of Prejudice and Racial Discrimination

Both white and African American students can perceive a cli-mate of racial discrimination and prejudice on their campus (Cabrera et al., 1999). However, the influence of such a perception on student assessments of their degree of academic and intellectual development differs between white and African American students. An indirect negative influence occurs for white students, whereas a direct negative effect occurs for African American students (Cabrera et al., 1999).

As stated, an abiding concern of the growth and development of its students represents one dimension of an institution's commitment to the welfare of its students. The academic and intellectual development of students provides a palpable index of the concern of a college or university for the growth and development of its students. Given that student perceptions of campus prejudice and racial discrimination negatively affect the growth and development of students (Cabrera et al., 1999), we might anticipate that such negative student perceptions will also wield a negative influence on student perceptions of the commitment of their institution to the welfare of its students.

Faculty Interest in Students and Good Teaching

Faculty members who evince a genuine interest in students contribute to the formation of student perceptions of the degree to which their college or university embraces an abiding concern for their growth and development. Likewise, a similar perception springs from taking courses from faculty who students view as outstanding teachers who are genuinely interested in teaching. Both faculty interest in students and good teaching also communicate the high value placed on students by their college or university. Taken together, these assertions lead to the expectation that both faculty interest in students and good teaching positively influence student perceptions of the commitment of their college or university to the welfare of its students.

Faculty Active Learning Practices

Active learning, an important pedagogical practice, entails any class activity that "involves students doing things and thinking about the things that they are doing" (Bonwell and Eison, 1991,

p. 2). Active learning includes discussion, the types of questions faculty ask students in class, role playing, cooperative learning, debates, and the types of questions faculty ask on examinations (Braxton, Milem, and Sullivan, 2000). Research demonstrates that the more frequently students observe faculty using active learning practices in their courses, the more they perceive that their college or university holds a commitment to the welfare of its students (Braxton, Jones, Hirschy, and Hartley, 2008).

Faculty Violations of Teaching Norms

Norms are prescribed or proscribed patterns of behavior (Merton, 1973). Because of the high degree of autonomy faculty hold in their teaching, norms safeguard the welfare of students as clients of teaching role performance, according to Braxton and Bayer (1999), who assert that seven inviolable norms (behaviors academics believe warrant severe sanctions) make up the normative structure of undergraduate college teaching.

Of these seven inviolable norms, six concern students as clients of undergraduate teaching. Of these six student-focused normative patterns, four entail proscribed behaviors that involve disrespect for students as individuals or the inequitable treatment of students by faculty: condescending negativism, personal disregard, moral turpitude, and particularistic grading. We expect that student observations of faculty violations of these four normative patterns wield a negative influence on student perceptions of the commitment of their college or university to student welfare.

To elaborate, condescending negativism rebukes the treatment of both students and colleagues in a condescending and demeaning way (Braxton and Bayer, 1999). Faculty violations of this norm display a lack of respect for students as individuals. Given that moral turpitude prohibits depraved, unprincipled acts by faculty, such as having a sexual relationship with a student, students who observe faculty violations of this normative pattern feel that equal consideration of all students in the class is impossible

(Braxton and Bayer, 1999). Violations of the norm of moral turpitude also convey a lack of respect for students as individuals (Svinicki, 1994). Since particularistic grading reproves the uneven or preferential treatment of students in the awarding of grades, faculty violations of this norm communicate to students that faculty favors some students over others (Braxton and Bayer, 1999). A lack of respect for students as individuals (Braxton and Bayer, 1999) emanates from faculty violations of the norm of personal disregard, as this normative orientation censures disrespect for the needs and sensitivities of students.

Possible Sources of Influence on Institutional Integrity

We turn our attention to the delineation of possible forces that influence student perceptions of the presence of institutional integrity at their residential college or university. As stated elsewhere in this chapter, institutional integrity constitutes an organizational characteristic that epitomizes the culture of a college or university. These possible forces include faculty interest in students, student reports of good teaching, the fulfillment of academic and social expectations for college, and student perceptions of prejudice and racial discrimination. With the exception of the fulfillment of academic and social expectations for college, we previously discussed these possible forces. However, in this section we turn our attention to the extension of the theory of student persistence in residential colleges and universities and the provision of literature-based rationales for these factors as possible sources of influence on student perceptions of the integrity of the college or university.

Faculty Interest in Students and Reports of Good Teaching

In Chapter 7, we describe the sample of residential colleges and universities we used to test the revised theory of student persistence in residential colleges and universities and to conduct our process of analytical cascading. Given that the colleges and universities in our sample espouse teaching as their primary mission, we might anticipate that students in such residential colleges and universities will expect their faculty to possess a genuine interest in students. We might also envisage students expecting good teaching from their professors. Accordingly, the more students perceive that faculty at their institution evince an interest in students, and the more they view faculty as good teachers, the stronger their beliefs about the institutional integrity of their college or university.

Fulfillment of Expectations for College

Student expectations for college develop from the images that they hold of the colleges and universities to which they make application. Institutional images include such attributes as the expected benefits and outcomes of attending a particular college or university, the perceived characteristics of the student body, and the perceived status of the institution within the hierarchy of colleges and universities (Clark et al., 1972). Students form the images of different colleges and universities through various information-gathering activities used during the college choice process. Information-gathering activities include obtaining information from colleges and universities, making campus visits, talking with admissions counselors, and speaking with college alumni (Hossler, Schmit, and Vesper, 1999). The accuracy of images developed through such information-gathering activities depends on consistency and truthfulness in the depiction of the academic and social life of students at a given college or university (Helland, Stallings, and Braxton, 2001–2002).

Institutional images developed through such information-gathering activities play a significant role in the student's decision to attend a particular college or university (Cook and Zallocco, 1983). Accordingly, students enter college with expectations for their college or university based on the images formed through the various information-gathering activities. If their expectations for college based on such images go unfulfilled, then first-year students will view their college or university as not exhibiting institutional integrity.

Student Perceptions of Prejudice and Racial Discrimination

As indicated in Chapter 7, the residential colleges and universities included in our sample also define themselves as religiously affiliated. Character development and moral development describe the cultures of religiously affiliated institutions (DeJong, 1992). Acts of prejudice and racial discrimination violate the cultural values embraced by such colleges and universities. Accordingly, the more students perceive that prejudice and racial discrimination exist at their college or university, the more negatively they view the institutional integrity at their college or university. Students perceive prejudice and racial discrimination as incongruent with the espoused mission of a religiously affiliated institution of higher education.

Chapter Summary

In this chapter, we presented a revision of Tinto's Interactionalist Theory to account for student persistence in residential colleges and universities. For our process of analytical cascading, described in Chapter 1, we also presented extensions of this theory to identify possible sources of influence on those core concepts of this theory found to be statistically significant, which we initially identified in Chapter 3 through our test of this theory. Because Tinto's Interactionalist Theory lacks explanatory power in commuter colleges and universities, the next chapter of this volume presents a theory to explain student persistence in commuter institutions.

6

A Theory of Student Persistence in Commuter Colleges and Universities

In this chapter, we describe the theory of student persistence in commuter colleges and universities constructed by Braxton, Hirschy, and McClendon (2004). In Chapter 9, we describe the results of our empirical test of this theory. Two factors warrant a separate theory of student persistence in commuter institutions. The conclusion of Braxton, Sullivan, and Johnson (1997) that Tinto's theory (1975) lacks explanatory power in commuter colleges and universities, coupled with the role of the external environment and the characteristics of social communities in commuter colleges and universities as previously delineated, constitute these two warranting factors.

The Theory and Its Derivation

The findings of research on student departure conducted in two- and four-year commuter colleges and universities provide the foundation for the generation of the formulations of this theory (Braxton, Hirschy, and McClendon, 2004). Some relevant research findings derived from studies in unspecified types of four-year colleges and universities also provide a basis for this theory. From these various research findings, which we note where germane, Braxton et al. (2004) constructed this theory using the previously delineated process of inductive theory construction. Because the persistence process for students enrolled in degree programs in two-year colleges resembles that of students in four-year colleges and universities, this theory applies to student persistence in both two-year and four-year commuter institutions. However, some of the formulations described herein stand as revisions to the 2004 statement of this theory advanced by Braxton, Hirschy, and McClendon. We note these revisions as pertinent.

The components of this theory of student departure in commuter institutions consist of student entry characteristics, the external environment, the campus environment, student academic and intellectual development, subsequent institutional commitment, and student persistence in the college or university. Figure 6.1 shows the longitudinal nature of the relationships among these components and their accompanying constructs. This figure includes the revisions we made to this theory presented in this chapter.

Student Entry Characteristics

Student entry characteristics play an important part in the persistence decisions of students enrolled in commuter colleges and universities. Some entry characteristics (e.g., academic ability and high school academic achievement) affect the student's initial level of commitment to the chosen college or university (Tinto, 1975, 1993; Braxton, Sullivan, and Johnson, 1997). The initial level of commitment to the institution also takes the form of an entry characteristic. This initial level of commitment also influences the student's level of commitment to the institution that develops as a result of attending the chosen institution (Tinto, 1975, 1993; Braxton, Sullivan, and Johnson, 1997).

Other student entry characteristics, such as students' motivation to attend college, their need for control, their sense of self-efficacy, their empathy, their need for social affiliation, their parents' educational level, and their engagement in anticipatory socialization prior to college entrance, emanate from the characteristics of the external environment and the campus

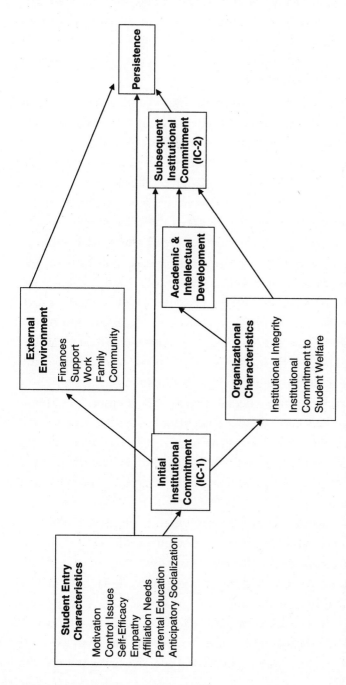

Figure 6.1 Theory of student persistence in commuter colleges and universities.

Source: Revision of Braxton, Hirschy, and McClendon (2004).

environment of commuter colleges and universities. Student entry characteristics directly influence student departure decisions in this institutional setting.

The External Environment

Entry characteristics also shape the way students perceive their experiences with the external environment. For example, the personality trait of empathy influences student perceptions of the demands of the external environment that impact their daily lives. Commuter students frequently have obligations distinct from attending college. For some, these obligations include work and family (Tinto, 1993). Conflicts between the commitments of both work and attending college may negatively affect the families of commuter students. Departure from college may result for those students aware of the negative effects of their college attendance on significant others. Students with the personality trait of empathy tend to be more likely to depart from commuter colleges and universities (Zhang and RiCharde, 1998). Thus, the greater the student's awareness of the effects of their actions and decisions on other people, the greater the student's likelihood of departure from college.

As a consequence, encouragement and support for attending college becomes crucial. Students who receive support and encouragement to attend college from significant others are less likely to depart (Schwartz, 1990; Mutter, 1992; Okun, Benin, and Brandt-Williams, 1996; Cabrera, Nora, Terenzini, Pascarella, and Hagedorn, 1999; Pike, Schroeder, and Berry, 1997). Thus, the greater the support the student receives from significant others for their college attendance, the greater their likelihood of their persistence in a commuter college or university.

The negative effects on families due to work while attending college diminishes if the financial costs of attending college are minimized. In turn, support and encouragement to attend college from significant others also increases if the financial costs of attending college are minimized. Thus, the lower the costs of college attendance incurred by the student, the greater their likelihood of persisting in college (St. John and Starkey, 1995).

The Campus Environment

In addition to the aspects of the campus environment shaped by student characteristics, organizational characteristics make up an additional dimension of the campus environment of commuter colleges and universities.

Student Characteristics and the Campus Environment

Student characteristics contribute to the shaping of the institutional environments—academic and social—of colleges and universities (Pascarella and Terenzini, 1991; Holland, 1997; Clark, 1972). Accordingly, the characteristics of students who commute to college determine to a large extent the environments of commuter colleges and universities. These characteristics also affect student perceptions of their experiences with the institutional environment of the commuter college or university.

Commuter students spend a very limited amount of time on the campus of a commuter college or university, and the time spent on campus typically involves attending class and meeting degree requirements (Tinto, 1993). Students hurry to attend their classes and hurry to leave the campus to go to work or to go home. Such time demands minimize the social involvement of commuting students. These forms of comings and goings create a "buzzing confusion." The order that exists comes from the daily schedule of classes meeting at their appointed times.

Student adjustment to the buzzing confusion that characterizes the campus environment of the commuter institution requires student motivation to make steady progress toward graduation and to graduate from college. According to Hagedorn, Maxwell, and Hampton (2001–2002), motivation to graduate from college exerts a positive influence on student persistence. Motivation to make steady progress toward college completion also positively impacts student retention (Hagedorn, Maxwell, and Hampton, 2001). Thus, motivation to graduate from college wields a positive influence on student persistence.

Given the role of external forces and the buzzing confusion that characterizes the commuter institution, students also need to believe that attending college will result in academic success and graduation. Put differently, commuter students must have high levels of self-efficacy, another entry student characteristic. Research tends to show that self-efficacy exerts a positive influence on student persistence (Zhang and RiCharde, 1998). Hence, the stronger a student's belief that they can achieve a desired outcome through their own efforts, the greater the student's likelihood of persistence in a commuter college or university.

The need for control constitutes another influential entry student characteristic that springs from the buzzing confusion of the campus environment of the commuter institution. This need relates to personal attributes such as locus of control and judging. Locus of control exerts a direct influence on student persistence, since students who attribute events or outcomes to their own efforts are more likely to depart than are students who attribute events to luck or fate (Bers, 1985). Stated another way, students with an internal locus of control are more likely to depart than students who hold an external locus of control. Judging also exerts a negative influence on the retention of students (Zhang and RiCharde, 1998). Judging reflects an individual's inclination to control the world through deliberate and planned decision making in contrast to a more flexible orientation (Zhang and RiCharde, 1998).

Those students with a high need for order may be especially challenged by the need to balance academic work with the demands of family and work responsibilities. Students who require order in their daily lives and have a need for control over events in their lives may experience difficulty adjusting to the confusing nature of the institutional environment. As a consequence, the greater a student's need for control and order in their daily life, the lower the student's likelihood of persistence.

In addition to the buzzing confusion that depicts the campus environment of the commuter institution, the lack of well-defined and ill-structured student social communities poses difficulties to students with a need for social affiliation. Students with such a need find this need unfulfilled given that such students are friendly, like to participate in activities with others, and hold a group orientation (Stern, 1970). Research tends to indicate that affiliation needs directly and negatively affect student persistence in nonresidential institutional settings (Pascarella and Chapman, 1983). Thus, the greater the student's need for social affiliation, the lower their likelihood of persistence in a commuter college or university.

Parental educational level, a student entry characteristic, also influences the meanings students attach to the poorly formed social communities of commuter colleges and universities. Student images of the ideal characteristics of colleges and universities come from a variety of sources, such as parents, teachers, high school college counselors, students, movies, television, and the media. "Residentiality" represents one element of the image of a college or university (Kamens, 1977). Residentiality depicts a symbolic role of higher education involving the physical and social isolation of students from their life prior to attending college (Kamens, 1977). The ill-defined structure of the social communities of the commuter institution provides a striking contrast to this notion of residentiality. Parents who attended college are more likely to hold residentiality as an important characteristic of a college or university. These formulations provide an explanation for findings by Halpin (1990) and Hagedorn, Maxwell, and Hampton (2001). Halpin found that students with fathers having higher levels of education are more likely to depart from a commuter college. Moreover, Hagedorn, Maxwell, and Hampton (2001) observed that parental educational level negatively affects student persistence through the first and second semesters of attendance. They used a combined measure of the educational level of the mother and the father. As a consequence, as parental educational level increases, the likelihood of student persistence in a commuter college or university decreases.

Students who engage in anticipatory socialization behaviors before enrolling in a commuter institution are also more likely to depart (Nora, Attinasi, and Matonak, 1990). Students who engage in such "getting ready behaviors" as forming early expectations for college and participating in pre-matriculation activities (Nora et al., 1990) learn that "residentiality" does not accurately depict day-to-day enrollment at a commuter institution. Consequently, the probability of student persistence in a commuter college or university decreases for students who engage in anticipatory socialization prior to entering college.

Organizational Characteristics

Characteristics of the commuter college or university as an organization also play an important part in the student persistence process. Commitment of the institution to student welfare and institutional integrity encompass such organizational characteristics (Braxton, Hirschy, and McClendon, 2004). We defined these two organizational characteristics in Chapter 5 in our description of the revised theory of student persistence in residential colleges and universities.

Students who perceive through the actions of organizational agents—administrators, faculty, and staff—that commitment to the welfare of students represents an abiding concern of their college or university develop a stronger subsequent level of commitment to their institution. Likewise, the actions of administrators, faculty, and staff provide students with opportunities to appraise the extent to which their institution remains true to its mission and goals. Greater levels of subsequent institutional commitment develop in students who perceive that their college or university exhibits such institutional integrity. Therefore, the more a student perceives that their college or university is committed to the welfare of its students, the greater the student's degree of subsequent commitment to their college or university. Moreover, the more a student perceives that their college or university exhibits institutional integrity, the greater the student's degree of subsequent commitment to their college or university.

We include a last proposition in the formulations of this theory as six of the six tests of this proposition in commuter colleges and universities received positive affirmation (Braxton and Lee, 2005). This proposition takes the following form: the greater the student's degree of subsequent commitment to their college or university, the greater the student's likelihood of persistence in a commuter college or university.

Herein, we postulate that students' perceptions of the commitment of their institution to the welfare of students and institutional integrity also influence their academic and intellectual development in a positive way. In their statement of this theory by Braxton, Hirschy, and McClendon (2004), such a linkage was not delineated. If students perceive that their college or university is committed to their welfare and exhibits institutional integrity, students are more likely to engage themselves more fully in their course work and course learning. Put in propositional terms, the more a student perceives that their college or university is committed to the welfare of its students, the greater the student's degree of academic and intellectual development. Additionally, the more a student perceives that their college or university exhibits institutional integrity, the greater the student's degree of academic and intellectual development.

These two revisions place the organizational characteristics of commitment of the institution to student welfare and institutional integrity as antecedents of academic development. These revisions improve the logical coherence of the formulations of this theory. In addition to these two revisions, we also revise the 2004 statement of this theory by changing the name of the construct of academic integration to academic and intellectual development. The rationale for this change involves the face validity of the typical approaches to the measurement of this construct in research studies. These measures typically include student perceptions of their intellectual growth and development and estimates of their grade-point average (Braxton and Brier, 1989; Cabrera, Castaneda, Nora, and Hengstler, 1992; Pascarella, Duby, and Iverson, 1983; Pascarella and Terenzini, 1980; Pascarella and Terenzini, 1983; Terenzini, Pascarella, Theophilides, and Lorang, 1985). These measures provide face validity for the operationalization of academic and intellectual development and not academic integration (Braxton, Milem, and Sullivan, 2000). Academic integration refers to a student's perception of their congruence with attitudes and values of the academic communities of the institution and a perception that they are not intellectually isolated (Braxton and Lien, 2000).

To further improve the logical coherence of this theory, we make an additional revision to the 2004 theory by placing academic and intellectual development as an antecedent to subsequent institutional commitment. The greater the degree of academic and intellectual development perceived by a student, the greater their degree of subsequent commitment to commuter college or university. This relationship receives empirical affirmation in seven out of ten tests of it conducted in commuter institutions (Braxton and Lien, 2000).

A final revision to the 2004 theoretical statement entails the removal of the role of academic communities—learning communities and active learning—from the "Internal Campus Environment" of its formulations. We make this alteration in the spirit of parsimony, as this alteration reduces the number of constructs and propositions. Moreover, we have accounted for the important role that the academic experiences of commuter students play in student persistence by positing relationships between the two organizational characteristics—commitment of the institution to student welfare and institutional integrity—and academic and intellectual development on one hand and academic and intellectual development and subsequent institutional commit- ment on the other hand. Figure 6.1 reflects these various revisions.

Given the vital role that academic and intellectual development and subsequent institutional commitment play in student persis- tence in commuter colleges and universities, we devote attention to the empirical testing of those propositions that concern these two critical aspects to student persistence in commuter colleges and universities. We also concentrate attention on propositions that posit direct relationships with student persistence. However, we do not test all of these propositions, because measures of these constructs are unavailable in the data source used.

With the preceding provisos in place, our empirical treatment of this theory entails the testing of the following 11 propositions generated by the preceding theoretical formulations:

1. As parental educational level increases, the likelihood of stu- dent persistence in a commuter college or university decreases.
2. The higher the student's level of motivation to graduate from college, the greater their likelihood of persisting in a commut- er college or university.
3. The lower the costs of college attendance incurred by the stu- dent, the greater their likelihood of persisting in a commuter college or university.
4. The greater the support the student receives from significant others for their college attendance, the greater their likelihood of persistence in a commuter college or university.
5. The greater the student's need for social affiliation, the lower their likelihood of persistence in a commuter college or university.
6. The more a student perceives that their college or university is committed to the welfare of its students, the greater the stu- dent's degree of academic and intellectual development.
7. The more a student perceives that their college or university exhibits institutional integrity, the greater the student's degree of academic and intellectual development.

8. The more a student perceives that their college or university is committed to the welfare of its students, the greater the student's degree of subsequent commitment to their college or university.

9. The more a student perceives that their college or university exhibits institutional integrity, the greater the student's degree of subsequent commitment to their college or university.

10. The greater the degree of academic and intellectual development perceived by a student, the greater the student's degree of subsequent commitment to a commuter college or university.

11. The greater the student's degree of subsequent institutional commitment, the greater the likelihood of the student's persistence in a commuter college or university.

Analytical Cascading: Extensions of the Theory of Student Persistence in Commuter Colleges and Universities

As we stated in Chapter 1, the findings that emerge from analytical cascading serve two purposes. The generation of recommendations for institutional practice constitutes one purpose. We contend that recommendations for levers of institutional action, or recommendations for institutional policy and practice, designed for commuter colleges and universities to improve their rates of student retention should rest on a rock-bed of findings derived from empirical research. The possible revision or refinement of the theory of student persistence in commuter colleges and universities forms the second reason for our engagement in the process of analytical cascading. We assert that research findings should provide the foundation for any revision or refinement of the theory of student persistence in commuter colleges and universities that we tested in this book.

As indicated in Chapters 3 and 9, our test of the theory of student persistence in commuter colleges and universities delineated academic and intellectual development, commitment of the institution to student welfare, institutional integrity, and support of significant others as statistically significant indirect forces in the student persistence in commuter colleges and universities. Accordingly, we concentrate our process of analytical cascading on those factors that also influence each of these four core concepts. In the next chapter, we present the operational definitions of these possible sources of influence.

Next, we present possible sources of influence on each of these four central concepts to student persistence in commuter colleges and universities, rationales for their possible influence, and their measurement.

Possible Sources of Influence on Academic and Intellectual Development

Through an extension of the theory of student persistence in commuter colleges and universities and based on previous research, we posit that various curricular arrangements and classroom practices positively influence the academic and intellectual development of students in commuter colleges and universities. These four possible forces include participation in a learning community, faculty use of active learning practices, the use of good practices in undergraduate education, and faculty teaching skills. In the following paragraphs, we describe each of these four possible forces and their literature-based rationales.

Participation in a Learning Community

Small communities form around specific courses. In particular, learning communities, a curricular arrangement, contribute to the formation of a community of the classroom. Learning communities involve the block scheduling of courses so that the same group of students takes a set of courses together (Tinto, 1997, 1998, 2000). A theme typically underlies the set of courses. Participation in a learning community wields a positive influence on student persistence in a commuter college or university (Tinto, 1997). Such participation also contributes to a student's academic and intellectual development (Braxton, Hirschy, and McClendon, 2004). Accordingly, we hypothesize that student participation in a learning community contributes in a positive way to the academic and intellectual development of students enrolled in a commuter college or university (Braxton et al., 2004).

Faculty Use of Active Learning Practices

Active learning constitutes a pedagogical practice employed by faculty members. As indicated previously in this chapter, active learning refers to those class activities that engage students in thinking about the subject matter of a course (Bonwell and Eison, 1991). Active learning enhances student course learning (Pascarella and Terenzini, 2005; Anderson and Adams, 1992; Chickering and Gamson, 1987; Johnson, Johnson, and Smith, 1991; McKeachie, Pintrich, YiGuang, and Smith, 1986). Accordingly, we hypothesize that the more frequently students perceive that faculty members use active learning practices in their courses, the greater the degree of academic and intellectual development of the student.

Faculty Use of Good Practices in Undergraduate Education

Chickering and Gamson (1987) delineate seven principles of good practice in undergraduate education. A robust body of research shows that faculty adherence to these seven principles positively impacts student learning (Sorcinelli, 1991). Accordingly, we might expect that the academic and intellectual development of students also increases when faculty adhere to these principles in their courses. We focus on four of the seven principles as possible influential forces on academic and intellectual development: encouragement of student-faculty contact, encouragement of cooperation among students, provision of prompt feedback, and the communication of high expectations. Time on task and respecting diverse talents and ways of knowing are two of the remaining three principles of good practice that we did not include, given that we do not have available measures of these two principles. Active learning constitutes the third principle. We do not include it under this category of factors as we concentrate on active learning earlier in this chapter.

The encouragement of faculty-student contact entails frequent interaction between students and faculty both in and out of class (Chickering and Gamson, 1987). Another principle of good practice encourages cooperation among students given that the sharing of ideas among students and reacting to the ideas of other students exerts a positive effect their learning (Chickering and Gamson, 1987). Appropriate feedback on student performance on course assignments enables students to appraise their understanding of course content (Chickering and Gamson, 1987). The provision of prompt feedback constitutes another principle of good practice. The communication of high expectations stands as the last of the four principles of practice that we include. This particular principle entails setting high standards for students, but also expecting them to meet these standards (Chickering and Gamson, 1987).

Faculty Teaching Skills

The organization's faculty teaching skills and preparation and instructional clarity enhance student course learning (Pascarella and Terenzini, 1991, 2005). Hence, we posit that the more frequently students observe these teaching skills in their classes, the greater the students' perceived level of academic and intellectual development.

Additional Possible Sources of Influence

In addition to curricular arrangements and classroom practices, academic advising, first-year student orientation, faculty interest in students, and student perceptions of good teaching at their college or university constitute four additional possible forces that may wield an influence on the academic and intellectual development of students in commuter colleges and universities.

Academic Advising

Grites (1979) defines academic advising as "a decision-making process during which students realize their maximum educational potential through communication and information exchanges with an advisor" (p. 1). Based on this definition, we might expect that academic advising facilitates the academic and intellectual development of students because of its emphasis on the realization of the academic potential of students. Accordingly, we might expect that the stronger the student's degree of satisfaction with academic advising at their institution, the greater they perceive their academic and intellectual development.

First-Year Student Orientation

As previously stated in this chapter, orientation programs for incoming first-year students strive to inform students about the academic and social life at the institution. Orientation topics include administrative and academic regulations, student organizations and activities, student services, and academic program design (Pascarella, Terenzini, and Wolfe, 1986). If an orientation program adequately prepares students for success in the academic environment of their college or university, then we might also expect such students to experience academic and intellectual development as a result of such successful preparation. As a consequence, we posit that student perceptions of such preparation by their first-year orientation program positively affect the academic and intellectual development of students enrolled in commuter colleges and universities.

Faculty Interest in Students and Good Teaching

In their book How College Affects Students (1991), Pascarella and Terenzini contend that a supportive social psychological context is a necessary condition for institutional impact on college students. Student academic and intellectual development represent such an institutional impact. A strong faculty emphasis on teaching and student development constitutes one of the characteristics of such a social psychological context. Thus, student perceptions of their faculty as good teachers and as interested in students reflect a faculty emphasis on teaching and student development. As a consequence, we anticipate that student perceptions of faculty interest in teaching and student perceptions of good teaching by their faculty wield possible positive influences on student perceptions of their academic and intellectual development.

Possible Sources of Influence on Commitment of the Institution to Student Welfare

We regard sources of influence as student participation in a learning community, faculty use of active learning practices, faculty use of good practices in undergraduate education, faculty teaching skills, and student course learning as the underlying mechanisms for academic and intellectual development. Communication by central administrators, faculty, staff, and clerical workers of the high value placed on students as individuals and a concern for the growth and development of students constitute the underlying mechanisms of influence on student perceptions of the commitment of the college or university to the welfare of its students. Moreover, academic advising, first-year student orientation, faculty interest in students, and student perceptions of good teaching at their college or university also may influence student perceptions of the commitment of their institution to student welfare, as these forces may communicate to students that their college or university places a high value on them as individuals and on their growth and development. A high value placed on students by the institution and an abiding concern for the growth and development of its students stand as two defining dimensions of the construct of the commitment of the institution to student welfare, as previously outlined in this chapter and by Braxton, Hirschy, and McClendon (2004).

Accordingly, we tested for the influence of these eight possible forces on student perceptions of their institution's level of commitment to the welfare of its students in our exercise of analytical cascading to identify statistically significant sources of influence on this core construct in commuter colleges and universities (see Chapter 9). Beyond these eight possible forces, we also mark out a set of possible institutional policies and practices that strive to meet the needs of commuting students. These institutional policies and practices flow from the formulations of the theory of student persistence in commuter colleges and universities described earlier in this chapter.

The external environment sculpts to a large extent the college experience of commuting students, as obligations such as work and family determine their daily activities (Tinto, 1993; Webb, 1990). As a consequence, commuter colleges and universities must accommodate the schedules of commuter students through such policies and practices as offering classes at times convenient to students; having university offices that serve students open at times convenient for students who work; providing "drop-in" child-care services; having physical facilities for students to study, type papers, and make copies of course materials; having a physical space open on weekends; having the university library open during the weekend; having eating facilities open during times convenient for commuting students; making commuting to and from campus as convenient as possible; having ample parking on campus for commuting students; and making parking convenient to the classes of students. The presence of these 10 practices clearly signals to commuter students the high value their college or university places on their attendance. Such a high value placed on the needs of commuting students by the institution contributes to their perception that their college or university embraces a commitment to the welfare of its students (Braxton, Hirschy, and McClendon, 2004).

Some additional institutional policies and practices that communicate an institutional concern for the welfare of its students include having a peer mentoring program, on-campus employment opportunities for students, course registration as a straightforward process, general-use computers with Internet access available throughout the campus, clear communication of institutional policies to students, clear communication of campus activities to students, and the use of technology to communicate information to students.

Possible Sources of Influence on Institutional Integrity

The teaching orientation of the commuter colleges and universities represented in this study and described in Chapter 7 suggests four possible forces that may affect student perceptions of institutional integrity of their college or university: faculty interest in students, good teaching by faculty members, and two faculty teaching skills—organization and preparation and instructional clarity. As explained previously in this chapter, institutional integrity pertains to congruence between the espoused mission and goals of a given college or university and the actions of administrators, faculty members, and staff of that college or university (Braxton, Hirschy, and McClendon, 2004). Each of these four possible forces can shape student perceptions of the extent to which their college or university exhibits institutional integrity. To elaborate, we presume that students in colleges and universities in general and those in teaching-oriented institutions in particular expect their faculty to possess a genuine interest in students. We also anticipate that students expect good teaching by their professors. Moreover, students in teaching-oriented institutions of higher learning also may think that the faculty members teaching them should exhibit organization and preparation as well as clarity in their instruction. Accordingly, the more students view faculty as good teachers and the more students perceive that faculty at their institution evince an interest in students, the greater their belief in the institutional integrity of their college or university. Likewise, the more students perceive the faculty teaching them as organized and prepared for class and clear in their instruction, the more they perceive their college or university as exhibiting institutional integrity.

In addition to these characteristics of faculty, academic advising and first-year student orientation constitute additional possible forces of influence on institutional integrity. Students in commuter colleges and universities might also expect that academic advising stands as a strong component of the academic environment at a teaching-oriented college or university. Moreover, they might also assume that their first-year orientation will prepare them for success in the academic environment of their college or university. Accordingly, the more students view academic advising as a strong component of the academic environment at their college or university and the more they regard first-year student orientation as preparing them for success in this environment, the more students view their college or university as possessing institutional integrity.

Commuter colleges and universities strive to serve commuter students. Because commuter students (in comparison with residential students) have been found to be less involved in campus co-curricular activities (Kuh, Gonyea, and Palmer, 2001), many colleges and universities make little effort to serve and engage commuter students. Research has found, however, that both residential and commuter students achieve greater academic success and higher levels of personal growth when engaged in campus-based educationally purposeful activities (Pascarella and Terenzini, 2005). In an effort to increase this type of engagement among their students, many commuter institutions adhere to a student-centered mission of being open and available when their students are available (Kezar and Kinzie, 2006).

Thus, the accommodation of the needs of commuter students constitutes an abiding concern of commuter colleges and universities. As previously expressed, the needs of commuter students arise from their family and work obligations. These obligations define the day-to-day activities of commuting students (Webb, 1990). The balancing of these obligations with taking courses necessitates the existence of institutional policies and practices that take family and work into account. Such policies and practices include offering classes at times convenient to students; having university offices that serve students open at times convenient for students who work; providing "drop-in" child-care services; having physical facilities for students to study, type papers, and make copies of course materials; having a physical space open on weekends; having the university library being open during the weekend; having eating facilities open during times convenient for commuting students; making commuting to and from campus as convenient as possible; having ample parking on campus for commuting students; and making parking convenient to the classes of students. The more students agree that these 10 institutional policies and practices exist at their college or university, the more they believe in the institutional integrity of their commuter college or university.

To recapitulate, we identified six possible forces related to the teaching orientation of the commuter colleges and universities included in this volume that may influence student perceptions of institutional integrity. Furthermore, we delineated 10 institutional policies designed to meet the needs of commuting students that may also influence student perceptions of institutional integrity. We outlined a total of 18 possible forces that influence student perceptions of institutional integrity.

Possible Sources of Influence on Support of Significant Others

Figure 6.1 demonstrates that Braxton, Hirschy, and McClendon (2004) view support from significant others as one defining aspect of the external environment of students enrolled in a commuter college or university. As stated previously in this chapter, one assumption of the theory of student persistence in commuter colleges and universities is that commuter students frequently have obligations distinct from attending college. For some students, such obligations include work and family (Tinto, 1993). The commitments of both work and attending college may negatively affect the families of commuter students. Thus, student encouragement and support for attending from significant others such as a parents, family members, and close friends becomes crucial.

We present an array of 17 factors that may influence student perceptions of the extent of their support for college attendance from their significant others. These factors include financial issues associated with college attendance, the academic experience of the focal student, institutional policies and practices that accommodate the needs of commuting students, and institutional efforts to make significant others feel welcomed at the institution, such as encouraging significant others to attend new student orientation and frequent communication of important information to significant others.

The financial costs of attending college may place burdens on significant others. The minimization of such costs may lessen the financial costs of college attendance for significant others. For example, financial support in the form of grants, loans, and work study may lead to support for college attendance from significant others. Working on and off campus constitute additional ways commuter students ease the financial burden of their college attendance for significant others.

Students who report to significant others that they receive academic advising that they regard as a strong component of the academic environment at their university may create an impression in significant others that the university cares about the academic progress of its students. Significant others who receive from the student reports of good teaching by faculty members and reports of faculty as interested in students may come to appreciate the educational benefits of taking courses at the university. Such an appreciation, in turn, may increase the support of significant others for college attendance.

The obligations of work and family create additional concerns for significant others. If policies and practices exist at a commuter college or university to ease the competing demands of work and attending class on significant others, then support from such significant others for college attendance may emerge. Such policies and practice include offering classes at times convenient to students, having university offices that serve students open at times convenient for students who work (provision of student services), having "drop-in" child-care services, making commuting to and from campus as convenient as possible, and having on-campus work opportunities. In addition, students who have reliable transportation to and from campus may also garner the support of significant others for their college attendance, because such reliable transportation may also make commuting easier and less of a time commitment.

Chapter Summary

In this chapter we described the formulations of a theory of student persistence in commuter colleges and universities. For our process of analytical cascading, described in Chapter 1, we also presented extensions of this theory to identify possible sources of influence on those core concepts of this theory found to be statistically significant, which we initially identified in Chapter 3 through our test of this theory, a test whose outcome we report in Chapter 9.

In the next chapter, we will describe the data source and research design we used to test the theory described in this chapter as well as the revised the revision of Tinto's theory for residential colleges and universities described in Chapter 5. We will also describe the data source and research design we used to conduct our process of analytical cascading pertinent to these two theories.

7

Design of the Studies

At base, we use two distinct studies in this volume. One study concentrates on understanding student persistence in residential colleges and universities, whereas the other study focuses on understanding student persistence in commuter colleges and universities. Both studies entail the empirical testing of a theory formulated to account for student persistence in each of these two distinct types of colleges and universities. We described these theories in Chapters 5 and 6.

In this chapter, we describe the design of these two studies. We describe the instruments used, the samples of the two studies, the variables used to test the respective theories, the variables used in analytical cascading, and the limitations of each of the two studies.

The Residential College and University Study

Two survey instruments were constructed for the residential college and university study: the *Fall Collegiate Experiences Survey* (FCES) and the *Spring Collegiate Experiences Survey* (SCES). Both of these instruments were designed to measure constructs of the revised theory for residential colleges and universities, which we described in Chapter 5. The FCES consists of 136 closed-ended items, and the SCES includes 137 closed-ended items.

These two instruments were also constructed to assist us in our exercise of analytical cascading. As indicated in Chapter 1, analytical cascading entails empirically identifying influences on those antecedents of social integration found to influence this core concept of the revised theory of student persistence in residential colleges and universities. These two instruments contain survey items that measure possible sources of influence on those antecedents of social integration found to wield a statistically significance influence on social integration that results from our test of the revised theory of student persistence in residential colleges and universities.

Both of these instruments rest on an extensive body of research literature (Bean, 1980, 1983; Berger, 1997; Berger and Braxton, 1998; Berger and Milem, 1999; Braxton and Brier, 1989; Braxton, Bray, and Berger, 2000; Braxton, Milem, and Sullivan, 2000; Braxton, Hirschy, and McClendon, 2004; Cabrera, Nora, and Castaneda, 1993; Cabrera, Stampen, and Hansen, 1990; Cabrera, Nora, Pascarella, Terenzini, and Hagedorn, 1999; Carver, Scheier, and Weintraub, 1989; Helland, Stallings, and Braxton, 2001–2002; Pascarella, Terenzini, and Wolfe, 1986; Voorhees, 1990).

Study Sample

The sample used in this study of student persistence in residential colleges and universities consists of a longitudinal panel design of 408 first-time, full-time, first-year students in eight residential and religiously affiliated colleges and universities. These eight institutions include one categorized as a master's college/university-I institution in the Carnegie Classification of Institutions (Carnegie Foundation for the Advancement of Teaching, 2003) and seven other institutions, one of which is a historically black university (HBCU). The residential nature of the colleges and universities included in this sample provided us with an adequate basis for the empirical testing of the revised theory of student persistence in residential colleges and universities described in Chapter 5.

Students were randomly selected at each of the eight colleges and universities to participate in this study. The data collection for this study consisted of the administration of the *Fall Collegiate*

Experiences Survey in fall 2002, the administration of the *Spring Collegiate Experiences Survey* in spring 2003, and the fall 2003 enrollment records of the eight participating colleges and universities. The two surveys were distributed to random samples of first-year students at each of the eight participating institutions. The longitudinal panel was constructed using the responses to the two surveys and the fall 2003 institutional enrollment records with student cases matched by a unique identification number across the three data collection points.

The sample of 408 students represents an aggregate response rate of 28.4 percent across the eight participating colleges and universities. Nearly 60 percent of the student respondents were female (59.8 percent, n = 244), and 12.8 percent were minority (n = 52). African American students at the one HBCU in the sample were considered "majority." Of the eight institutions from which the sample was drawn, one is a masters I, four are baccalaureate-general, and three are baccalaureate-liberal arts. In fall 2002, the average SAT composite score for these eight colleges and universities was 1048 with a range of 820 to 1230. The average full-time equivalent enrollment of these eight institutions in fall 2002 was 1,594 students ranging from a low of 696 to a high of 3,242 students. The average size for classes that typically enroll first-year students is 19 students, which ranged from a low of 12 to a high of 23 students.

Due to the relatively low response rate in this study, cases from two of the eight institutions were weighted to ensure some degree of representativeness to their respective campus populations on gender. In the case of the first institution, male respondents were weighted by a factor of 1.22. The application of this weight resulted in the percentage of male students in the sample corresponding to the percentage of males in the population of the first institution. For the second institution, male respondents were weighted by a factor of 1.68. This adjustment also resulted in the percentage of males students in the sample matching the percentage of males in the population of the second institution.

Research Design: Test of the Theory of Student Persistence in Residential Colleges and Universities

As indicated previously, an empirical test of the revised theory of student persistence in residential colleges and universities constitutes one the principle objectives of this volume. In Chapter 5, we list the eight propositions derived from this theory that provide the basis for the research design used to test this theory. For the sake of the clarity of our research design, we again list these eight propositions:

1. The greater the student's belief that they have the ability to pay for the cost of attending the chosen college or university, the greater the student's degree of social integration.
2. The more a student perceives that the institution is committed to the welfare of its students, the greater the student's level of social integration.
3. The more a student perceives the potential for community on campus, the greater the student's level of social integration.
4. The more a student perceives that the institution exhibits institutional integrity, the greater the student's level of social integration.
5. The greater the student's use of proactive adjustment strategies, the greater the student's level of social integration.
6. The greater the level of psychological energy that a student invests in various social interactions at their college or university, the greater the student's degree of social integration.
7. The greater the student's degree of social integration, the greater their level of subsequent commitment to the college or university.
8. The greater the level of subsequent commitment to the institution, the more likely the student persists in college.

The testing of these eight propositions required the following sets of variables: student entry characteristics (gender, race/ethnicity, parental educational level, parental income, and average grades earned in high school), on-campus residence, initial institutional commitment, ability to pay, commitment of the institution to student welfare, communal potential, institutional integrity, proactive social adjustment, psychosocial engagement, social integration, subsequent institutional commitment, and student persistence. A rigorous testing of these eight propositions requires the inclusion of the five student entry characteristics and initial institutional commitment because of their role in the revised theory portrayed in Figure 5.1 of Chapter 5. Put differently, the testing of this theory would be incomplete without the inclusion of these variables. Nevertheless, initial goal commitment was unavailable to us and is not included in the testing of this theory. We included on-campus residences, as some students in these eight colleges and universities lived off campus during their first year in college. The college experience varies significantly between students who live on campus and off campus (Braxton, Hirschy, and McClendon, 2004; Chickering, 1974). Thus, we needed to hold constant the influence of on-campus residence in our testing of these eight propositions. Table A.1 of Appendix A shows the operational definitions of these sets variables, and Table A.2 displays the means and standard deviations for these variables.

Student Entry Characteristics

Our measures of the five student entry characteristics—gender, race/ethnicity, parental educational level, parental income, and average grades earned in high school—and on-campus residence are face valid and straightforward. The specific measures of the five student entry characteristics are shown in Table A.1 of Appendix A.

Initial Institutional Commitment

We measured initial institutional commitment as a student's ranking of their institution of enrollment as their first choice = 4, second choice = 3, third choice = 2, or fourth choice = 1 of an institution to attend. This item was included in the *Fall Collegiate Experiences Survey*. Our measure of this variable corresponds that used by Berger and Milem (1999) and Berger and Braxton (1998) in their research to measure initial institutional commitment.

Ability to Pay

We appraised ability to pay using a student's response to the survey item: "Do you have any concern about your ability to finance your college education?" (none = 1, some = 2, major = 3). This item was included in the *Fall Collegiate Experiences Survey*. Cabrera, Stampen, and Hansen (1990) viewed satisfaction with the costs of attending the college or university of enrollment as the ability to pay. The extent of students' concern for financing their college education reflects their degree of satisfaction with the costs of attending a particular college or university.

Proactive Social Adjustment

We restricted our measurement of proactive social adjustment to a focus on the stress coping strategy termed "positive reinterpretation and growth" (Carver, Scheier, and Weintraub, 1989). As indicated in Chapter 5, proactive social adjustment involves the recognition by students that they need to adjust in a proactive way to the demands and pressures that social interactions place on them during their first year in college (Braxton, Hirschy, and McClendon, 2004). Coping with the stress of challenging situations by viewing stress in a positive way entails the use of positive reinterpretation and growth as a coping strategy. We measure positive reinterpretation and growth using a composite of four survey items based on the research of Carver, Scheier, and Weintraub (1989) and Braxton, Bray, and Sullivan (1999). We obtained these four items from the *Fall Collegiate Experiences Survey*.

Psychosocial Engagement

As indicated in Chapter 5, psychosocial engagement refers to the amount of psychological energy required by social interactions with peers and participation in extracurricular activities of first-year college students (Braxton, Hirschy, and McClendon, 2004). Accordingly, we plumb psychosocial engagement using a composite of six forms of peer interaction and extracurricular activity, such as talking with or discussing course content with other students outside of class; studying or socializing with a friend; attending campus movies, plays, concerts, and/or recitals; participating in social activities with members of the Greek system; going out on a date with another student; and drinking beer, wine, or liquor. Students were asked to indicate how frequently they engaged in these six forms (never = 1 to very often = 5). Table A.1 exhibits these items that were included in the *Fall Collegiate Experiences Survey*. We assert that such forms of peer interaction and participation in extracurricular activities require varying degrees of psychological investment by students. These measures correspond to those used by Milem and Berger (1997) and Berger and Milem (1999) to assess fall peer involvement.

Communal Potential, Institutional Integrity, and Commitment of the Institution to Student Welfare

We developed new measures for communal potential, institutional integrity, and commitment of the institution to student welfare. The definitions of these constructs advanced in Chapter 5 provided the basis for the development of the survey items used to measure these constructs. We measured communal potential using a composite of nine survey items that appeared on the *Fall Collegiate Experiences Survey*. Our measure of institutional integrity takes the form of a composite of five survey items obtained from the *Spring College Experiences Survey*. We used a composite of 10 survey items derived from the *Spring College Experiences Survey* to construct our measure of commitment of the institution to student welfare. Table A.1 shows the survey items of these three composite measures.

Social Integration

Social integration mirrors the student's perception of their degree of social affiliation with others and their degree of congruency with the attitudes, beliefs, norms, and values of the social communities of a college or university (Durkheim, 1951; Tinto, 1975). Accordingly, we measured social integration using a composite of seven items that were included on the *Spring College Experiences Survey*. Table A.1 shows these seven items. This measurement of social integration resonates with measures of this construct used in previous research (Pascarella and Terenzini, 1980; Pascarella, Terenzini, and Wolfe, 1986; Braxton and Brier, 1989; Cabrera, Castaneda, Nora, and Hengstler, 1992; Cabrera, Nora, and Castaneda, 1993; Berger and Milem, 1999).

Subsequent Institutional Commitment

We used a composite of two items to measure subsequent institutional commitment. These two items were included in the *Spring Collegiate Experiences Survey*. We specify these two items in Table A.1. These are the same two items used in previous research to measure subsequent institutional commitment (Pascarella and Terenzini, 1980; Pascarella, Terenzini, and Wolfe, 1986; Braxton and Brier, 1989; Cabrera, Castaneda, Nora, and Hengstler, 1992; Berger and Braxton, 1998; Berger and Milem, 1999).

Student Persistence

This variable was plumbed as the student's decision to reenroll for fall 2003 (not enrolled = 0, enrolled = 1) in the same institution that they entered in fall 2002. Data source for this enrollment status was provided by the eight participating residential colleges and universities.

Research Design: Analytical Cascading

In Chapter 5, we extended the theory of student persistence in residential colleges and universities and used previous research to delineate possible sources of influence on psychosocial engagement, commitment of the institution to student welfare, and institutional integrity. As indicted in Chapter 3, these three antecedents of social integration wield statistically significant influences on this core concept to the theory of student persistence in residential colleges and universities. In this section, we describe the measurement of these possible forces. Table A.3 of Appendix A presents the operational definitions of these possible forces and Table A.4 displays their means and standard deviations.

Academic Advising

We measure satisfaction with academic advising using the following item from the *Fall Collegiate Experiences Survey*: "Academic advisement is a strong component of the academic environment here" (strongly disagree = 1 to strongly agree = 4).

Ability to Pay

We assessed ability to pay using a student's response to the survey item, "Do you have any concern about your ability to finance your college education?" (none = 1, some = 2, major = 3).

Communal Potential

We used the same measure of this variable that we used in our test of the theory of student persistence in residential colleges and universities. See Table A.1 for the operational definition of communal potential.

Cultural Capital

We treat cultural capital as a student entry characteristic. We define it as the extent of student involvement during their last year in high school in various cultural activities that require cultural knowledge, such as visiting an art museum, attending a symphony concert, or traveling abroad. These activities, which represent the type of cultural knowledge possessed by the middle and upper classes, are considered aspects of cultural capital (Bourdieu, 1986). Table A.3 displays illustrative items that make up our composite measure of cultural capital. We obtained these measures from the *Fall Collegiate Experiences Survey*.

Fall First-Year Student Orientation

We measured the possible influence of fall first-year student orientation using student responses to the survey item on the *Fall Collegiate Experiences Survey*: "Freshmen orientation adequately prepared me for success in the social environment" (strongly disagree = 1 to strongly agree = 4).

Faculty Active Learning Practices

In Table A.3, we show the six survey items that make up the composite scale we used to measure the possible source of influence of active learning practices used by faculty. We attained these six items from the *Spring Collegiate Experiences Survey*.

Faculty Interest in Students and Good Teaching

We measure these two possible forces using composite scales we developed. We labeled one scale "Faculty Interest in Students" and the other scale "Student Reports of Good Teaching." Both scales consist of two items derived from the *Spring Collegiate Experiences Survey*. We display the survey items that make up these two scales in Table A.3.

Faculty Violations of Teaching Norms

In Table A.3, we exhibit the specific items identifying behaviors for each of the following four normative patterns: faculty violations of norm of condescending negativism, personal disregard, moral turpitude, and particularistic grading. We derived these specific behaviors from the *Spring Collegiate Experience Survey*.

Fulfillment of Expectations for College

Following the research of Helland, Stallings, and Braxton (2001–2002), we used two indicators to assess the fulfillment of student expectations for college: fulfillment of academic expectations and fulfillment of social expectations. We display the specific survey items that make up these two composite measures in Table A.3. We derived these survey items from the *Spring Collegiate Experience Survey*.

Organizational Behavior

In Chapter 5, we posited communication, fairness, and participation in decision making as forms of organizational behavior that serve as possible sources of influence. We exhibit the indicators we used in Table A.3. We derived the specific items of these three composite scales from the research of Bean (1980, 1983). We obtained these survey items from the *Spring Collegiate Experiences Survey*.

Proactive Social Adjustment

We used the same measure of student use of positive reinterpretation and growth to plumb proactive social adjustment that we used in our test of the theory of student persistence in residential colleges and universities. See Table A.1 for the operational definition of this item.

Sense of Community in Residence Halls

Table A.3 shows the three composite scales and the specific survey items of these scales that we used to measure identity, solidarity, and interaction in residence halls. We obtained these specific items from the *Fall Collegiate Experiences Survey*.

Student Perceptions of Prejudice and Racial Discrimination

We derived our measure of campus prejudice and racial discrimination from the research of Cabrera, Nora, Pascarella, Terenzini, and Hagedorn (1999). This measure takes the form of a composite scale made up of eight specific items included in the *Spring Collegiate Experiences Survey*. We display these eight specific items in Table A.3.

Data Analysis Design for Theory Testing and Analytical Cascading

We describe the statistical design we used to test the revised theory of student persistence in residential colleges and universities in Appendix B. There we also explain the statistical design we used in our process of analytical cascading. We utilized multivariate statistical procedures using the 0.05 level of statistical significance in executing these statistical designs.

Limitations to the Residential College and University Study

Here we present a set of four limitations to our residential college and university study. These limitations temper our recommendations for policy and practice advanced in previous chapters of this volume as well as the conclusions we draw from the findings presented in Chapter 8. These limitations are as follows:

1. Our sample of residential colleges and universities is best characterized as a non-probability sample. The eight religiously affiliated private residential colleges and universities included in our sample were not randomly selected from the population of such colleges and universities. These eight institutions were purposively selected because they agreed to participate in this study. Because this sample is a non-probability sample, we cannot make inferences of some degree of certitude to these respective populations. Nevertheless, this sample of institutions contains specific institutions that strongly resemble the residential colleges and universities that make up these populations. Although this is not a representative sample, we do have confidence that these institutions share sufficient similarities with other institutions of higher education, and we believe that we can expect our theory testing and analytical cascading to be applicable in these settings as well.

2. Although the eight residential colleges and universities were not randomly selected from their respective populations, the students who completed the survey instruments were randomly selected from the population of students at their college or university. However, this second limitation pertains to the response rates obtained. For the residential college and university sample, we obtained a response rate of 28.4 percent across

the eight institutions. This response rate raises questions about the extent of bias that may exist in this sample. However, this limitation is blunted to some degree as we conclude that little bias exists in this sample, because cases from two of the eight institutions were weighted to ensure some degree of representativeness to their respective campus populations on gender. We describe this process in more detail in chapter in the section "Study Sample."

3. Our test of the revised theory of student persistence in residential colleges and universities focuses only on first- to second-year student persistence. As a consequence, it does not take into account later re-enrollments at the focal institution or persistence beyond the first year of attendance (Eckland, 1964).

4. Several composite scales we used to measure factors in either the testing of the theory of student persistence in residential colleges and universities in our process of analytical cascading pertaining to those factors important to student persistence in residential colleges and universities have Cronbach alpha reliability values that suggest low internal consistency, as exhibited in Tables A.1 and A.3. The composite scales and their Cronbach alpha reliability values are psychosocial engagement ($r = 0.64$), subsequent institutional commitment ($r = 0.36$), identity as a dimension of a sense of community in residence halls ($r = 0.62$), interaction as a sense of community in residence halls ($r = 0.59$), solidarity as a sense of community in residence halls ($r = 0.51$), and active learning ($r = 0.59$).

Despite these reliability values, we view the use of these composite measures as tenable for three reasons. First, the items used in these scales are identical to the items used in other studies that used these concepts. Thus, we continue to use the items that make up these scales to maintain a consistency in the conduct of research on student persistence. Second, the primary result of low internal consistency reliability is attenuation of the effects of these measures (Carmines and Zeller, 1979). As a consequence of such attenuation, the regression coefficients obtained for these composite variables may be underestimated. The third reason is that Cronbach alpha estimates are generally viewed as conservative estimates of reliability (Carmines and Zeller, 1979).

The Commuter College and University Study

The *University Students' Experience Survey* was the survey instrument constructed for the *Commuter College and University Study*. This instrument was designed to measure constructs of the theory of student persistence in commuter colleges and universities that we outlined in Chapter 6. The *University Students' Experience Survey* consists of 137 closed-ended items.

This instrument was also constructed to assist us in our exercise of analytical cascading. As indicated in Chapter 1, analytical cascading entails empirically identifying influences on those core concepts of the theory of student persistence in commuter colleges and universities found to be statistically significant through our empirical test of this theory. As initially indicated in Chapter 3, our test of this theory identified academic and intellectual development, commitment of the institution to student welfare, institutional integrity, and supports of significant others as statistically significant indirect forces in student persistence in commuter colleges and universities. As a consequence, we focus our process of analytical cascading on these four core concepts.

We used an extensive body of theory and research to develop the *University Students' Experience Survey*. This body of research includes the work of Braxton, Bray, and Berger (2000); Braxton, Hirschy, and McClendon (2004); Braxton, Jones, Hirschy, and Hartley (2008); Braxton, Milem, and Sullivan (2000); Chickering and Gamson (1987); Dunphy, Miller, Woodruff, and Nelson (1987); Pascarella and Terenzini (1980); Pascarella, Terenzini, and Wolfe (1986); Stern (1970); Tinto, (1997, 1998, 2000); and Voorhees (1990).

Study Sample

The data source for the testing of the theory of student persistence in commuter colleges and universities as well as the process of analytical cascading consists of a longitudinal panel design of 714 students enrolled at five publicly supported commuter colleges and universities who have completed two or fewer semesters at their college or university and who live at home with their parents, with their spouse or partner, or by themselves.

We selected five state-supported four-year institutions to participate in this study from high- and low-performing states in terms of their student persistence and bachelor's degree completion, as reported in *Measuring Up 2006: The National Report Card on Higher Education* published by the National Center for Public Policy and Higher Education. Of the five institutions participating in this study, three are located in low-performing states and two are in high-performing states.

During the second semester of the 2007–2008 academic years, site coordinators at each of the five commuter institutions drew a sample of 600 first-year students. Thus, the initial sample for this data source consisted of 3,000 first-year students. Site coordinators obtained their sample of 600 students through a cluster sampling design. The first stage of this cluster sampling design consisted of a random selection of courses from a list of courses that typically enroll large numbers of first-year students at each of five participating commuter institutions. The second stage of this cluster sampling design entailed the administration of the *University Students' Experience Survey* to students enrolled in these randomly selected courses.

The administrations of the *University Students' Experience Survey* resulted in a sample of 1,596 students who completed the instrument for an aggregate response rate of 53.2 percent across the five participating institutions. The lowest rate of response was

30.3 percent, whereas the highest was 72.3 percent. By restrict-
ing our analytical sample to those students who completed two
or fewer semesters at their college or university and who live at
home with their parents, their spouse or partner, or on their own,
the useable sample of 714 students was derived from the sample
of 1,596 students who completed the *University Students' Experience Survey*.

Coordinators at each of the five participating commuter colleges
and universities used institutional enrollment records to ascertain
the fall 2008 enrollment status—returned or did not return—
for each of the students who completed the *University Students'
Experience Survey* at their institution. We obtained the measure of
student persistence used in Chapter 9 using this information.

Research Design: Test of the Theory of Student Persistence in Commuter Colleges and Universities

As previously stated, an empirical test of the theory of student
persistence in commuter colleges and universities stands as one of
the principle objectives of this volume. In Chapter 6, we delineated the 11 propositions derived from this theory that guide the
research design used to test this theory. For the sake of the clarity of
our research design, we again list these 11 propositions here:

1. As parental educational level increases, the likelihood of student persistence in a commuter college or university decreases.
2. The higher the student's level of motivation to graduate from
   college, the greater their likelihood of persisting in a commuter college or university.
3. The lower the costs of college attendance incurred by the student, the greater their likelihood of persisting in a commuter
   college or university.
4. The greater the support the student receives from significant
   others for their college attendance, the greater their likelihood
   of persistence in a commuter college or university.

5. The greater the student's need for social affiliation, the lower their likelihood of persistence in a commuter college or university.

6. The more a student perceives that their college or university is committed to the welfare of its students, the greater the student's degree of academic and intellectual development.

7. The more a student perceives that their college or university exhibits institutional integrity, the greater the student's degree of academic and intellectual development.

8. The more a student perceives that their college or university is committed to the welfare of its students, the greater the student's degree of subsequent commitment to their college or university.

9. The more a student perceives that their college or university exhibits institutional integrity, the greater the student's degree of subsequent commitment to their college or university.

10. The greater the degree of academic and intellectual development perceived by a student, the greater their degree of subsequent commitment to a commuter college or university.

11. The greater the student's degree of subsequent institutional commitment, the greater the likelihood of their persistence in a commuter college or university.

The testing of these 11 propositions required the following array of variables: student entry characteristics (gender, race/ethnicity, parental educational level, and average grades earned in high school), full- or part-time attendance status, costs of college attendance, need for social affiliation, motivation to graduate from college, support from significant others, institutional integrity, institutional commitment to the welfare of students, academic and intellectual development, subsequent institutional commitment, and student persistence. Table A.5 of Appendix A exhibits the operational definitions of these sets variables, and Table A.6 presents the means and standard deviations for these variables. Unless otherwise noted, the specific measures of each variable were taken from the *University*

Students' Experience Survey and are shown in Table A.5. The ordering of these variables follows Figure 6.1 of Chapter 6.

Student Entry Characteristics

Our measures of the four student entry characteristics—gender, race/ethnicity, parental educational level, and average grades earned in high school—are face valid. The specific measures of these four student entry characteristics are shown in Table A.5.

Full or Part-Time Attendance Status

We used the following item to measure the student's attendance status: "What is your current enrollment status?" (full-time student = 1, part-time student = 0).

Costs of College Attendance

We measured this variable using the student's degree of agreement with the statement, "I am satisfied with the amount of financial support (grants, loans, work study) I have received while attending this institution" (strongly disagree = 1 to strongly agree = 4).

Need for Social Affiliation

We used a scale developed by Stern (1970) to measure the student's need for social affiliation. This scale consists of 10 survey items that measure the likes and dislikes of students that pertain to various social interactions. Students indicate the extent of their agreement with such statements as, "I enjoy going to the park or beach with a crowd," "I enjoy leading an active social life," "I enjoy meeting a lot of people," and "I enjoy belonging to a social group" (strongly disagree = 1 to strongly agree = 4).

Motivation to Graduate from College

Hagedorn, Maxwell, and Hampton (2000–2001) conceptualized motivation to graduate from college as the level of importance an individual places on their graduation from college. Accordingly, we appraised this level of importance of graduating from college using the student's degree of agreement with the statement, "I am determined to finish college regardless of the obstacles that get in my way" (strongly disagree = 1 to strongly agree = 4).

Support from Significant Others

We used a composite of two survey items measuring student agreement with the statements, "The people closet to me (e.g., parents, family members, close friends, significant other) approve of my attendance at this university," and "The people closet to me (e.g., parents, family members, close friends, significant other) encourage me to get a college degree" (strongly disagree = 1 to strongly agree = 4) to measure support from significant others.

Institutional Integrity

We use the formulations of Braxton, Hirschy, and McClendon (2004) regarding the construct of institutional integrity to develop our measure. We measured student perceptions of institutional integrity using a composite scale of five items. Our test of the revised theory of student persistence in residential colleges and universities used these same five items to measure institutional integrity. These five items include such statements as, "The actions of the administration are consistent with the stated mission of this institution," "The institution almost always does the right thing," "The values of this institution are communicated clearly to the campus community," "The rules of this institution appear in harmony with the values the institution espouses," and "The decisions made at this institution rarely conflict with the values it espouses." Students used a four-point scale to record their level of agreement with each of these statements (strongly disagree = 1 to strongly agree = 4).

Institutional Commitment to the Welfare of Students

We use the formulations of Braxton, Hirschy, and McClendon (2004) pertaining to the construct of institutional commitment to the welfare of students to develop our measures of this construct. To measure student perceptions of how committed their college or university is to the welfare of its students, we used a composite scale made up of nine statements that included "Most student services staff (e.g., dean of students office, student activities, housing, etc.) are genuinely interested in students," "Most other college/university staff (e.g., registrar, student accounts, financial aid, etc.) are genuinely interested in students," "I have experienced negative interactions with faculty members (reverse scored)," "I have experienced negative interactions with student services staff (reverse scored)," "I have experienced negative interactions with other college/university staff (reverse scored)," "Faculty members treat students with respect," "Student services staff treat students with respect," "Other college/university staff treat students with respect," and "I know where to go if I need more information about a policy." Students used a four-point scale to record their level of agreement with each of these statements (strongly disagree = 1 to strongly agree = 4). We derived these nine survey items the *University Students' Experience Survey*. We used these same nine items to assess student perceptions of the commitment of the institution to student welfare in our test of the revised theory of student persistence in residential colleges and universities. We, however, did not include the item, "Most of the campus religious leaders (e.g., chaplain, priest, rabbi, etc.) are genuinely interested in students," which we included in our composite measure of commitment of the institution to student welfare used in our test of the revised theory of student persistence in residential colleges and universities.

Academic and Intellectual Development

We measured this construct using a composite of three survey items measuring student perceptions of their academic and intellectual development: satisfaction with the academic experience at their university, satisfaction with the extent of their intellectual development since enrolling, and the increase in their interest in ideas and intellectual matters since coming to their university. Students used a four-point scale to register their level of agreement with each of these three statements (strongly disagree = 1 to strongly agree = 4). In our measurement of academic and intellectual development, we derived these three items from the research of Braxton and Brier (1989); Cabrera, Castaneda, Nora, and Hengstler (1992); Pascarella, Duby, and Iverson (1983); Pascarella and Terenzini (1980, 1983); and Terenzini, Pascarella, Theophilides, and Lorang (1985).

Subsequent Institutional Commitment

We measure the student's level of subsequent institutional commitment using a composite of two survey items that measure student agreement with the statements, "It is not important for me to graduate from this university (reversed scored)," and "I am confident that I made the right decision in choosing to attend this university" (strongly disagree = 1 to strongly agree = 4). These items are the same two items used in previous research to measure subsequent institutional commitment (Pascarella and Terenzini, 1980; Pascarella, Terenzini, Wolfe, 1986; Braxton and Brier, 1989; Cabrera, Castaneda, Nora, and Hengstler, 1992; Berger and Braxton, 1998; Berger and Milem, 1999). We also used these same two items to operationalize subsequent institutional commitment in our test of the revised theory of student persistence in residential colleges and universities.

Student Persistence

We measured student persistence as whether the student returned to the same university in the fall of 2008 (did return in fall 2008 = 1, did not return in fall 2008 = 0). Site coordinators at each of the five participating commuter institutions provided us with this information from which we constructed this variable.

Research Design: Analytical Cascading

In the previous chapter, we extended the theory of student persistence in commuter colleges and universities and used previous research to demarcate possible sources of influence on academic and intellectual development, commitment of the institution to student welfare, institutional integrity, and support of significant others given that our test of the theory of student persistence in commuter colleges and universities delineated these core concepts as statistically significant indirect forces in the student persistence in commuter colleges and universities (see Chapter 9).

In this section, we describe the measurement of these possible forces. Table A.7 of Appendix A presents the operational definitions of these possible forces and Table A.8 exhibits means and standard deviations. Unless otherwise noted, we obtained the specific survey items used to measure these possible forces from the *University Students' Experience Survey.*

Academic Advising

We measured satisfaction with academic advising using the student's degree of agreement with the statement, "Academic advising is a strong component of the academic environment at this university" (strongly disagree = 1 to strongly agree = 4). Table A.7 displays this item.

Faculty Interest in Students and Good Teaching

We used the same scales as we used in our process of analytical cascading to delineate possible sources of influence on student perceptions of the commitment of the institution to student welfare and on student perceptions of institutional integrity in residential colleges and universities. We exhibit the survey items that make up these two scales in Table A.7.

Faculty Use of Active Learning Practices

We measured faculty use of active learning practices using the same variables as we used to measure active learning in our process of analytical cascading to identify possible sources of influence on student perceptions of the commitment of their institution to student welfare in residential colleges and universities. Table A.7 lists the survey items we used to construct the composite scale that measures faculty use of active learning practices. In this case, we derived these items from the *University Students' Experience Survey*.

Faculty Use of Good Practices in Undergraduate Education

We measured the following four of Chickering and Gamson's (1987) principles of good practice in undergraduate education: encouragement of student-faculty contact, encouragement of cooperation among students, provision of prompt feedback, and communication of high expectations. We display the measures we used to tap each of these four principles of good practice in undergraduate education in Table A.7.

Faculty Teaching Skills

Table A.7 shows the composite scales we constructed to measure the teaching skills of organization and preparation and instructional clarity. In developing these two composite scales, we used the same measures used by Braxton, Bray, and Berger (2000).

Financial Support (Costs of College Attendance)

We used the same measure we used in the test of theory of student persistence in commuter colleges and universities to plumb financial support. See Table A.5.

Institutional Policies and Practices

In Chapter 6, we pointed to possible institutional policies and practices that strive to meet the needs of commuting students. Examples of these policies and practices are as follows: clear communication of institutional policies to students; clear communication of campus activities to students; course registration as a straightforward process; having ample parking on campus for commuting students; having "drop-in" child-care services; having eating facilities open during times convenient for commuting students; having on-campus employment opportunities for students; having general-use computers with Internet access available throughout the campus; having parking convenient to the classes of students; having a physical space open on weekends; having a peer mentoring program; having physical facilities for students to study, type papers, and make copies of course materials; having university library open during the weekend; having university offices that serve students open at times convenient for students who work; making commuting to and from campus as convenient as possible; offering classes at times convenient to students, and the use of technology to communicate information to students. We measure each of these institutional policies and practices using items included in on the *University Students' Experience Survey*. We show these items and their response scales in Table A.7.

Reliable Transportation

We measured student perceptions of the degree to which they have reliable transportation to and from campus using student level of agreement with the following statement: "I have reliable transportation to and from campus" (strongly disagree = 1 to strongly agree = 4). Table A.7 exhibits this measure.

Data Analysis Design for Theory Testing and Analytical Cascading

We describe the statistical design we used to test the theory of student persistence in commuter colleges and universities in Appendix B. There we also explain the statistical design we used in our process of analytical cascading. We utilized multivariate statistical procedures using the 0.05 level of statistical significance in executing these statistical designs.

Limitations to the Commuter College and University Study

In this section, we present a set of five limitations to our commuter college and university study. These limitations moderate our recommendations for policies and practices advanced in previous chapters of this volume as well as the conclusions we draw from the findings presented in Chapter 9. These limitations are as follows:

1. Our sample of commuter colleges and universities is best described as a non-probability sample. The five commuter colleges and universities that make-up our sample were purposely selected because they were located in either a high-performing or a low-performing state in terms of their student persistence and bachelor's degree completion reported in *Measuring Up 2006: The National Report Card on Higher Education* published by the National Center for Public Policy and Higher Education. Of the five institutions participating in this study, three are located in low-performing states and two in high-performing states. Because this sample is a non-probability sample, we cannot make inferences of some degree of certitude to these respective populations. Nevertheless, this sample of commuter institutions contains specific institutions that strongly resemble the commuter colleges and universities that make up these populations. Although this is not a representative sample, we do have confidence that these institutions share sufficient similarities with other institutions of their type so that we can expect the results of our theory testing and analytical cascading to be applicable in these settings.

   Although the five commuter colleges and universities were not randomly selected from their respective populations, this limitation is tempered to some degree because the students who completed the *University Students' Experience Survey* were randomly selected from the population of students at their college or university.

2. The second limitation pertains to the response rates obtained. For the commuter college and university sample, we obtained a response rate of 53.2 percent across the five institutions. This response rate raises questions about the extent of bias that may

exist in this sample. However, in our review of the demographic characteristics of the populations sampled in the commuter institutions, we found that the demographic profile of our sample was similar to the demographic profile of the entire institution in almost all cases. In only two institutions were Z-tests of differences in proportions statistically significant for a demographic category between the full sample and our sample.

3. Our test of the theory of persistence in commuter colleges and universities was incomplete. The *University Students' Experience Survey* we used to test the theory of student persistence in commuter colleges and universities did not include survey items to test all of the propositions of the theory described in Chapter 6. For example, we are unable to test those propositions that pertain to such concepts as need for control, self-efficacy, empathy, and anticipatory socialization behaviors. Nevertheless, we were able to test propositions pertaining to academic and intellectual development and subsequent institutional commitment, two critical aspects to theory of student persistence in commuter colleges and universities. In addition, we were able to test proposition 11 that posits a direction relationships between subsequent institutional commitment and student persistence. Although the test of the theory of student persistence in commuter colleges and universities is incomplete, our test of this theory does include the key concepts and their associated propositions.

4. Our test of the theory of student persistence in commuter colleges and universities focuses only on first- to second-year student persistence. As a consequence, it does not take into account later re-enrollments at the focal institution or persistence beyond the first year of attendance (Eckland, 1964).

5. The Conbrach alpha reliability estimate for the composite scale measuring subsequent institutional commitment in our test of the theory of student persistence in commuter colleges and universities is 0.18. Despite the low level of internal

consistency of this measure, we retained the two items used in this composite scale, because these items, which are displayed in Table A.5, are identical to the items used to measure this variable in our test of the theory of student persistence in residential colleges and universities (see Table A.1). Moreover, these items are also the same two items used in previous research to measure subsequent institutional commitment (Pascarella and Terenzini, 1980; Pascarella, Terenzini, and Wolfe, 1986; Braxton and Brier, 1989; Cabrera, Castaneda, Nora, and Hengstler, 1992; Berger and Braxton, 1998; Berger and Milem, 1999). Thus, we continue to use the items that make up this scale to maintain a consistency in the conduct of research on student persistence. Despite the attenuation of the variance in subsequent institutional commitment, the regression coefficient obtained, as reported in Chapter 9, is statistically significant. In addition to these reasons, our finding, which we report in Chapter 9, that subsequent institutional commitment positively affects student persistence in commuter colleges and universities, joins the ranks of six previous tests of this relationship in commuter institutions that also empirically support it (Braxton and Lee, 2005).

Part III

Key Factors in Student Persistence in Residential and Commuter Colleges and Universities

8

Student Persistence in Residential Colleges and Universities

In this chapter, we describe the findings of our test of the revised theory of college student persistence in residential colleges and universities. We presented the formulations of this theory in Chapter 5. Through this description, we develop an understanding of those factors that either directly or indirectly contribute to students' decisions to return to their college or university in the fall of their second year of attendance.

Our Test of the Revised Theory of Student Persistence in Residential Colleges and Universities

In the following paragraphs, we provide details on the findings that emerged from our empirical test of the revised theory of student persistence in residential colleges and universities. We derive these details from the results of the multivariate analysis we conducted to test this theory, details that we display in Table C.1 of Appendix C, "Multivariate Analyses Results Tables." We describe the specifics of this multivariate analysis in Section 8.1 of Appendix B, "Technical Appendix for Statistical Procedures." We organize these findings by the three core concepts of social integration, subsequent institutional commitment, and student persistence.

Social Integration

As indicated in Chapter 5, the revised theory of student persistence in residential colleges and universities posits that commitment of the institution to student welfare (proposition 2), institutional integrity (proposition 4), and psychosocial engagement (proposition 6) exerts a positive influence on social integration. Through our test of these three propositions, we learned that commitment of the institution to student welfare, institutional integrity, and psychosocial engagements exert their expected influence on social integration. More specifically, the more a student perceives that the institution is committed to the welfare of its students, the greater the student's level of social integration. Likewise, the more a student perceives that their institution exhibits institutional integrity, the greater the student's level of social integration. Put differently, the more students perceive that the actions of their college or university coincide with its goals and mission, the greater their level of social integration. Moreover, greater levels of student psychosocial engagement also lead to greater degrees of social integration for them. These three statistically significant factors exert relatively equal degrees of influence on social integration given the similarities in the standardized regression coefficients identified for each of these factors (see Table C.1). In contrast, three of the other hypothesized antecedents to social integration fail to wield their expected influence. To elaborate, ability to pay (proposition 1), communal potential (proposition 3), and proactive social adjustment (proposition 5) bear little or no association with social integration.

In addition to commitment of the institution to student welfare, institutional integrity, and psychosocial engagement, the student's race/ethnicity and whether or not they live on campus during their first year of college also wield statistically significant influences on social integration. More specifically, Caucasian students and students who live on campus experience greater degrees of social integration.

Subsequent Institutional Commitment

As indicated in Chapter 5, proposition 7 of the revised theory of student persistence in residential colleges and universities postulates that social integration positively influences the student level of subsequent commitment to their college or university. Our expectation receives some degree of empirical affirmation given the statistically significant relationship between social integration and subsequent institutional commitment identified. Expressed in different words, the greater the student's degree of social integration, the greater their level of subsequent commitment to their college or university. This finding adds to our confidence in the reliability of this particular relationship as the vast majority of empirical tests of this relationship in residential colleges and universities (16 out of 19) generate empirical support (Braxton and Lee, 2005).

Initial institutional commitment and commitment of the institution to student welfare also positively influence the extent to which students espouse commitment to their institution following a semester's worth of experience in attending their particular college or university. Thus, the greater the student's initial level of commitment to their college or university, the greater their subsequent level of commitment. Moreover, the more the student perceives that their college or university is committed to the welfare of its students, the greater their degree of subsequent commitment to their college or university. The positive influence of the commitment of the institution to student welfare on both social integration and subsequent institutional commitment suggest the centrality of this factor to the persistence of first-year students in residential colleges and universities.

Student Persistence

Subsequent institutional commitment positively affects student persistence, as proposition 8 asserts. Put differently, as the student's level of subsequent commitment to their college or university increases, the likelihood of their persistence in college also increases.

Moreover, this positive influence of subsequent institutional com-mitment on student persistence also emerges as reliable knowledge given that 11 of 13 previous tests empirically verify this relationship (Braxton and Lee, 2005). We also learned that, like subsequent in-stitutional commitment, the student's initial level of commitment to their college or university also positively affects the likelihood of student persistence in a residential college or university.

Overall Appraisal of Empirical Support for the Revised Theory of Student Persistence in Residential Colleges and Universities

Our test of the revised theory of college student persistence in residential colleges and universities (Braxton, Hirschy, and McClendon, 2004) provides empirical support for this theory. We make this assertion given that our test resulted in empirical support for five of the eight propositions of this theory (propositions 2, 4, 6, 7, and 8). Moreover, two of the five supported propositions prevail as propositions indispensable to the logical and empirical coherence of this theory. These critical, empirically supported propositions are the positive influence of social integration on subsequent in-stitutional commitment (proposition 7) and the positive influence of subsequent institutional commitment on student persistence (proposition 8). Without empirical backing for these two proposi-tions, the theory would fail to provide any basis for an explanation of student persistence in residential colleges and universities.

In addition to the empirical support provided for these two indispensable propositions, three of the six antecedents of social integration and their attendant propositions posited by this theory also garner empirical affirmation. Phrased differently, commitment of the institution to student welfare (proposition 2), institutional integrity (proposition 4), and psychosocial engagement (proposi-tion 6) constitute three empirically supported antecedents to so-cial integration. Because of its critical importance to this theory, a knowledge of factors that influence social integration stands as an essential condition to the ability of this theory to account for student persistence. Without empirical support for antecedents of social integration, the theory would be incomplete. With support for antecedents of social integration, the explanatory power of this revised theory garners additional strength.

As indicated in Chapter 5, this theory also delineates ability to pay (proposition 1), communal potential (proposition 3), and proactive social adjustment (proposition 5) as antecedents of social integration. However, our test of this theory failed to provide such support.

Significant Influences on Psychosocial Engagement, Commitment of the Institution to Student Welfare, and Institutional Integrity

A deepening of our knowledge and understanding of student persistence in residential colleges and universities results from a delineation of factors that influence each of these three empirically verified antecedents of social integration: psychosocial engagement, commitment of the institution to student welfare, and institutional integrity. See the statistical design (Appendix B, sections 8.2, 8.3, 8.4, and 8.5) and results (Tables C.2, C.3, and C.4 of Appendix C) of the multivariate analyses we conducted. As stated previously in this volume, we call the process of empirically identifying such factors "analytical cascading." Beyond improvement in the explanatory power of the revised theory of student persistence in residential colleges and universities, the delineation of such empirically supported sources of influence will provide a basis for the development of institutional policies and practices designed to improve institutional retention rates for first-year students in residential colleges and universities.

Significant Influences on Psychosocial Engagement

In Chapter 5, we extended the revised theory of student persistence in residential colleges and universities to identify factors that may influence psychosocial engagement or the amount of psychological energy students invest in interactions with their peers and in participation in extracurricular activities during the fall semester of their first year in college. These possible sources of influence on psychosocial engagement included ability to pay, communal potential, cultural capital, first-year orientation as preparation for success in the institution's social environment, proactive social adjustment, and three dimensions—identity, interaction and solidarity—of a sense of community in residence halls. In Section 8.2 of Appendix B, we describe the multivariate analyses conducted to identify statistically significant forces of influence on psychosocial engagement. Table C.2 shows the results of this multivariate analysis.

Communal potential, cultural capital, and two dimensions (identity and interaction) of a sense of community in residence halls emerge as statistically significant sources of influence on psychosocial engagement. However, ability to pay, proactive social adjustment, and first-year orientation as preparation for success in the institution's social environment, plus solidarity as a sense of community in residence halls, each fail to influence psychosocial engagement in a statistically significant way. We discuss each of the significant influences on psychosocial engagement in the following paragraphs.

Communal Potential

We learned from our process of analytical cascading that the more students perceive that a subgroup of students exists within the various communities of their college or university that hold values, beliefs, and goals similar to their own, the greater their level of psychosocial engagement. Although our test of the revised theory of student persistence in residential colleges and universities failed to confirm the role of communal potential as an antecedent to social integration, we found that communal potential, instead, tends to act as an antecedent to psychosocial engagement. Communal potential acts as an antecedent to psychosocial engagement because the experiences a student has with their peers in residences halls (Berger, 1997), the classroom (Tinto, 1997, 2000), and student peer groups (Newcomb, 1966) tend to shape the perceptions they hold regarding their potential for community. Accordingly, the more the student perceives that a subgroup of students exists within the various communities of their college or university that hold values, beliefs, and goals similar to their own, the greater the student's willingness to expend the psychological energy needed to participate in a wide range of extracurricular activities and social interactions with peers.

Cultural Capital

Through our multivariate statistical analysis, we learned that cultural capital positively influences psychosocial engagement. Put in different words, students with higher levels of cultural capital tend to expend greater degrees of psychological energy than their peers with lower levels of cultural capital. As stated in Chapter 5, Bourdieu and Boltanski (1981) point to involvement in cultural activities, such as reading books and attending concerts, plays, and museums as one aspect of cultural capital. The possession of cultural capital provides students with self-esteem and social self-confidence that makes possible their fuller participation in a wide range of extracurricular activities and social interactions with peers. Their levels of cultural capital equip them with cultural knowledge, mannerisms, and attitudes that create a high level of social comfort in such social exchanges. Such social exchanges require the investment of psychological energy. As a consequence, the greater the student's level of cultural capital, the greater the extent of their psychosocial engagement.

Sense of Community in Residence Halls

Identity and interaction constitute two dimensions of a sense of community in residence halls that influence psychosocial engagement in a statistically significant positive manner. To elaborate, identity pertains to the degree to which students view themselves as members of a community in their residence hall. Put differently, they "identify with and attach importance to the community in their living unit" (Berger, 1997, p. 445). Interaction concerns the frequency and intensity of face-to-face interactions among the residents of a residence hall (Berger, 1997). Identity and interaction influence psychosocial engagement given these dimensions of a sense of community in residence halls help "newcomers to find an early physical, social, and academic anchor during the transition to college life" (Tinto, 1993, p. 125). Thus, the greater the degrees to which students identify with and attach importance to the community in their residence hall, the greater their degree of psychosocial engagement. Moreover, the greater the frequency and intensity of face-to-face interactions among residents of a student's residence hall, the greater their extent of psychosocial engagement.

Communal Potential and Its Significant Sources of Influence

As indicated, communal potential wields a statistically significant positive influence on the psychosocial engagement of first-year students in residential colleges and universities. Given the role communal potential plays in fostering student psychosocial engagement, we engage in further analytical cascading to identify those factors that shape student perceptions of their communal potential.

We posit that ability to pay, cultural capital, first-year student orientation, proactive social adjustment, and the three dimensions of a sense of community in residence halls—identity, solidarity, and interaction—influence student perceptions of their degree of communal potential at the residential college or university that they chose to attend. To elaborate on these possible sources of influence on communal potential, we first posit that ability to pay may exert such an influence, because students who express fewer financial concerns may feel more inclined to interact with peers and participate in extracurricular activities. Such social exchanges enable students to appraise their likelihood of establishing membership in a community of students at their residential college or university. These formulations stand as an extension of the above formulations and those of Chapter 5.

Cultural capital bestows self-esteem and social self-confidence on students that permits them to participate fully in a wide range of extracurricular activities and social interactions with peers. Their levels of cultural capital equip them with cultural knowledge, mannerisms, and attitudes that create a high level of social comfort in such social exchanges. Because of such social exchanges, students with higher levels of cultural capital come to view themselves as able to find a subgroup of students at their college or university that hold values, beliefs, and goals similar to their own.

If students perceive that the fall first-year student orientation adequately prepared them for success in their institution's social environment, they will feel equipped to interact with peers and participate in extracurricular activities. Through such interactions, students assess their likelihood of communal potential.

Proactive social adjustment may also lead to varying degrees of communal potential. Through an extension of our formulations for the influence of proactive social adjustment on psychosocial engagement, we assert that students who respond to the stresses that social interactions create in a proactive way through the coping strategy of positive reinterpretation and growth (Carver, Scheier, and Weintraub, 1989) possess the level of psychological energy needed to engage in such social exchanges as interacting with student peers and participating in extracurricular activities. These social exchanges enable students to gauge their likelihood of communal potential.

Student views on their likelihood of communal potential also emerge from their experiences with a sense of community in their residence halls. Given that identity as a dimension of the community pertains to the degree to which students "identify with and attach importance to the community in their living unit" (Berger, 1997, p. 445), a student's communal potential emerges from such an identity. The importance students attach to their living unit leads them to anticipate finding a community of students in which to establish membership. Communal potential also springs from a sense of solidarity in the residence hall given that solidarity entails the sharing of similar beliefs and goals and an eagerness to work together to solve problems in a residence halls (Berger, 1997). Interaction as a dimension of community in the residence hall also forms perceptions of communal potential. As stated previously in this chapter, interaction concerns the frequency and intensity of face-to-face interactions among the residents of a residence hall (Berger, 1997). Frequent and intense face-to-face interactions with student peers in the residence halls enable students to form beliefs about their likelihood of finding peers with beliefs, goals, and values similar to their own. Thus, we anticipate that these three dimensions of community positively affect student perceptions of their communal potential.

We use a multivariate statistical procedure to determine the influence of ability to pay, cultural capital, first-year student orientation, proactive social adjustment, and the three dimensions of a sense of community in residence halls on student perceptions of their likelihood of communal potential. We describe the specifics of this multivariate analysis in Section 8.3 of Appendix B.

We learned that cultural capital, first-year student orientation as preparation for success in the social environment, proactive social adjustment, identity as a sense of community in their residence hall, solidarity as a dimension of a student's sense of community in their residence hall, and interaction as a dimension of a student's sense of community in their residence hall each positively affects student perceptions of their communal potential. We also learned from this regression analysis that Caucasian students tend to express a greater likelihood of communal potential than do first-year students of color, and that students with lower average high school grades tend to express lower likelihoods of their communal potential.

Of these sources of significant influence on communal potential, cultural capital exerts the strongest degree of influence. However, we also learned that ability to pay fails to wield a statistically significant influence on communal potential.

Significant Influences on Commitment of the Institution to Student Welfare

As indicated in Chapter 5, we extended the revised theory of student persistence in residential colleges and universities to identify factors that may influence student perceptions of the commitment of the institution to student welfare. These possible sources of influence included academic advising; faculty interest in students; good teaching; faculty active learning practices; fall first-year orientation as preparation for success in the institution's academic environment; organizational behaviors including communication, fairness, and participation in decision making; student perceptions of prejudice and racial discrimination at their institution; and student observations of faculty violations of teaching norms. In Section 8.4 of Appendix B we describe the multivariate analyses conducted to identify statistically significant forces of influence on commitment of the institution to student welfare. We exhibit the results of this multivariate analysis in Table C.3 of Appendix C.

As a result of our analysis, we identify the organizational behavior of fairness in the administration of rules and regulations, faculty interest in students, and student-reported good teaching by faculty members as sources of influence that each tend to positively affect student perceptions of the commitment of their college or university to student welfare. Clearly, faculty interest in students wields the largest influence given the value of the standardized regression coefficient for this force (see Table C.3). In contrast, we learned that student perceptions of prejudice and racial discrimination on their campus and student observations of violations by faculty of the norm of condescending negativism as factors that adversely influence student perceptions of the commitment of their institution to the welfare of its students. In addition, we also identified parental educational level as a positive influence on commitment of the institution to student welfare. More explicitly, as a student's parents' educational level increases, the more positive the student's perceptions of the commitment of their institution to the welfare of its students.

We also learned from our multivariate analysis that such possible forces as academic advising, fall student orientation as preparation for success in the institution's academic environment, the organizational behaviors of communication and participation in decision making, faculty use of active learning practices, and faculty violations of the norms of moral turpitude, particularistic grading, and personal disregard each fail to influence student perceptions of the commitment of their college or university to student welfare. The failure of faculty use of active learning practices to influence commitment of the institution to student welfare constitutes a striking finding given previous research by Braxton, Jones, Hirschy, and Hartley (2008) that observed a positive influence of such faculty teaching practices. Our analysis included the other possible influences on commitment of the institution to student welfare, whereas the research by Braxton, Jones, Hirschy, and Hartley (2008) focused only on the influence of active learning on commitment of the institution to the welfare of its students. The moderation of the influence of active learning on the commitment of the institution to student welfare by the forces included in our analysis may account for the differences between our analysis and that of Braxton et al. (2008).

We discuss each of the significant influences on commitment of the institution to student welfare in the following paragraphs. These significant influences include faculty interest in students, the organizational behavior of fairness in the administration of rules and regulations, student perceptions of prejudice and racial discrimination on their campus, student-reported good teaching by faculty members, and violations by faculty of the norm of condescending negativism.

Faculty Interest in Students

An abiding concern for the growth and development of its students and the high value the institution places on its students constitute two key aspects of the commitment of the institution to student welfare (Braxton, Hirschy, and McClendon, 2004). We asserted in Chapter 5 that faculty members who evince a genuine interest in students contribute to the formation of student perceptions of the degree to which their college or university embraces an abiding concern for their growth and development. Moreover, taking courses from such faculty also communicates the high value placed on students by their college or university. As a consequence, the more the student perceives that faculty members at their college or university show a genuine interest in students, the more favorable the student's perceptions of the commitment of the institution to student welfare.

Organizational Behavior of Fairness

As stated in Chapter 5, organizational behavior concerns the actions of faculty, administrators, staff, and clerical workers at a given college or university (Berger, 2001–2002). Students observe actions involving fairness in the administration of rules and requirements in making decisions regarding matters of importance to students. If students feel that rules and regulations pertinent to them are fairly administered, then they come to perceive that their institution treats students in an equitable way. Such treatment constitutes a key aspect of the commitment of an institution to the welfare of its students (Braxton, Hirschy, and McClendon, 2004). Thus, the more the student perceives that their college or university fairly administers its rules and regulations, the more favorable the student's perception of the commitment of their college or university to the welfare of its students.

Student Perceptions of Prejudice and Racial Discrimination on Campus

Our findings indicate that the student who views prejudice and racial discrimination as existing on their campus tends to hold more negative perceptions of the commitment of their institution to the welfare of its students. The more the student perceives that prejudice and racial discrimination exists on their campus, the more likely they come to regard their college or university as not treating students in an equitable manner or with respect as individuals.

Student Reports of Good Teaching by Faculty Members

The positive influence of student reports of good teaching by faculty members on student perceptions of the commitment of the institution to student welfare stems from the student's perception that their institution not only exhibits an abiding concern for the growth and development of its students, but also highly values students. As we assert in Chapter 5, such perceptions develop from taking courses from faculty who students view as outstanding teachers and genuinely interested in teaching.

Violations by Faculty of the Norm of Condescending Negativism

The undergraduate college teaching norm of condescending negativism rebukes the treatment of both students and colleagues in a condescending and demeaning way (Braxton and Bayer, 1999). As we posit in Chapter 5, faculty violations of this norm display a lack of respect for students as individuals. As a consequence, the greater the frequency of which the student observes faculty violations of the norm of condescending negativism, the less favorable the student's perception of the commitment of their institution to the welfare of its students.

Significant Influences on Institutional Integrity

We extended the revised theory of student persistence in residential colleges and universities to identify factors that may influence student perceptions of the integrity of their college or university. The possible sources of influence we delineated through these theoretical extensions include faculty interest in students, fulfillment of academic and social expectations for college, student perceptions of prejudice and racial discrimination, and student reports of good teaching by faculty. We describe the multivariate analyses conducted to identify statistically significant forces of influence on institutional integrity in Section 8.5 of Appendix B. In Table C.4 of Appendix C we show the results of this multivariate analysis.

Through our multivariate statistical procedure, we delineate three forces that influence institutional integrity in a statistically significant way. Student perceptions of faculty interest in students and fulfillment of academic expectations for college tend to influence student perceptions of institutional integrity positively, whereas student perceptions of prejudice and racial discrimination on their campus tend to affect such perceptions negatively. Of these three significant forces, faculty interest in students clearly exerts the greater degree of influence given the magnitude of its standardized regression coefficient (see Table C.4). Our multivariate analysis also indicated that student reports of good teaching bear little or no association with student perceptions of institutional integrity. We discuss each of the significant influences on commitment of the institution to student welfare following paragraphs.

Faculty Interest in Students

In our extension of the revised theory of student persistence in residential colleges and universities in Chapter 5, we stated that each of the eight residential colleges and universities represented in the *Residential College and University Study* of this volume espouses teaching as its primary institutional mission. Because of the importance of teaching as an institutional mission, we might anticipate that students in such colleges and universities expect an interest in them by their professors. Accordingly, the more the student views faculty at their college or university as interested in students, the stronger the student's beliefs about the institutional integrity of their college or university.

Fulfillment of Expectations for College

In Chapter 5, we posited that student expectations for college develop from the images that they hold of the colleges and universities to which they make application. Students form the images of different colleges and universities through various information-gathering activities used during the college choice process. The accuracy of images developed through such information-gathering activities depends on consistency and truthfulness in the depiction of the academic and social life of students at a given college or university (Helland, Stallings, and Braxton, 2001–2002). Institutional images developed through such information-gathering activities play a significant role in the student's decision to attend a particular college or university (Cook and Zallocco, 1983). Accordingly, students enter college with expectations for their college or university based on the images formed through the various information-gathering activities. If their expectations for college based on such images are fulfilled, then first-year students will view their college or university as exhibiting institutional integrity. Thus, the more the student perceives that their academic expectations for college have been fulfilled, the more positive the student's perception of the degree to which their college or university exhibits institutional integrity.

Student Perceptions of Prejudice and Racial Discrimination

We have stated elsewhere in this volume that the residential colleges and universities represented define themselves as religiously affiliated. Given that character development and moral development describe the cultures of religiously affiliated institutions (DeJong, 1992), acts of prejudice and racial discrimination violate the cultural values embraced by such colleges and universities. As a consequence, the more the student perceives that prejudice and racial discrimination exist at their college or university, the more negatively the student views the institutional integrity at their college or university. Students perceive prejudice and racial discrimination as incongruent with the espoused mission of a religiously affiliated institution of higher education.

In Summary

In this section of this chapter, we offer a summary of our findings from our test of the revised theory of student persistence in residential colleges and universities and from our analytical cascading conducted to identify significant influences on the key antecedents of social integration: psychosocial engagement, commitment of the institution to student welfare, and institutional integrity. This summary provides a foundation for the recommendations for policy and practice in residential colleges and universities that we presented in Chapter 3. This summary also affords a foundation for the conclusions and recommendations for theory and research we advance in Chapter 10.

Summary of the Test of the Revised Theory

We found empirical support for the revised theory of student persistence in residential colleges and universities. Of the eight propositions of this theory tested, we found support for five of them. More explicitly, the student's level of psychosocial engagement, their perceptions of the commitment of the institution to student welfare, and their perceptions of the extent of institutional integrity exhibited by their college or university each tend to influence the student's level of social integration in a positive way. The student's level of social integration, in turn, positively influences their degree of subsequent commitment to the institution. The greater the level of the student's subsequent commitment to their institution, the greater their likelihood of persistence to the fall of their second year of college. However, we failed to confirm the hypothesized positive influence of three antecedents of social integration—ability to pay, communal potential, and proactive social adjustment. We base some of the recommendations for policy and practice for residential institutions found in Chapter 3 on the positive influence of psychosocial engagement, commitment of the institution to student welfare, and institutional integrity on social integration.

Summary of Findings from Analytical Cascading

The findings we obtained from our process of analytical cascading to identify significant influences on psychosocial engagement, commitment of the institution to student welfare, and institutional integrity serve two purposes. The drawing of implications for the revision of the theory of student persistence in residential colleges and universities constitutes one purpose, whereas providing a foundation for the development of recommendations for institutional policy and practice stands as the other purpose.

Implications for Theory Revision

Our test of the revised theory of student persistence in residential colleges and universities failed to support propositions 3 and 5. Proposition 3 posited a positive influence of communal potential on social integration, whereas proposition 5 hypothesized a positive relationship between proactive social adjustment and social integration. Through our process of analytical cascading, we found that communal potential positively influences psychosocial engagement and that proactive social adjustment wields a positive effect on communal potential. Thus, these two concepts play roles in student persistence in residential colleges and universities that differ from what was expected in the theory of student persistence in residential colleges and universities. Nevertheless, they do play a part in this process. As a consequence, the roles played by communal potential and proactive social adjustment, which our findings delineate, suggest a reordering of some aspects of the theory. We discuss such reorder in Chapter 10. As indicated in Chapter 1 and elsewhere in this volume, theory revision constitutes one of the primary purposes of analytical cascading.

Implications for the Development of Policies and Practices

Our process of analytical cascading found that cultural capital, faculty espousal of a genuine interest in students, sense of community in residence halls, and student perceptions of prejudice and racial discrimination on campus constitute significant sources of influence on more than one key concept in the student persistence process in residential colleges and universities. More specifically, cultural capital positively affects both psychosocial engagement and communal potential. Student reports of faculty espousing a genuine interest in students wield a positive influence on student perceptions of both commitment of the institution to student welfare and institutional integrity. Dimensions of a sense of community in a student's residence hall bear a positive relationship with both psychosocial engagement and communal potential. Identity and interaction relate positively to psychosocial engagement, whereas identity, interaction, and solidarity—aspects of a sense of community in residence halls—bear a positive association with communal potential. In contrast to these positive relationships, student perceptions of prejudice and racial discrimination on their campus negatively influence student perceptions of the commitment of their college or university to the welfare of its students and institutional integrity. These findings provide a foundation for the development of policies and practices for implementation in residential colleges and universities that we put forth in Chapter 3.

Other findings also provide the groundwork for the development of policies and practices outlined in Chapter 3. These findings include the positive influences of communal potential on psychosocial engagement, proactive social adjustment on communal potential, and first-year student orientation as preparation for success in the social environment on communal potential. Additional findings include those factors that positively influence commitment of the institution to student welfare, such as student reports of good teaching by faculty and organizational behavior in the form of fair administration of rules and regulations. Moreover, the positive influence of the fulfillment of academic expectations for college on institutional integrity, as well as the negative relationships between student perceptions of prejudice and racial discrimination on their campus and faculty, and violations of the teaching norm of condescending negativism on student perceptions of the commitment of the institution to student welfare constitute additional findings that contribute to policies and practices for residential colleges and universities to increase their retention rates, which we present in Chapter 3.

In the next chapter, we present the results of our test of theory of student persistence in commuter colleges and universities as well as the results of our analytical cascading process to identify significant influences on the core concepts of academic and intellectual development, commitment of the institution to student welfare, institutional integrity, and support of significant others for college attendance. We also provide a summary of findings that provides the underpinning for the policies and practices designed to increase student retention in commuter colleges and universities that we discussed in Chapter 3.

9

Student Persistence in Commuter Colleges and Universities

I n this chapter, we describe the findings of our test of the theory of college student persistence in commuter colleges and universities that we described in Chapter 6. Through this presentation of findings, we develop an understanding of those factors that either directly or indirectly contribute to the student's decision to return to a commuter college or university in the fall of their second year of attendance.

Our Test of the Theory of Student Persistence in Commuter Colleges and Universities

In this section of this chapter, we present the findings that transpired from our empirical test of the theory of student persistence in commuter colleges and universities. We derive the details of the results of the multivariate analysis we conducted to test this theory. We show these details in Table C.5 in Appendix C and Section 9.1 of Appendix B. We organize these findings by the three core concepts of academic and intellectual development, subsequent institutional commitment, and student persistence.

Academic and Intellectual Development

As specified in Chapter 6, two propositions (6 and 7) of the theory of student persistence in commuter colleges and universities concern student perceptions of their degree of academic and intellectual development attained through their collegiate attendance. Both of these propositions garner empirical support. Specifically, the more a student perceives that their college or university exhibits institutional integrity, the greater the student's degree of academic and intellectual development. Second, the more a student perceives that their college or university is committed to the welfare of its students, the greater the degree of the student's academic and intellectual development. Given the similarities in the standardized regression coefficients (see Table C.5) identified for each two factors, it appears that these factors wield similar degrees of influence, although a somewhat greater degree of influence is obtained for commitment of the institution to student welfare. In addition to these two important sources of influence, women college students and students attending college on a full-time time basis tend to perceive less academic and intellectual development than their counterparts.

Subsequent Institutional Commitment

Two statistically significant factors positively shape the level of commitment commuting students espouse for their college or university as an outcome of their attendance. Put differently, two of the three propositions (9 and 10) pertinent to subsequent institutional commitment received empirical affirmation. To elaborate, the more a student perceives that their college or university exhibits institutional integrity, the greater the student's degree of subsequent commitment to their college or university (proposition 9). Likewise, the greater the degree of academic and intellectual development perceived by a student, the greater their degree of subsequent commitment to a commuter college or university (proposition 10). We anticipated that commitment of the institution to student welfare would wield a positive influence on subsequent institutional commitment. However, this proposition (8) failed to receive statistically significant support.

Beyond the delineation of academic and intellectual development and institutional integrity as factors that form subsequent commitment to a commuter college or university, other sources of statistically significant influence emerge from our multivariate analysis. Student entry characteristics such as being a student of color, average high school grades, and parental educational level tend to show a negative association with subsequent institutional commitment. In contrast, attending college on a full-time basis, being satisfied with the costs of attending their college or university, and having the support of significant others to attend college tend to exert positive influences on subsequent institutional commitment.

Student Persistence

As anticipated by proposition 11, subsequent institutional commitment exerts a positive influence on student persistence in a commuter college or university. In addition to the positive influence of subsequent institutional commitment on student persistence, attending college on a full-time basis also positively relates to student persistence in a commuter college or university.

In stark contrast to the empirical support provided proposition 11, the other five propositions (1 to 5) pertaining directly to student persistence failed to receive statistically significant affirmation. In more specific terms, parental educational level (proposition 1), motivation to graduate from college (proposition 2), costs for attending college (proposition 3), support from significant others (proposition 4), and the need for social affiliation (proposition 5) each bear little or no relationship to student persistence. However, parental education level, costs for attending college, and support from significant others each tends to exhibit a relationship with subsequent institutional commitment rather than with persistence as postulated by the theory of student persistence in commuter colleges and universities.

Overall Appraisal of Empirical Support for the Theory of Student Persistence in Commuter Colleges and Universities

In Limitation 3 of the "Limitation to the Commuter College and University Study" section of Chapter 7, we state that we did not fully test the theory of student persistence in commuter colleges and universities. However, we did test 11 of the key propositions of this theory as delineated in Chapter 6. Our test of these 11 propositions resulted in empirical verification for 5 of them. As a consequence, we view our test of this theory as bestowing partial empirical support for the theory of student persistence in commuter colleges and universities proposed by Braxton, Hirschy, and McClendon (2004) and revised in Chapter 6.

We offer this tepid appraisal given that we garnered empirical support for most of the propositions pertinent to academic and intellectual development (two of three) and subsequent institutional commitment (two of three), the two critical facets of student persistence in commuter colleges and universities. As we stated in Chapter 6, we view academic and intellectual development and subsequent institutional commitment as critical facets of student persistence in commuter colleges and universities. Commuter students spend their time on campus attending classes and meeting degree requirements (Tinto, 1993). Thus, commuter students characterize their collegiate experience principally in terms of the degree of academic and intellectual development they experience because of their course work.

The importance of subsequent institutional commitment emanates from its posited direct role in influencing student persistence decisions. The positive influence of subsequent institutional commitment on student persistence also bolsters the degree of support ascribed to this theory. Without empirical support for the linkage between academic and intellectual development and subsequent institutional commitment, as well as the linkage between subsequent institutional commitment and student persistence, this theory would lack any empirical footing as an explanation of student persistence in commuter colleges and universities.

As delineated in Chapter 6, the theory of student persistence in commuter colleges and universities also hypothesized direct influences of parental educational level (proposition 1), motivation to graduate from college (proposition 2), costs for attending college (proposition 3), support from significant others (proposition 4), and the need for social affiliation (proposition 5) on student persistence. Our test, however, failed to confirm the expected relationships.

Significant Influences on Core Factors

An expansion of our knowledge and understanding of student persistence in commuter colleges and universities requires an empirical delineation of factors that influence commitment of the institution to student welfare, institutional integrity, and academic and intellectual development. We will also concentrate attention on the delineation of factors that influence support for college attendance by significant others because of its positive influence on subsequent institutional commitment.

The pattern of findings that result from such analytical cascading will contribute to the explanatory power of the theory of student departure from commuter colleges and universities. Moreover, these empirically supported sources of influence also provide a foundation for the development of institutional policies and practices designed to improve institutional retention rates for commuter college students. We presented these recommendations for policies and practices for commuter colleges and universities in Chapter 3.

We derive these significant influences from the results of the multivariate analyses we conducted. We describe the statistical design used to conduct these multivariate analyses in Appendix B (Sections 9.2 to 9.5). We display the results of these multivariate analyses in Tables C.6 to C.9 of Appendix C.

Significant Influences on Academic and Intellectual Development

In Chapter 6 we extended the revised theory of student persistence in commuter colleges and universities to pinpoint factors that may influence student perceptions of their academic and intellectual development. The identified possible sources of influence on academic and intellectual development included such curricular arrangements and classroom practices as participation in a learning community, faculty use of active learning practices, the use of good practices in undergraduate education, and faculty teaching skills. Academic advising, faculty interest in students, first-year student orientation as adequate preparation for academic success, and student perceptions of good teaching at their college or university constitute additional theoretically relevant possible sources of influence. In Section 9.2 of Appendix B, we describe the multivariate analysis conducted to identify statistically significant forces of influence on student perceptions of their academic and intellectual development. We display the results of this multivariate analysis in Table C.6 of Appendix C.

From the results of this multivariate analysis, we empirically delineate six forces that influence the academic and intellectual development of commuting students in a positive way. These statistically significant forces of influence include such forms of curricular arrangements and classroom practices as student participation in a learning community, faculty use of active learning practices, and faculty teaching skills of instructional clarity and organization and preparation. However, none of the principles of good practice in undergraduate education, which are forms of classroom practices demarcated by Chickering and Gamson (1987), emerge as statistically significant sources of influence on academic and intellectual development.

In addition to these forms of curricular arrangements and classroom practices, academic advising, faculty interest in students, and first-year student orientation as adequate preparation for academic success stand as three additional statistically significant forces that positively shape such student perceptions. We discuss each of the significant influences on student perceptions of their academic and intellectual development in the following paragraphs.

Academic Advising

Academic advising stands as "a decision-making process during which students realize their maximum educational potential through communication and information exchanges with an advisor" (Grites, 1979, p. 1). As a consequence, academic advising fosters the academic and intellectual development of students given its emphasis on the realization of the academic potential of students. Our finding that academic advising positively affects the student's perception of their academic and intellectual development resonates with these assertions about academic advising.

Faculty Interest in Students

Pascarella and Terenzini (1991) assert that a supportive social psychological context stands as a necessary condition for institutional impact on college students, such as the academic and intellectual development of students. A strong faculty emphasis on teaching and student development constitutes one of the characteristics of such a social psychological context. Thus, student perceptions of their faculty as genuinely interested in students reflect a faculty emphasis on teaching and student development. As a consequence, the more the student perceives that faculty evince a genuine interest in students, the greater the student's reported level of academic and intellectual development.

Faculty Teaching Skills

The faculty teaching skills of organization and preparation and instructional clarity enhance student course learning (Pascarella and Terenzini, 1991, 2005). As a consequence, the more frequently students observe these teaching skills displayed by faculty in their

classes, the greater their perceived level of academic and intellectual development.

Faculty Use of Active Learning Practices

Active learning entails the use of class activities that engage students in thinking about the subject matter of a course (Bonwell
and Eison, 1991). Active learning enhances student course learning (Pascarella and Terenzini, 2005; Anderson and Adams, 1992;
Chickering and Gamson, 1987; Johnson, Johnson, and Smith,
1991; McKeachie, Pintrich, Yi Guang, and Smith, 1986). Our
findings resonate with this assertion, as we found that the more
frequently students perceive that faculty members use active learning practices in their courses, the greater the students' degree of
academic and intellectual development.

First-Year Student Orientation

Orientation programs for first-year students inform students about
such topics as administrative and academic regulations, student organizations and activities, student services, and academic program
design (Pascarella, Terenzini, and Wolfe, 1986). If an orientation
program adequately prepares students for success in the academic
environment of their college or university, then we might expect
students to experience academic and intellectual development as
a result of such successful preparation. Our findings offer empirical
support for this contention given that we found that the more the
student believes that their first-year student orientation adequately
prepared them for success in the academic environment of their
university, the greater their perceived level of academic and intellectual development.

Student Participation in a Learning Community

Learning communities involve the block scheduling of courses, so
that the same group of students takes a set of courses together (Tinto,
1997, 1998, 2000). A theme typically underlies the set of courses.

Participation in a learning community wields a positive influence on student persistence in a commuter college or university (Tinto, 1997). Such participation also makes a contribution to a student's academic and intellectual development (Braxton, Hirschy, and McClendon, 2004). As a consequence, student participation in a learning community tends to influence their perceptions of their own academic and intellectual development in a positive way.

Significant Influences on Commitment of the Institution to Student Welfare

We extended, in Chapter 6, the revised theory of student persistence in commuter colleges and universities to demarcate factors that may influence student perceptions of the commitment of their institution to the welfare of its students. These demarcated possible sources of influence consist of student participation in a learning community, faculty use of active learning practices, the use of good practices in undergraduate education, faculty teaching skills, academic advising, first-year student orientation, faculty interest in students, and student perceptions of good teaching at their college or university. We also extend this theory to suggest that institutional policies and practices may also shape student perceptions of the commitment of their college or university to the welfare of its students. These 10 policies and practices involve (1) offering classes at times convenient to students; (2) having university offices that serve students open at times convenient for students who work; (3) having "drop-in" child-care services; (4) having physical facilities for students to study, type papers, and make copies of course materials; (5) having a physical space open on weekends; (6) having the university library be open during the weekend; (7) having eating facilities open during times convenient for commuting students; (8) making commuting to and from campus as convenient as possible; (9) having ample parking on campus for commuting students; and (10) having parking convenient to the classes of students. An additional seven institutional policies and practices include having a peer mentoring program, having on-campus employment opportunities for students, course registration as a straightforward process, having general-use computers with Internet access available throughout the campus, clear communication of institutional policies to students, clear communication of campus activities to students, and the use of technology to communicate information to students.

We describe the multivariate analysis we conducted to identify statistically significant forces of influence on student perceptions of the commitment of their college or university to the welfare of its students in Appendix B, Section 9.3. Table C.7 of Appendix C shows the results of this multivariate analysis.

From our multivariate analysis, we learned that the faculty teaching skills of organization and preparation and instructional clarity positively influence student perceptions of the commitment of their college or university to the welfare of its students. Moreover, academic advising and having faculty interested in students also have some positive bearing on student perceptions of the commitment of their institution to student welfare.

However, only 3 of the 17 delineated possible institutional policies and practices tend to shape, to a small degree, positive student perceptions of the commitment of their college or university to the welfare of its students. Having ample parking on campus for commuting students, university offices that serve students (e.g., financial aid, counseling, registrar) being open at convenient times for working students, and having general-use computers with Internet access available throughout the campus constitute these institutional policies and practices. In the paragraphs that follow, we discuss each of these significant influences on commuter student perceptions of the commitment of their college or university to the welfare of its students.

Academic Advising

The existence of academic advising as a strong component of the academic environment of a college or university signifies to students that their college or university places a high value on them as individuals and on their growth and development. A high value placed on students by the institution and an abiding concern for the growth and development of its students stand as two defining dimensions of the construct of the commitment of the institution to student welfare (Braxton, Hirschy, and McClendon, 2004). Hence, the more students perceive that academic advising is a strong component of the academic environment of their college or university, the more they perceive that their institution espouses a commitment to the welfare of its students.

Faculty Interest in Students

A college or university with faculty who demonstrate a genuine interest in students conveys to students that the institution places a high value on them as individuals and on their growth and development, two defining characteristics of a college or university committed to the welfare of its students. Thus, the more the student perceives that faculty at their institution hold a genuine interest in students, the more favorable the student's perception of the commitment of their college or university to the welfare of its students.

Faculty Teaching Skills

The faculty teaching skills of organization and preparation and instructional clarity increase student course learning (Pascarella and Terenzini, 1991, 2005). Given that the student's course learning increases because of such faculty teaching skills, the student will come to view such faculty members as being concerned about the growth and development of students. Such a perception leads to the formation of favorable outlook on the commitment of the college or university to the welfare of its students. As a result, the more frequently the student observes the teaching skills of organization and preparation and instructional clarity in their classes, the more favorable their perception of the commitment of their college or university to the welfare of its students.

Institutional Policies and Practices

As stated elsewhere in this volume, obligations such as work and family shape the daily activities of many commuting students (Tinto, 1993; Webb, 1990). As a result, commuter colleges and universities must accommodate the schedules of commuter students through such policies and practices as having ample parking on campus for commuting students, having university offices that serve students (e.g., financial aid, counseling, registrar) being open at convenient times for working students, and having general-use computers with Internet access available throughout the campus. The existence of such policies and practices by a commuter college or university demonstrates to the student that the institution places a high value on the needs of its students. As a consequence, the student comes to view their college or university as committed to the welfare of its students.

Significant Influences on Institutional Integrity

In Chapter 6 we offered some formulations to extend the revised theory of student persistence in commuter colleges and universities to delineate factors that may influence student perceptions of the extent to which their commuter college or university exhibits institutional integrity. Through these formulations, we identified such factors as academic advising faculty interest in students, good teaching by faculty members, faculty teaching skills of organization and preparation and instructional clarity, and first-year student orientation as possible forces of influence on institutional integrity. As postulated in Chapter 6, these possible influences stem from the teaching-oriented missions of the five commuter colleges and universities included in this volume.

These formulations also suggest 12 institutional policies and practices that may also shape student perceptions of institutional integrity. These 12 policies and practices include offering classes at times convenient to students; having university offices that serve students open at times convenient for students who work; having "drop-in" child-care services; having physical facilities for students to study, type papers, and make copies of course materials; having a physical space open on weekends; having the university library open during the weekend; having eating facilities open during times convenient for commuting students; making commuting to and from campus as convenient as possible; having ample parking on campus for commuting students; having parking convenient to the classes of student; making course registration a straightforward process; and having general-use computers with Internet access available throughout the campus. These policies and practices strive to meet the needs of commuting students.

We describe the multivariate analysis we conducted to identify statistically significant forces of influence on student perceptions of institutional integrity in Appendix B, Section 9.4. We display the results of this analysis in Table C.8 in Appendix C. Through this multivariate analysis, we found that of the six possible factors emanating from the teaching orientation of the commuter colleges and universities included in this volume, only student reports of good teaching wields little or no influence on student perceptions of institutional integrity. More explicitly, the more students agree that academic advising is a strong component of the academic environment at their college or university and the more they regard first-year student orientation as preparing them for success in this environment, the more they perceive their college or university as exhibiting institutional integrity. Additionally, the more students perceive that faculty at their institution show an interest in students, the greater their belief in the institutional integrity of their college or university. Likewise, the more students perceive faculty as organized and prepared for class and clear in their instruction, the more students perceive that their college or university demonstrates institutional integrity.

Institutional policies and practices that accommodate the needs of commuting students also emerged from our multivariate analyses

as affecting student perceptions of institutional integrity in a positive way. Having classes offered at times convenient for students,
provision of student services or having offices that serve students
(e.g., counseling, financial aid, registrar) open at times convenient
for working students, and having ample parking on campus for
commuting students positively affect such student perceptions of
the integrity of their institution.

In our extension of the theory of student persistence in commuter colleges and universities advanced in Chapter 6 we pointed
out that the five commuter colleges and universities that make up
the sample for the *Commuter College and University Study* espouse
a teaching-oriented institutional mission. The teaching orientation of these commuter colleges and universities gives rise to student expectations that faculty at their college or university should
demonstrate a genuine interest in students. Moreover, students in
teaching-oriented institutions of higher learning may also expect
that faculty members should possess such teaching skills as being
prepared and well-organized and clear in their instruction. Students in these five commuter colleges and universities might also
expect that academic advising prevails as a strong component of
the academic environment at a teaching-oriented college or university. They might also assume that their first-year orientation will
prepare them for success in the academic environment of their college or university. If the student finds these expectations met, then
the student would regard the institution as being true to its mission
as a teaching institution. Because institutional integrity concerns
the congruence between the espoused mission and goals of a giv-
en college or university and the actions of administrators, faculty
members, and staff of that college or university (Braxton, Hirschy,
and McClendon, 2004), the student then would hold an affirming
view of the institutional integrity of their college or university.

In extending the theory of student persistence in commuter
colleges and universities of Chapter 6, we also note that many
commuter institutions adhere to a student-centered mission of

being open and available when their students are available (Kezar and Kinzie, 2006). Efforts to accommodate the needs of commuter students resonate with such a student-centered mission. Accordingly, commuter institutions that possess such policies and practices as having classes offered at times convenient for students, having offices that serve students (e.g., counseling, financial aid, registrar) open at times convenient for working students, and having ample parking on campus for commuting students serve the needs of commuter students. The more the student agrees that these institutional policies and practices exist at their college or university, the more they believe in the institutional integrity of their commuter college or university. Such a favorable perception of institutional integrity stems from the congruence of such policies and practices with the mission of serving the needs of commuter students.

Significant Influences on the Support of Significant Others

Given that commuter students frequently have work and family obligations distinct from attending college, encouragement and support for attending college from such significant others as parents, family members, and close friends becomes crucial.

We offer, in Chapter 6, an extension of the theory of student persistence in commuter colleges and universities to ascertain possible sources of influence on support from significant others for college attendance. These delineated possible sources of influence include financial issues or college costs associated with college attendance, the academic experience of the focal student, institutional policies and practices that accommodate the needs of commuting students, and institutional efforts to make significant others feel welcomed at the institution.

In Section 9.5 of Appendix B, we describe the multivariate analysis we conducted to identify statistically significant forces of influence on support from significant others. We show the results of our analysis in Table C.9 of Appendix C.

We empirically identified four forces that influence support from significant others in a statistically significant way. The significant positive forces of influence are student reports of faculty being interested in students, having classes offered at times convenient to the student, having reliable transportation to and from campus, and student impressions that their family is welcomed at their university. We discuss each of these forces in the following paragraphs.

Faculty Interest in Students

In our theoretical extensions of Chapter 6, we postulated that significant others who receive reports of faculty who demonstrate a genuine interest in students and their children, spouse, or partner may come to appreciate the educational benefits of taking courses at the university. Such an appreciation, in turn, increases the support of significant others for college attendance. Hence, the more the student perceives that faculty at their institution embrace a genuine interest in students, the greater the level of support they receive from significant others for their college attendance.

Institutional Policies and Practices

According to our theoretical extensions of Chapter 6, the obligations of work and family that accompany college attendance by a child, spouse, or partner create anxiety for significant others. If policies and practices exist at the commuter college or university attended that strive to ease the burdens on significant others of work and attending class, then support from such significant others for college attendance may emerge. Such policies and practices include offering classes at times convenient to these students. The more the student agrees that such a policy or practice exists at their college or university, the greater the level of support they receive from significant others for college attendance. In addition, students who have reliable transportation to and from campus also garner the support of significant others for their college attendance, because such reliable transportation makes commuting easier and less of a time commitment.

Family Feels Welcomed on Campus

Feeling welcomed on the campus of the student's college or university may also positively affect support from significant others for college attendance. General impressions such as significant others feeling welcomed at university events and the individual commuter student perceiving that their family is welcomed on campus may create such a feeling. Thus, the more the student perceives that their significant others (spouse/partner, children, parents) feel welcomed at events at their college or university, the greater the level of support from significant others for college attendance.

Forces That Make Family Members Feel Welcomed

Of the influences on the support of significant others for college attendance, the positive influence of student impressions that their family is welcomed at their university invites further engagement in analytical cascading. In this case, we focus on the delineation of forces that shape such impressions. Through such a focus, policies and practices aimed to make family members feel welcome might spring forth. Such policies and practices include having "drop-in" child-care services, the college or university having a website that contains information for significant others, encouragement by the university for significant others to attend the orientation for new students, the impression that significant others feel welcomed at university events, and the frequent communication of important information to significant others.

We performed a multivariate analysis to ascertain which of these possible policies and practices demonstrate a statistically significant relationship with student impressions that their family is welcome at their university. We describe this multivariate analysis in Section 9.6 of Appendix B.

We learned from this multivariate analysis that having a web-site containing information for significant others, encouragement by the university for significant others to attend the orientation for new students, and the impression that significant others feel welcomed at university events tend to contribute in a positive way to the impression of students that their family is welcomed at their university.

In Summary

In this chapter, we offer a summary of our findings from our test of the theory of student persistence in commuter colleges and universities and from analytical cascading conducted to identify significant influences on the key dimensions to this theory of academic and intellectual development, commitment of the institution to student welfare, institutional integrity, and support from significant others for college attendance. This summary presents the ground-work for the recommendations for policy and practice in commuter colleges and universities that we presented in Chapter 3. This summary also provides the underpinning for the conclusions and recommendations for theory and research we put forth in Chapter 10.

Summary of the Test of the Revised Theory

We regard our test of this theory as conferring partial empirical support for the theory of student persistence in commuter colleges and universities proposed by Braxton, Hirschy, and McClendon (2004) and revised in Chapter 6. We proffer such a moderate assessment given that we acquired empirical support for two of the three propositions relevant to academic and intellectual development as well as two of the three propositions pertinent to subsequent institutional commitment. We also found empirical affirmation for proposition 11 that posits that subsequent institutional commitment positively influences student persistence in a commuter college or university. However, we failed to find support for those propositions regarding parental educational level (proposition 1), motivation to graduate from college (proposition 2), costs for attending college (proposition 3), support from significant others (proposition 4), and the need for social affiliation (proposition 5), as each bear little or no relationship to student persistence.

Put in more narrative terms, we learned that the more a student perceives that their college or university exhibits institutional integrity, the greater the student's degree of academic and intellectual development. Moreover, the more a student perceives that their college or university is committed to the welfare of its students, the greater their degree of academic and intellectual development. Likewise, the greater the degree of academic and intellectual development perceived by a student, the greater their degree of subsequent commitment to a commuter college or university. In addition, the more a student perceives that their college or university exhibits institutional integrity, the greater the student's degree of subsequent commitment to their college or university. In turn, the greater the subsequent commitment to the institution espoused by the student, the greater their likelihood of persistence in a commuter college or university. We derived some of the recommendations for policy and practice for commuter colleges and universities that we put forth in Chapter 3 on such findings as the positive influences of commitment of the institution to student welfare and institutional integrity on academic and intellectual development and the positive influences of academic and intellectual development and institutional integrity on subsequent institutional commitment.

Implications for Theory Revision

Our test of the theory of student persistence in commuter colleges and universities proved unsuccessful in providing empirical support for those propositions concerning the relationship between parental educational level (proposition 1), motivation to graduate from college (proposition 2), costs for attending college (proposition 3), support from significant others (proposition 4), the need for social affiliation (proposition 5), and student persistence. Each of these propositions hypothesized a direct relationship with student persistence. However, our test of this theory identified statistically significant associations between parental educational level, costs for attending college, support from significant others, and subsequent institutional commitment. We found little or no relationship between motivation to attend college and the need for social affiliation and subsequent institutional commitment. More specifically, we learned that parental educational level negatively influences subsequent institutional commitment and not student persistence, as predicted by proposition 1. We also learned that costs for attending college and support from significant others to attend college both influence subsequent institutional commitment in a positive way, and not student persistence, as postulated by propositions 3 and 4. Thus, the part these three constructs—parental educational level, costs for college attendance, and support from significant others—plays in student persistence in commuter colleges and universities suggests a rearrangement of some aspects of the theory. We discussed such reorder in Chapter 10.

Summary of Findings from Analytical Cascading

The findings we acquired from our method of analytical cascading to identify significant influences on student perceptions of their academic and intellectual development, student perceptions of the commitment of their institution to the welfare of its students, student perceptions of institutional integrity, and student perceptions of their degree of support from significant others for college attendance afford us an empirically based foundation for the development of recommendations for institutional policy and practice for implementation by commuter colleges and universities wishing to increase their institution's student retention rate. In the next section, we outline implications for the development of such institutional policies and practices that we draw from our configuration of findings derived from analytical cascading.

Implications for the Development of Policies and Practices

Our process of analytical cascading found that academic advising, faculty espousal of a genuine interest in students, and the faculty teaching skills of instructional clarity and organization and preparation stand as significant sources of influence on the chief concepts of academic and intellectual development, student perceptions of the commitment of the institution to student welfare, and student perceptions of institutional integrity in the student persistence process in commuter colleges and universities. In each case, these sources of influence bear a direct and positive association with each of these core concepts. In addition to these three critical concepts, faculty espousal of a genuine interest in students also affects support from significant others in a positive manner. First-year student orientation as adequate preparation for academic success also constitutes an additional positive source of influence on the core concepts of academic and intellectual development and institutional integrity.

In addition to these sources of influence, three institutional policies and practices play a part in positively influencing core concepts of the theory of student persistence in commuter colleges and universities. More specifically, having ample parking on campus for commuting students and having university offices that serve students (e.g., financial aid, counseling, registrar) open at convenient times for working students each positively influence student perceptions of the commitment of their institution to the welfare of its students as well as student perceptions of degree of integrity displayed by their college or university. Moreover, offering classes at times convenient for students bears a positive relationship both with institutional integrity and support from significant others for college attendance.

In addition to these findings, several other findings provide the basis for the development of institutional policies and practices for implementation by commuter colleges and universities. More specifically, we learned that such curricular arrangements and teaching practices as student participation in a learning community and faculty use of active learning practices positively influence student perceptions of their academic and intellectual development. We also delineated the following two institutional policies and practices that affect student perceptions of the integrity of their institution: having general-use computers with Internet access available throughout the campus, and having ample parking on campus for commuting students. Moreover, support from significant others for college attendance also benefits from students having reliable transportation to and from campus and taking measures to help the family members of the attending student feel welcome at the university. Our findings suggest that measures such as having a website that contains information for significant others, encouragement by the university for significant others to attend the orientation for new students, and making significant others feel welcomed at university events tend to shape a positive view of students that their family is welcomed at their institution. These assorted findings contributed to the development of the institutional policies and practices for implementation by commuter colleges and universities that we outlined in Chapter 3.

10

Conclusions and a Call
for Further Research

In this chapter, we offer conclusions derived from our pattern of findings obtained through theory testing and analytical cascading. We also present some implications for theory as well as some recommendations for further research. However, the limitations to both the *Residential College and University Study* and the *Commuter Colleges and Universities Study* delineated in Chapter 7 shape the conclusions, implications for theory, and recommendations for further research presented in this chapter.

Conclusions

We present six conclusions that we derive from both our theory testing and analytical cascading.

1. *Robust empirical support for the revised theory of student persistence in residential colleges and universities obtains.*

Our test of the revised theory of college student persistence in residential colleges and universities (Braxton, Hirschy, and McClendon, 2004) imparts robust empirical support for this theory. We make this assertion given that our test of this theory resulted in empirical support for five of the eight propositions of this theory. Moreover, two of the five supported propositions prevail as propositions indispensable to the logical and empirical coherence of this theory. These critical, empirically supported propositions are the positive influence of social integration on subsequent institutional commitment and the positive influence of subsequent institutional commitment on student persistence. Without empirical backing for these two propositions, the theory would fail to provide any basis for an explanation of student persistence in residential colleges and universities.

In addition to the empirical support provided for these two indispensable propositions, three of the six antecedents of social integration, and their attendant propositions, posited by this theory also garner empirical affirmation. Commitment of the institution to student welfare, institutional integrity, and psychosocial engagement constitute these three antecedents to social integration. The further explanatory power of this theory rests on empirical affirmation for these three antecedents of social integration. Without empirical support for antecedents of social integration, the theory would be incomplete.

Moreover, the explanatory power of this revised theory garners additional strength because of the empirical support provided by our pattern of findings for three of the six antecedents of social integration. Empirical support for the role of the commitment of the institution to student welfare, institutional integrity, and psychosocial engagement as positive influences on social integration imparts such additional explanatory power. Because of its critical importance to this theory, a knowledge of factors that influence social integration stands as an essential condition to the ability of this theory to account for student departure. Without antecedents to social integration, the theory would be incomplete.

However, our test of this theory failed to provide empirical affirmation for communal potential and proactive social adjustment as antecedents of social integration. Nevertheless, our process of analytical cascading revealed that communal potential positively influences psychosocial engagement and that proactive social adjustment influences communal potential. Thus, the placement of communal potential and proactive social adjustment in the logical flow of this theory requires adjustment. We discuss this adjustment in the upcoming section of this chapter, "Implications for Theory."

2. *Partial empirical support for the theory of student persistence in commuter colleges and universities exists.*

As indicated in the third limitation of the *Commuter Colleges and Universities Study* described in Chapter 7, we did not fully test the theory of student persistence in commuter colleges and universities. However, we did test 11 of the key propositions of this theory. We delineate these 11 propositions in Chapter 6. Our test of these 11 propositions resulted in empirical verification for 5 of them. As a consequence, we conclude that our test of this theory bestows partial empirical support for the theory of student persistence in commuter colleges and universities proposed by Braxton, Hirschy, and McClendon (2004) and revised in Chapter 6.

Despite this tepid appraisal, this theory warrants further testing. To elaborate, we garnered empirical support for most of the propositions pertinent to academic and intellectual development (two of three) and subsequent institutional commitments (two of three), the two critical facets of student persistence in commuter colleges and universities. As we stated in Chapter 6, we view academic and intellectual development and subsequent institutional commitment as critical facets of student persistence in commuter colleges and universities. Commuter students spend their time on campus attending classes and meeting degree requirements (Tinto, 1993). Thus, commuter students characterize their collegiate experience principally in terms of the degree of academic and intellectual development they experience because of their course work. The importance of subsequent institutional commitment emanates from its posited direct role in influencing student persistence decisions.

Beyond support for propositions germane to these two critical aspects, the positive influence of subsequent institutional commitment on student persistence also bolsters the degree of support ascribed to this theory. Without empirical support for the linkage between academic and intellectual development and subsequent institutional commitment as well as the linkage between subsequent institutional commitment and student persistence, this theory would lack any empirical footing as an explanation of student persistence in commuter colleges and universities. As a consequence, this theory merits further testing and does not warrant abandonment. We discuss the further testing of this theory later this chapter.

3. *Direct and indirect reliable relationships in influencing student persistence have been identified.*

Our testing of the two theories identified relationships that contribute to a body of reliable knowledge concerning factors that play either a direct or an indirect role in influencing student persistence. Two such reliable factors emerged from our testing of the theory of student persistence in residential colleges and universities. The positive influence of social integration on subsequent institutional commitment joins the ranks of the other 16 of 19 tests, as of 2005, that empirically affirm this relationship in residential colleges and universities (Braxton and Lee, 2005).[1] Moreover, the positive influence of subsequent institutional commitment on student persistence also emerges as reliable knowledge given that 11 of 13 previous tests empirically verify this relationship.

Our testing of the theory of student persistence in commuter colleges and universities likewise identified two relationships that add to our body of reliable knowledge about student persistence. The positive influence of academic and intellectual development on subsequent institutional commitment joins seven of ten tests previously conducted that affirm this relationship in commuter colleges and universities (Braxton and Lien, 2000).[2] Likewise, the positive relationship between subsequent institutional commitment and student persistence joins the ranks of the six other affirming tests of this relationship in commuter colleges and universities (Braxton and Lee, 2005).

4. *Organizational culture plays an indirect role in student persistence.*

The organizational culture of commuter and residential colleges and universities plays an important, albeit indirect, role in influencing student persistence in these two types of colleges and universities. As previously discussed in this volume, such organizational attributes as commitment of the institution to student welfare and institutional integrity reflect the culture of a college or university. We learned through our testing of the theory of residential colleges and universities (Chapter 8) that commitment of the institution to student welfare positively influences both social integration and subsequent institutional commitment, whereas institutional integrity positively influences social integration.

In commuter colleges and universities, institutional integrity wields a positive influence on both academic and intellectual development and subsequent institutional commitment, whereas commitment of the institution to student welfare influences academic and intellectual development in a positive way. We discerned these relationships through our testing of the theory of student persistence in commuter colleges and universities (Chapter 9).

5. *Faculty play a critical role in student persistence.*

We characterize the role of college and university faculty members as critical to student persistence. Tinto (2012) and Habley, Bloom, and Robbins (2012) offer a similar assertion. We ground this conclusion in findings we derived from our process of analytical cascading (Chapters 8 and 9). To elaborate, we note that the student perception that faculty at their institution hold a genuine interest in students wields a positive influence on their views of the commitment of their institution to student welfare and of its institutional integrity both commuter and residential colleges and universities. From analytical cascading, we also found that faculty who display a genuine interest in students also positively influence the academic and intellectual development of students (Chapter 9) as well as the support they receive from significant others for college attendance(Chapter 9) in commuter colleges and universities.

Faculty teaching role performance also indirectly contributes to student persistence. In residential colleges and universities, good teaching by faculty positively affects student perceptions of the commitment of the institution to student welfare (Chapter 8), whereas student reports of violations of the teaching norm of condescending negativism influences such perceptions in a negative way (Chapter 8). In commuter colleges and universities, such aspects of faculty teaching role performance as the use of active learning practices in class and the teaching skills of instructional clarity, organization, and preparation influence academic and intellectual development in an affirmative way. In such institutions, these teaching skills also positively influence both student perceptions of commitment of the institution to student welfare and institutional integrity.

6. *Direct influences on student persistence elude us.*

The empirical delineation of factors that directly influence student persistence in both residential and commuter colleges and universities elude us (see Tables C.1 and C.5 in Appendix C). Aside from our finding of a direct, positive influence of subsequent institutional commitment on student persistence in both residential and commuter colleges and universities, our test of the theory of student persistence in residential colleges and universities identified only initial institutional commitment as an additional positive direct influence on first-year student persistence in this type of college or university (Chapter 8). Moreover, the theory of student persistence in commuter colleges and universities delineated five propositions— parental educational level, motivation to graduate from college, the costs of college attendance, support from significant others for college attendance, and need for social affiliation—that predict a direct influence on student persistence. However, the testing of these five propositions failed to demonstrate a direct influence on student persistence in commuter colleges and universities (Chapter 9). Nevertheless, the testing of the proposition predicting a positive direct influence of subsequent institutional commitment on student persistence bore fruit, as did the identification of attending college full time as a direct influence on student persistence (Chapter 9).

Thus, the phenomenon of student persistence presents itself as difficult to predict and directly control. Thus, we characterize this phenomenon as slow to respond to such efforts. As a consequence, accounting for student persistence as well as the development of policies and practices to improve student retention requires a complexity of factors to influence this tricky phenomenon indirectly. Fortunately, the two theories described and tested in this volume model such complexity. Moreover, the multitude of levers of action we presented in Chapter 3 also addresses this need to view student persistence as a complex matter.

Implications for Theory

We divide our discussion of implications for theory into two categories. One category presents revisions for the two theories tested in this volume, whereas the second category offers some theoretical possibilities derived from findings of this book.

Implications for Theory Revision: Residential Colleges and Universities

As previously stated, our test of the theory of student persistence in residential colleges and universities provides strong empirical support for this theory. Nevertheless, findings that resulted from this theory test as well as from the process of analytical cascading indicate the need for revision of the theory of student persistence in residential colleges and universities.

Figure 10.1 graphically depicts the suggested revisions. The first revision entails the removal of proactive social adjustment and communal potential as direct antecedents of social integration as currently posited in this theory. This revision emanates from the failure of our test of this theory to find a statistically significant positive influence on communal potential and proactive social adjustment on social integration (Chapter 8). However, psychosocial engagement, commitment of the institution to student welfare, and institutional integrity remain as direct antecedents to social integration given that the test of this theory yielded the expected positive influence of these three factors on social integration.

The second revision involves the placement of communal potential as a direct source of influence on psychosocial engagement. Our process of analytical cascading delineated communal potential as a positive source of influence on psychosocial engagement (Chapter 8).

The third revision centers on the placement of proactive social adjustment as a direct influence on communal potential. This revision stems from our finding, derived from analytical cascading, that proactive social adjustment wields a positive influence on communal potential.

The addition of cultural capital to this theory stands as a fourth revision. We view cultural capital as a student entry characteristic that influences communal potential and psychosocial engagement, both in a positive way. We recommend this addition based on our finding that cultural capital positively influences both communal potential and psychosocial engagement.

A narrative form of these revisions reads as follows: A student's level of cultural capital equips the student to participate in conversations with peers in their residence halls, in their classes,

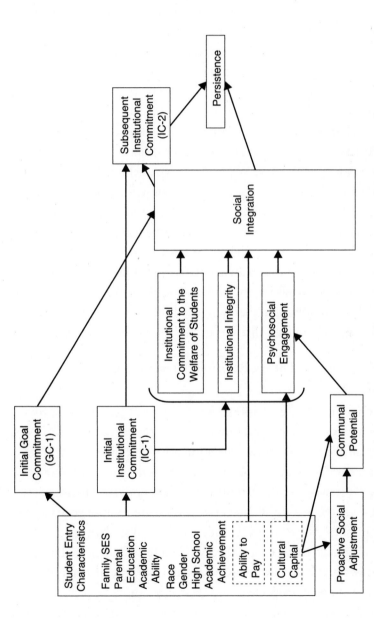

Figure 10.1 Toward a revision of the theory of student persistence in residential colleges and universities.

and in clubs and organizations. Accordingly, students with higher levels of cultural capital perceive that they will find a group of students with which they hold similar attitudes, beliefs, and values. As a consequence, cultural capital positively influences students' perceptions of their communal potential. Cultural capital also enables students to commit more fully the psychological energy necessary to engage in social interactions with their student peers and participate in extracurricular activities. Thus, cultural capital wields a positive influence on a student's level of psychosocial engagement.

In addition to the possession of varying degrees of cultural capital, the proactive adjustment of students also influences their degree of communal potential. Students who acknowledge that they need to approach stressful social situations with peers in a positive, proactive way can socially interact with their student peers in an unencumbered manner. As a consequence, proactive social adjustment by students enables them to gauge their likelihood of communal potential in an accurate way. Students who perceive communal potential for themselves are more likely to invest the levels of psychological energy needed for social interaction with student peers and participation in extracurricular activities.

Implications for Theory Revision: Commuter Colleges and Universities

We offer very minor revisions in the theory of student persistence in commuter colleges and universities. These revisions center on the placement of parental educational level, satisfaction with the costs for college attendance, and support from significant others for college attendance. As described in Chapter 6, the theory of student persistence in commuter colleges and universities posits direct relationships between these three factors and student persistence. However, our testing of this theory (Chapter 9) indicates that each of these factors influences subsequent institutional commitment and not student persistence.

The directions of these influences mirror those expected for student persistence. Specifically, we learned that parental educational level negatively affects subsequent institutional commitment, satisfaction with the costs of college positively influences subsequent institutional commitment, and support from significant others contributes in a positive way to shaping the subsequent institutional commitment of students. Accordingly, we recommend the placement of parental educational level, satisfaction with college costs, and support from significant others as sources of direct influence on subsequent institutional commitment and not persistence.

A Theoretical Possibility

We offer a suggestion for theory development. This suggestion delineates possible additions to the theory of student persistence in residential colleges and universities. This possible addition entails the placement of academic and intellectual development as an outcome of the commitment of the institution to student welfare. The rationale for this possible placement stems from the assertions of our fifth conclusion that stress the important, but indirect, role faculty members play in the persistence of students in residential colleges and universities. To elaborate, students who view faculty at their institution as genuinely interested in students and report good teaching by faculty also tend to perceive their college or university as committed to the welfare of students. Moreover, we found that commitment of the institution to student welfare positively influences academic and intellectual development in commuter colleges and universities. By extension, we might also find that student perceptions of the commitment of their institution to student welfare results in their academic and intellectual development in residential colleges and universities.

The vital role played by faculty, coupled with the influence of an institutional commitment to student welfare, brings academic dimensions back into the picture in residential colleges and universities. This perspective stands in stark contrast to the contention of Braxton, Hirschy, and McClendon (2004) that the role of academic integration (academic and intellectual development) stands as problematic in residential colleges and universities. Nevertheless, the findings of this volume offer a new perspective on the role of academics in residential colleges and universities. By suggesting such a view, we remain steadfast in asserting a strong role for social integration in the persistence of students in residential colleges and universities, a role well supported by our test of the theory of student persistence in residential colleges and universities.

A Call for Further Research

In this section of this chapter, we offer six recommendations for further research.

1. *Test the theory of student persistence in residential institutions in a variety of residential institutions that are not religiously affiliated.*

Scholars should test the theory of student persistence in residential colleges and universities in a variety of residential colleges and universities other than religiously affiliated institutions. Residential institutions across the spectrum of the Carnegie Classification of Institutions should serve as the settings for such theory testing. In particular, public and private research universities should serve as settings for theory testing. We recommend research universities because of Hermanowicz's (2003) finding concerning a "culture of enforced student success" in the research university with the highest retention rate. Given his finding, we might expect considerable institutional variation in the role of commitment of the institution to student welfare in research universities. Scholars may elect to test the initial version of this theory as described in Chapter 5 or test the revision to this theory outlined in this chapter and illustrated by Figure 10.1. Scholars should also pursue, if possible, the process of analytical cascading to identify those forces that influence empirically supported factors of the theory.

Such further theory testing should work toward adding to our body of reliable knowledge about factors important to student persistence in residential colleges and universities. We discussed such a body of reliable knowledge in our third conclusion.

2. *Test the theory of student persistence in commuter colleges and universities in a variety of four- and two-year commuter institutions.*

Scholars should test the theory of student persistence in a different set of commuter colleges and universities than the five institutions used in our test of this theory. In particular, two-year community colleges should serve as a setting for such theory testing given that Braxton, Hirschy, and McClendon (2004) posited this theory as applicable to both two- and four-year commuter institutions. Our test of this theory included only four-year institutions. Scholars may choose to test the theory of student persistence in commuter colleges and universities as postulated in Chapter 6 or may elect to test the theory with the minor revisions we offer here. Nevertheless, in conducting either test, scholars should work to conduct a complete test of this theory by including such psychological characteristics and processes as empathy, need for control and order in one's daily life, and sense of personal self-efficacy—factors we were unable to include in our test of this theory. If possible, scholars should also engage in the process of analytical cascading to identify those forces that influence empirically supported factors of the theory.

Furthermore, further theory testing should endeavor to add to our body of reliable knowledge those factors important to student persistence in commuter colleges and universities. We discussed such a body of reliable knowledge in our third conclusion.

3. *Future research on student persistence in commuter colleges and universities should include the Chickering and Gamson Principles of Good Practice.*

In our process of analytical cascading to identify forces that influence academic and intellectual development and the commitment of the institution to student welfare in commuter colleges and universities, we failed to detect empirical support for the influence of faculty use of four of the principles of good practice delineated by Chickering and Gamson (1987) on both of these factors of importance to student persistence in such colleges and universities. Encouragement of student-faculty contact, encouragement of cooperation among students, provision of prompt feedback, and the communication of high expectations constitute these four principles. We offer formulations for the possible influence of these principles of good practice in Chapter 6. Given these formulations, future research on student persistence in commuter colleges and universities should focus on the influence of these principles of good practice on such factors as academic and intellectual development and the commitment of the institution to student welfare.

4. *Future research on student persistence in residential institutions should include faculty teaching skills.*

Through our process of analytical cascading, we found that the teaching skills of instructor clarity, organization, and preparation positively influence student perceptions of their academic and intellectual development (Chapter 9), their perceptions of institutional integrity, and their perceptions of the commitment of the institution to student welfare in commuter colleges and universities (Chapter 9). We did not have measures of these two teaching skills available for analytical cascading to identify forces that influence commitment of the institution to student welfare and institutional integrity in residential colleges and universities. Future research in residential colleges and universities should include measures of these teaching skills. These measures are exhibited in Table A.3 of Appendix A.

5. *Future research on student persistence in commuter colleges and universities should include student perceptions of campus prejudice and racial discrimination.*

As we indicated in Chapter 8, our process of analytical cascading identified a student's perceptions of prejudice and racial discrimination on their campus as holding negative relationships with student perceptions of the commitment of their institution to the welfare of its students and student perceptions of the institutional integrity of their college or university in residential colleges and universities. We did not have a measure of student perceptions of prejudice and racial discrimination on their campus available for analytical cascading to identify forces that influence commitment of the institution to student welfare and institutional integrity in commuter colleges and universities. Future research in commuter colleges and universities should include such a measure, as shown in exhibited in Table A.3 of Appendix A.

6. *Assessment of the efficacy of policies and practices developed to increase institutional retention rates should occur.*

Chapters 2 and 3 of this volume present a vast array of levers of action. Pascarella (1986) recommends the empirical assessment of the efficacy of policies and practices developed to increase institutional retention rates. We concur with his recommendation. Through such appraisals, reliable knowledge about levers of institutional action may result. Reliable knowledge leads to the delineation of best practices.

Closing Thoughts

The key concluding thought for those policymakers pursuing improved college completion is that this goal ought not to be considered unattainable. Policymakers working with college and university leaders fundamentally changed the system of higher education in the latter half of the 20th century, allowing a previously unimaginable number of students to enroll in higher education. Many at the time thought that these students would not or could not benefit from higher education because they were not "college material." Now we face the challenge of ensuring that students are able to complete their educational goals. It is simply not the case that these students are not college material. Instead, with a focus on effective interventions that recognize the complexity of various higher education environments, more students than ever before can complete their objectives.

For the scholarly community, much work remains in our study of college student persistence. The conclusions, implications for theory, and suggestions for further research point the way for such work.

The practice communities at the level of individual colleges and universities must not lose track of the role of student persistence as a portal to other forms of student success. If students fail to persist, then their attainment of forms of student success such as academic attainment through student learning, acquisition of general education, development of academic competence (e.g., writing and speaking in a clear manner), development of cognitive skills and intellectual dispositions, occupational attainment, preparation for adulthood and citizenship, personal accomplishments (e.g., work on the college newspaper, election to student office), and personal development (Braxton, 2008) appear unattainable. Although the enactment of the multitude of levers of action we outlined in Chapter 3 seeks to increase institutional rates of student retention, the enactment of these levers of action also indirectly contributes to student success in ways other than their persistence.

Endnotes

1. The analysis conducted by Braxton and Lee (2005) focused only on single institutional tests of these relationships. Although the samples of residential and commuter colleges and universities are multi-institutional, we view our tests of the two theories as single-institutional. We assert that these two aggregated samples are the product of separate, discrete studies of student persistence. At each institution, a longitudinal panel design with data collected at different points in time from a randomly selected sample of students was used. Moreover, the variables of both theories were measured phenomenologically within the context of each of the participating colleges and universities. Thus, the reported behaviors of students are nested within the context of each of the participating colleges and universities. Moreover, the recorded perceptions of students stem from their own experiences and their interpretations of such experiences with their particular college or university.

2. The analysis conducted by Braxton and Lien (2000) focused on academic integration. However, academic integration and academic and intellectual development are interchangeable, because the indicators typically used to measure academic integration, at base, measure academic and intellectual development. See Chapter 6 for more details on this matter.

Appendix A

Design of the Studies Tables

We developed this appendix to serve as a companion to Chapter 7. This appendix includes Tables A.1 to A.8, which exhibit such details as our operational definitions of the variables used to test the two theories, the variables used in analytical cascading, the Cronbach reliability estimates of those variables measured as composite variables, and the means and standard deviations of all of the variables used. Tables A.1 to A.4 pertain to the testing of the theory of student persistence in residential colleges and universities and to analytical cascading for this theory, whereas Tables A.5 to A.8 relate to the testing of the theory of student persistence in commuter colleges and universities and to analytical cascading for this theory.

Table A.1   Description of the Variables Used to Test the Revised Theory of Student Persistence in Residential Colleges and Universities

Variable Name	Operational Definition
Gender	Student gender (male = 0; female = 1). Item on the *Fall Collegiate Experiences Survey*.
Race/ethnicity	White Caucasian students = 1, other racial/ethnic groups = 0. Survey items on the *Fall Collegiate Experiences Survey*.
Parental education level	Level of parental educational attainment (grammar school or less for both parents = 2 to graduate work for both parents = 16). Composite variable is sum of two items: father's level of educational attainment and mother's level. Survey items on the *Fall Collegiate Experiences Survey*.
Average grades in high school	Self-reported high school cumulative grade average (D or lower = 1 to A or A+ = 10). Item on the *Fall Collegiate Experiences Survey*.
On-campus residence	Living on campus in a residence hall or a fraternity or sorority house = 1; off campus with family or without family = 0. Survey item on the *Fall Collegiate Experiences Survey*.
Initial institutional commitment	Ranking of student's college choice (fourth choice or more = 1 to first choice = 4). Item on the *Fall Collegiate Experiences Survey*.
Proactive social adjustment	Composite of four items that ask students what they usually do when they experience a stressful event. These actions are as follows: try to grow as a person as a result of the experience, try to see it in a different light to make it seem more positive, look for something good in what is happening, and learn something from the experience. Cronbach's alpha = 0.75. Survey items from the *Fall Collegiate Experiences Survey*.
Psychosocial engagement	Self-reported estimates of how frequently during the fall semester the student talked with or discussed course content with other students outside of class; studied or socialized with friends; attended campus movies, plays, concerts, and/ or recitals; participated in social activities with members of the Greek system; gone out on a date with another student; drank beer, wine, or liquor (never = 1 to very often = 5). Cronbach's alpha = 0.64. Survey items on the *Fall Collegiate Experiences Survey*.

Table A.1   (continued)

Variable Name	Operational Definition
Communal potential	Composite of nine items measuring student's perceptions of the potential for community among peers on campus: like the way students treat each other, satisfied with student presence on campus during weekends, believe that there are peers on campus student would like to know better, believe groups of peers exist that student would like to get involved with, can see several ways to make connections with peers on campus, recognize many students seen on campus, confident that there are peers on campus with whom student shares important values, peers seem to deal with conflicts constructively, peers encourage academic success (strongly disagree = 1 to strongly agree = 4). Cronbach's alpha = 0.78. Survey items on the *Fall Collegiate Experiences Survey*.
Institutional integrity	Composite of five items measuring student perceptions that the institution exhibits integrity: the actions of the administration are consistent with the stated mission of this institution, the institution almost always does the right thing, the values of this institution are communicated clearly to the campus community, the rules of this institution appear in harmony with the values the institution espouses, the decisions made at this institution rarely conflict with the values it espouses (strongly disagree = 1 to strongly agree = 4). Cronbach's alpha = 0.87. Survey items from the *Spring Collegiate Experiences Survey*.
Commitment of the institution to student welfare	Composite of 10 items measuring student perceptions that the institution is committed to the welfare of students: most student services staff (e.g., dean of students office, student activities, housing, etc.) are genuinely interested in students; most other college/university staff (e.g., registrar, student accounts, financial aid, etc.) are genuinely interested in students; most of the campus religious leaders (e.g., chaplain, priest, rabbi, etc.) are genuinely interested in students; have experienced negative interactions with faculty members (reverse scored); have experienced negative interactions with student services staff (reverse scored); have experienced negative interactions with other college/university staff (reverse scored); faculty members treat students with respect; student services staff treat students with respect; other college/university staff treat students with respect; know where to go if need more information about a policy (strongly disagree = 1 to strongly agree = 4). Cronbach's alpha = 0.86. Survey items from the *Spring Collegiate Experiences Survey*.

(continued)

Table A.1 *(continued)*

Variable Name	Operational Definition
Social integration	Composite of seven items measuring the degree of student's integration into the campus social system: interpersonal relationships with other students have had influence on intellectual growth; developed close personal relationships with peers; peer relationships have had influence on personal growth, values, and attitudes; difficulty making friends (reverse scored); few peers would listen to personal problems (reverse scored); peer friendships have been satisfying; student's attitudes and values differ from that of peers (reverse scored) (strongly disagree = 1 to strongly agree = 4). Cronbach's alpha = 0.79. Items on the *Spring Collegiate Experiences Survey*.
Subsequent institutional commitment	Composite of two items measuring degree of subsequent commitment to college of enrollment: not important to graduate from this college (reverse scored), made the right decision in choosing to attend this college (strongly disagree = 1 to strongly agree = 4). Cronbach's alpha = 0.36. Items derived from the *Spring Collegiate Experiences Survey*.
Student persistence	Student's decision to reenroll at institution for fall 2003. Data source for enrollment status provided by participating institutions (not enrolled = 0, enrolled = 1).

Table A.2   Means and Standard Deviations for Variables Used in the Testing of the Revised Theory of Student Persistence in Residential Colleges and Universities

Variable Name	Mean	Standard Deviation
Gender	0.60	0.49
Race/ethnicity	0.81	0.39
Parental education level	10.21	3.32
Parental income	8.74	2.94
Average grades in high school	8.20	1.75
On-campus residence	0.87	0.33
Initial institutional commitment	3.54	0.80
Ability to pay	1.83	0.66
Proactive social adjustment	3.14	0.58
Psychosocial engagement	2.66	0.47
Communal potential	3.06	0.40
Institutional integrity	2.94	0.52
Commitment of the institution to student welfare	3.11	0.47
Social integration	3.07	0.47
Subsequent institutional commitment	3.07	0.73
Student persistence	0.89	0.31

Table A.3   Description of the Variables Related to Analytical Cascading for Residential Colleges and Universities

Variable Name	Operational Definition
Academic advising	Student response to the survey item on the *Fall Collegiate Experiences Survey*: "Academic advisement is a strong component of the academic environment here" (strongly disagree = 1 to strongly agree = 4).
Communication	Composite of six items measuring student perceptions of how well informed they are about academic rules, social rules, course requirements, graduation requirements, changes to academic rules/requirements, and changes to social rules (very poorly informed = 1 to very well informed = 5). Cronbach's alpha = 0.88. Survey items on the *Spring Collegiate Experiences Survey*.
Cultural capital	Self-reported estimates of how frequently the student engaged in cultural activities in senior year of high school, such as private art or music lessons; participated in band, choir, dance, drama, or musical; visited art or history museums; studied a foreign language, read for pleasure, took a dance class outside of school; attended a symphony concert, ballet, or opera performance; performed volunteer work; and borrowed books from the public library (never = 1 to very frequently = 5). Cronbach's alpha = 0.81. Survey items on the *Fall Collegiate Experiences Survey*.
Dimension of community in residence halls: identity	Composite of four items measuring student agreement with such statements as, "My residence hall floor is a good place to live," "I feel at home on my residence hall floor," "I care about what my neighbors on my residence hall floor think about my actions," and "It is important for me to live on my particular residence hall floor" (strongly disagree = 1 to strongly agree = 4). Cronbach's alpha = 0.62. Survey items from the *Fall Collegiate Experiences Survey*.
Dimension of community in residence halls: interaction	Composite of four items measuring student agreement with such statements as, "I can recognize all of the people who live on my residence hall floor," "Very few of my neighbors on my residence hall floor know me" (reverse scored), "I have no influence over what my residence hall floor is like" (reverse scored), and "People on my residence hall floor generally do not get along with each other" (reverse scored) (strongly disagree = 1 to strongly agree = 4). Cronbach's alpha = 0.59. Survey items from the *Fall Collegiate Experiences Survey*.

Table A.3   (continued)

Variable Name	Operational Definition
Dimension of community in residence halls: solidarity	Composite of three items measuring student agreement with such statements as, "People on my residence hall floor do not share the same values" (reverse scored), "My neighbors and I want the same thing for our residence hall floor," and "If there is a problem on my residence hall floor people who live there can get it solved" (strongly disagree = 1 to strongly agree = 4). Cronbach's alpha = 0.51. Survey items from the *Fall Collegiate Experiences Survey*.
Faculty interest in students	Composite of two items measuring student agreement with such statements as, "Most faculty members I have had contact with are genuinely interested in students," and "Most of the faculty I have had contact with are interesting in helping students grow in more than just academic areas" (strongly disagree = 1 to strongly agree = 4). Cronbach's alpha = 0.70. Survey items from the *Spring Collegiate Experiences Survey*.
Faculty use of active learning practices	Composite of six times measuring the frequency in which the following activities were engaged in: "Instructors engage me in classroom discussion or debate of course ideas and concepts"; "Instructors' questions in class ask me to point out fallacies in basic ideas, principles, or points of view in the course"; "Instructors' questions in class ask me to argue for or against a particular point of view"; "Few exams require me to argue for or against a particular point of view" (reverse scored); "Course papers or research projects require me to argue for or against a particular point of view and defend my argument"; and "Course papers require me to propose a plan for a research project or experiment" (never = 1 to very often = 4). Cronbach's alpha = 0.59. Survey items derived from the *Spring Collegiate Experiences Survey*.
Faculty violations of the norm of condescending negativism	Composite of the frequency of four faculty behaviors personally known to the student during the academic year: expressions of impatience with a slow learner, making condescending remarks to students in class, criticizing the academic performance of a student in front of other students, and treating an advisee in a condescending manner (never = 1 to frequently = 4). Cronbach's alpha = 0.83. Survey items from the *Spring Collegiate Experience Survey*.

(continued)

Table A.3   (continued)

Variable Name	Operational Definition
Faculty violations of the norm of moral turpitude	Composite of the frequency of two faculty behaviors personally known to the student during the academic year: frequently attends class while obviously intoxicated and makes suggestive sexual comments to a student enrolled in the course (never = 1 to frequently = 4). Cronbach's alpha = 0.87. Survey items from the *Spring Collegiate Experience Survey*.
Faculty violations of the norm of particularistic grading	Composite of the frequency of three faculty behaviors personally known to the student during the academic year: allows personal friendships with a student to intrude on the objective grading of their work; social, personal, or other nonacademic characteristics of students are taken into account in the awarding of grades; and stated policies about late work and incompletes are not universally applied to all students (never = 1 to frequently = 4). Cronbach's alpha = 0.78. Survey items from the *Spring Collegiate Experience Survey*.
Faculty violations of the norm of personal disregard	Composite of the frequency of four faculty behaviors personally known to the student during the academic year: frequently uses profanity in class, usually dismisses class early, practices poor personal hygiene and regularly has offensive body odor, and routinely comes late to class (never = 1 to frequently = 4). Cronbach's alpha = 0.68. Survey items from the *Spring Collegiate Experience Survey*.
Fairness	Composite of six items measuring student perceptions of how fairly at their institution the following are done: enforcement of academic rules, enforcement of social rules, grading, awarding scholarships, assigning housing to students, and assigning office/activity space to student groups (not at all = 1 to a very great extent = 5). Cronbach's alpha = 0.79. Survey items from the *Spring Collegiate Experiences Survey*.
Fall first-year student orientation as preparation for academic success	Student response to the survey item on the *Fall Collegiate Experiences Survey*: "Freshmen orientation adequately prepared me for success in the academic environment" (strongly disagree = 1 to strongly agree = 4).
Fall first-year student orientation as preparation for social success	Student response to the survey item on the *Fall Collegiate Experiences Survey*: "Freshmen orientation adequately prepared me for success in the social environment" (strongly disagree = 1 to strongly agree = 4).
Fulfillment of academic	Composite of three items measuring student comparisons of how satisfied they thought they would be when deciding

Table A.3   (*continued*)

Variable Name	Operational Definition
expectations for college	to attend their college or university with their current level of satisfaction for the following: the quality of faculty for their courses, the number of students in their classes, and the quality of courses in the field they want (much worse than I thought = 1 to much better than I thought = 5). Cronbach's alpha = 0.80. Survey items from the *Spring Collegiate Experiences Survey*.
Fulfillment of social expectations for college	Composite of three items measuring student comparisons of how satisfied they thought they would be when deciding to attend their college or university with their current level of satisfaction for the following: the day-to-day personal relations I would have with other students, my social life, and overall the degree to which I feel that I fit into the social environment here (much worse than I thought = 1 to much better than I thought = 5). Cronbach's alpha = 0.83. Survey items from the *Spring Collegiate Experiences Survey*.
Participation in decision making	Composite of eight items measuring student perceptions of how much say they feel they actually have in making the following decisions: kinds of course assignments, amount of course assignments, making academic rules/requirements, changing academic rules/requirements, making social rules, changing social rules, making rules in the residence halls (if applicable), and changing the rules in the residence halls (if applicable) (no say = 1 to a great deal of say = 5). Cronbach's alpha = 0.92. Survey items from the *Spring Collegiate Experiences Survey*.
Student perceptions of prejudice and racial discrimination on their campus	A composite of eight items measuring student agreement with such statements as, having observed discriminatory words, behaviors, or gestures directed at minority students here; having observed discriminatory words, behaviors, or gestures directed at majority students here; feeling there is a general atmosphere of prejudice among students; having encountered racism while attending this institution; having heard negative words about people of my own race or ethnicity while attending classes; feeling there is a general atmosphere of prejudice among academic staff here; feeling there is a general atmosphere of prejudice among nonacademic staff here; and having been singled out in class and having been treated differently than other students because of my race (strongly disagree = 1 to strongly agree = 4). Cronbach's alpha = 0.90. Survey items from the *Spring Collegiate Experiences Survey*.

(continued)

Table A.3   (continued)

Variable Name	Operational Definition
Student reports of good teaching	Composite of two items measuring student agreement with such statements as, "Few of the faculty members I have had contact with are genuinely outstanding or superior teachers," and "Few of the faculty members I have had contact with are genuinely interested in teaching" (both items reverse scored) (strongly disagree = 1 to strongly agree = 4). Cronbach's alpha = 0.85. Items on the *Spring Collegiate Experiences Survey*.

Table A.4   Means and Standard Deviations for Variables Related to Analytical Cascading for Residential Colleges and Universities

Variable Name	Mean	Std. Dev.
Academic advising	3.03	0.72
Communication	3.67	0.73
Cultural capital	2.20	0.60
Dimensions of community in residence halls: identity	2.82	0.56
Dimensions of community in residence halls: interaction	3.07	0.54
Dimensions of community in residence halls: solidarity	2.72	0.55
Faculty interest in students	3.21	0.60
Faculty use of active learning practices	2.77	0.58
Faculty violations of the norm of condescending negativism	1.46	0.61
Faculty violations of the norm of moral turpitude	1.19	0.52
Faculty violations of the norm of particularistic grading	1.55	0.67
Faculty violations of the norm of personal disregard	1.66	0.54
Fairness	3.56	0.67
Fall first-year student orientation as preparation for academic success	2.58	0.86
Fall first-year student orientation as preparation for social success	2.66	0.87

Table A.4 (continued)

Variable Name	Mean	Std. Dev.
Fulfillment of academic expectations for college	3.61	0.76
Fulfillment of social expectations for college	3.62	0.82
Participation in decision making	2.54	0.82
Student perceptions of prejudice and racial discrimination on campus	1.84	0.62
Student reports of good teaching	2.74	0.88

Table A.5 Description of Variables Used to Test the Theory of Student Persistence in Commuter Colleges and Universities

Variable Name	Operational Definition
Gender	Student gender (male = 0; female = 1). Survey item from the *University Student's Experience Survey*.
Race/ethnicity	White Caucasian students = 1, other racial/ethnic groups = 0. Survey item on the *University Student's Experience Survey*.
Parental education level	Level of parental educational attainment (grammar school or less for both parents = 2 to graduate work for both parents = 16). Composite variable is sum of two items: father's level of educational attainment and mother's level. Survey items derived from the *University Student's Experience Survey*.
Average grades in high school	Student response to the question, "What were your average grades in high school?" (D or lower = 1 to A or A+ = 10).
Attendance status	Student response to the question, "What is your current enrollment status?" (full time student =1, part time student = 0). Survey item from the *University Student's Experience Survey*.
Costs of college attendance	Student agreement with the statement, "I am satisfied with the amount of financial support (grants, loans, work-study) I have received while attending this institution" (strongly disagree = 1 to strongly agree = 4). Survey item from the *University Student's Experience Survey*.
Need for social affiliation	Composite of 10 survey items that measure the likes and dislikes of students that pertain to various social interactions. Students indicate the extent of their agreement with such statements as, "I enjoy going to the park or beach with a crowd," "I enjoy leading an active social life," "I enjoy meeting a lot of people," and "I enjoy belonging to a social group" (strongly disagree = 1 to strongly agree = 4). Cronbach's alpha = 0.87. Survey items from the *University Student's Experience Survey*.

(continued)

Table A.5 *(continued)*

Variable Name	Operational Definition
Motivation to graduate from college	Student agreement with the statement, "I am determined to finish college regardless of the obstacles that get in my way (strongly disagree = 1 to strongly agree = 4). Survey item from the *University Student's Experience Survey*.
Support from significant others	Composite of two survey items measuring student agreement with the statements, "The people closest to me (e.g., parents, family members, close friends, significant other) approve of my attendance at this university," and "The people closest to me (e.g., parents, family members, close friends, significant other) encourage me to get a college degree (strongly disagree = 1 to strongly agree = 4). Cronbach's alpha = 0.69. Survey items derived from the *University Student's Experience Survey*.
Institutional integrity	Composite of five items measuring student perceptions that the institution exhibits integrity: the actions of the administration are consistent with the stated mission of this institution, the institution almost always does the right thing, the values of this institution are communicated clearly to the campus community, the rules of this institution appear in harmony with the values the institution espouses, the decisions made at this institution rarely conflict with the values it espouses (strongly disagree = 1 to strongly agree = 4). Cronbach's alpha = 0.84. Survey items from the *University Student's Experience Survey*.
Institutional commitment to student welfare	Composite of nine measuring student perceptions that the institution is committed to the welfare of students: most student services staff (e.g., dean of students office, student activities, housing, etc.) are genuinely interested in students, most other college/university staff (e.g., registrar, student accounts, financial aid, etc.) are genuinely interested in students, have experienced negative interactions with faculty members (reverse scored), have experienced negative interactions with student services staff (reverse scored), have experienced negative interactions with other college/university staff (reverse scored), faculty members treat students with respect, student services staff treat students with respect, other college/university staff treat students with respect, know where to go if need more information about a policy (strongly disagree = 1 to strongly agree = 4). Cronbach's alpha = 0.31. Survey items from the *University Student's Experience Survey*.
Academic and intellectual development	Composite of three survey items measuring student perceptions of their academic and intellectual development: satisfaction with the academic experience at their university,

Table A.5   (continued)

Variable Name	Operational Definition
	satisfied with the extent of their intellectual development since enrolling, and their interest in ideas and intellectual matters has increased since coming to their university (strongly disagree = 1 to strongly agree = 4). Cronbach's alpha = 0.78. Survey items derived from the *University Student's Experience Survey*.
Subsequent institutional commitment	Composite of two survey items measuring student agreement with the statements, "It is not important for me to graduate from this university" (reverse scored), and "I am confident that I made the right decision in choosing to attend this university" (strongly disagree = 1 to strongly agree = 4). Cronbach's alpha = 0.18. Items derived from the *University Student's Experience Survey*.
Student persistence	Return to university in fall 2008 (did return in fall 2008 = 1 to did not return in fall 2008 = 0). Institutional records.

Table A.6   Means and Standard Deviations for Variables Related to the Test of the Theory of Student Persistence in Commuter Colleges and Universities

Variable Name	Mean	Std. Dev.
Gender	0.55	0.49
Race/ethnicity	0.83	0.38
Parental educational level	8.75	3.03
Average grades in high school	7.28	2.14
Attendance status	0.83	0.38
Costs of college attendance	2.65	0.99
Need for social affiliation	2.90	0.56
Motivation to graduate from college	3.68	0.53
Support from significant others	3.59	0.53
Institutional integrity	2.94	0.49
Commitment of the institution to student welfare	3.00	0.46
Academic and intellectual development	3.15	0.54
Subsequent institutional commitment	2.96	0.67
Student persistence	0.73	0.44

Table A.7   Description of Variables Related to Analytical Cascading for Commuter Colleges and Universities

Variable Name	Operational Definition
Academic advising	Student agreement with the statement, "Academic advising is a strong component of the academic environment at this university" (strongly disagree = 1 to strongly agree = 4). Survey item from the *University Student's Experience Survey*.
Ample parking on campus for commuting students	Student agreement with the statement, "There is ample parking on campus for commuting students" (strongly disagree = 1 to strongly agree = 4). Survey item from the *University Student's Experience Survey*.
Clear communication of campus activities to students	Student agreement with the statement, "Campus activities are clearly communicated to me" (strongly disagree = 1 to strongly agree = 4). Survey item from the *University Student's Experience Survey*.
Clear communication of institutional policies to students	Student agreement with the statement, "The policies of this institution are clearly communicated to me" (strongly disagree = 1 to strongly agree = 4). Survey item from the *University Student's Experience Survey*.
Commuting to and from campus as convenient as possible	Student agreement with the statement, "This institution attempts to make commuting to and from campus as convenient as possible" (strongly disagree = 1 to strongly agree = 4). Survey item from the *University Student's Experience Survey*.
Course registration as a straightforward process	Student agreement with the statement, "Registration for classes at this institution is a straightforward process" (strongly disagree = 1 to strongly agree = 4). Survey item from the *University Student's Experience Survey*.
Drop-in child-care services	Student response to the statement, "This university has drop-in child-care services for enrolled students" (yes = 1; no, not sure = 0). Survey item from the *University Student's Experience Survey*.
Eating facilities open during times convenient for commuting students	Student agreement with the statement, "Eating facilities are open during convenient times for commuting students" (strongly disagree = 1 to strongly agree = 4). Survey item from the *University Student's Experience Survey*.

Table A.7   (*continued*)

Variable Name	Operational Definition
Faculty interest in students	Composite of two survey items measuring student agreement with such statements as, "Most faculty members I have had contact with are genuinely interested in students," and "Most of the faculty I have had contact with are interested in helping students grow in more than just academic areas" (strongly disagree = 1 to strongly agree = 4). Cronbach's alpha = 0.62. Survey items from the *University Student's Experience Survey*.
Faculty teaching skill of instructional clarity	Composite of five survey items registering student perceptions of the frequency in which things happen in classes they have taken or are currently taking this academic year, such as instructors give clear examples, instructors make good use of examples and illustrations to get across difficult points, instructors effectively review and summarize the material, instructors interpret abstract ideas and theories clearly, and instructors answer students' questions in a way that helps students understand the material (never = 1 to very often = 4). Cronbach's alpha = 0.84. Survey items derived from the *University Student's Experience Survey*.
Faculty teaching skill of organization and preparation	Composite of five survey items registering student perceptions of the frequency in which things happen in classes they have taken or are currently taking this academic year, such as presentation of class materials is well-organized, instructors are well prepared for class, instructors use class time effectively, course requirements are clearly explained, instructors have a good command of what they are teaching (never = 1 to very often = 4). Cronbach's alpha = 0.87. Survey items derived from the *University Student's Experience Survey*.
Faculty use of active learning practices	Composite of five survey items registering student perceptions of the frequency in which things happen in classes they have taken or are currently taking this academic year, such as "Instructors engage me in classroom discussions or debate"; "Instructors' questions in class ask me to point out fallacies in basic ideas, principles, or points of view presented in the course"; "Instructors' questions in class ask me to argue for or against a particular point of view"; "Course papers or research projects require me to argue for or against a particular point of view and defend my argument"; and "Course papers require me to propose a plan for a research project or experiment" (never = 1 to very often = 4). Cronbach's alpha = 0.72. Survey items derived from the *University Student's Experience Survey*.

(*continued*)

Table A.7 (*continued*)

Variable Name	Operational Definition
Family feels welcomed on campus	Student agreement with the statement, "I feel as though my family is welcomed on this campus" (strongly disagree = 1 to strongly agree = 4). Survey item from the *University Student's Experience Survey*.
First-year student orientation	Student agreement with the statement, "First-year student orientation adequately prepared me for success in the academic environment of this university" (strongly disagree = 1 to strongly agree = 4). Survey item from the *University Student's Experience Survey*.
General-use computers with Internet access available throughout the campus	Student agreement with the statement, "General-use computers with access to the Internet are available throughout this campus" (strongly disagree = 1 to strongly agree = 4). Survey item from the *University Student's Experience Survey*.
Hours employed off campus	Student response to the question, "During this academic year, approximately how many hours per week were you employed off-campus?" (none = 1 to more than 35 = 9). Survey item from the *University Student's Experience Survey*.
Hours employed on campus	Student response to the question, "During this academic year, approximately how many hours per week were you employed on-campus?" (none = 1 to more than 35 = 9). Survey item from the *University Student's Experience Survey*.
Important information communicated to significant others	Student agreement with the statement, "The university frequently communicates important information to my parents/spouse" (strongly disagree = 1 to strongly agree = 4). Survey item from the *University Student's Experience Survey*.
Library open during the weekend	Student response to the statement, "The university library is open during the weekend" (yes = 1; no, not sure = 0). Survey item from the *University Student's Experience Survey*.
Offering classes at times convenient to students	Student agreement with the statement, "Classes at this institution are offered at times which are convenient to me" (strongly disagree = 1 to strongly agree = 4). Survey item from the *University Student's Experience Survey*.
Offices serve students open at times convenient for students who work (provision of student services)	Student agreement with the statement, "University offices that serve students (e.g., financial aid, counseling, registrar) are open at times convenient for students who work while attending this university" (strongly disagree = 1 to strongly agree = 4). Survey item from the *University Student's Experience Survey*.

Table A.7   (continued)

Variable Name	Operational Definition
On-campus employment opportunities for students	Student response to the statement, "This university has on-campus employment opportunities for enrolled students" (yes = 1; no, not sure = 0). Survey item from the *University Student's Experience Survey*.
Parking convenient to the classes of students	Student agreement with the statement, "Parking on campus is convenient to my classes" (strongly disagree = 1 to strongly agree = 4). Survey item from the *University Student's Experience Survey*
Participation in a learning community	Student response to the statement, "Since entering this university I have taken two or more courses with the same group of students. The two or more courses had an underlying theme" (yes = 1; no, not sure = 0). Survey item from the *University Student's Experience Survey*.
Peer mentoring program	Student response to the statement, "This university has a peer mentoring program" (yes = 1; no, not sure = 0). Survey item from the *University Student's Experience Survey*.
Physical facilities for students to study, type papers, and make copies of course materials	Student response to the statement, "This university has physical facilities for students to study, type papers, and to make copies of various course materials" (yes = 1; no, not sure = 0). Survey item from the *University Student's Experience Survey*.
Physical space open on weekends	Student response to the statement, "This university has a physical space open for students during the weekends" (yes =1; no, not sure = 0). Survey item from the *University Student's Experience Survey*.
Principles of good practice: cooperation among students	Composite of two survey items registering student perceptions of the frequency in which things happen in classes they have taken or are currently taking this academic year, such as instructors requiring students to work in groups and instructors requiring students to work in cooperative groups to do course assignments (never = 1 to very often = 4). Cronbach's alpha = 0.86. Survey items derived from the *University Student's Experience Survey*.
Principles of good practice: encouragement of faculty-student contact	One survey item that registers student perceptions of the frequency in which things happen in classes they have taken or are currently taking this academic year in which instructors encourage students to drop by their offices just to visit (never = 1 to very often = 4). Survey item derived from the *University Student's Experience Survey*.

(continued)

Table A.7 (continued)

Variable Name	Operational Definition
Principles of good practice: prompt feedback	One survey item that registers student perceptions of the frequency in which things happen in classes they have taken or are currently taking this academic year in which instructors return examinations and papers within a week (never = 1 to very often = 4). Survey item derived from the *University Student's Experience Survey*.
Principles of good practice: setting of high expectations for students	Composite of three survey items registering student perceptions of the frequency in which things happen in classes they have taken or are currently taking this academic year, such as instructors telling students that they expect them to work hard in their classes, instructors emphasizing the importance of holding high standards for academic achievement, and instructors explaining to students what will happen if they do not complete their work on time (never = 1 to very often = 4). Cronbach's alpha = 0.76. Survey items derived from the *University Student's Experience Survey*.
Reliable transportation to and from campus	One item measuring student agreement with the statement, "I have reliable transportation to and from campus" (strongly agree = 1 to strongly disagree = 4). Survey item from the *University Student's Experience Survey*.
Reports of good teaching by faculty	One item measuring student agreement with the statement, "Few of the faculty members I have had contact with are genuinely outstanding or superior teachers" (strongly agree = 1 to strongly disagree = 4). Survey item from the *University Student's Experience Survey*.
Significant others encouraged to attend new student orientation	Student agreement with the statement, "The university encourages significant others (e.g., spouse/life partner, parents) to attend the orientation for new students" (strongly disagree = 1 to strongly agree = 4). Survey item from the *University Student's Experience Survey*.
Significant others welcomed at on-campus events	Student agreement with the statement, "My significant others (e.g., spouse/life partner, parents) feel welcomed at events at this university" (strongly disagree = 1 to strongly agree = 4). Survey item from the *University Student's Experience Survey*.
Technology to communicate information to students	Student agreement with the statement, "Technology (e.g., e-mail, institutional website, etc.) is effectively used by this university to communicate information to students" (strongly disagree = 1 to strongly agree = 4). Survey item from the *University Student's Experience Survey*.

Table A.7   (*continued*)

Variable Name	Operational Definition
Website for significant others	Student response to the statement, "This university has a website that contains information for the significant others (e.g., parents, spouse/life partner) of enrolled students" (yes = 1; no, not sure = 0). Survey item from the *University Student's Experience Survey*.

Note: All composite variables are computed as the mean of the items included in the composite.

Table A.8   Means and Standard Deviations for Variables Related to Analytical Cascading for Commuter Colleges and Universities

Variable Name	Mean	Std. Dev.
Academic advising	2.89	0.81
Ample parking on campus for commuting students	2.22	0.99
Clear communication of campus activities to students	2.89	0.83
Clear communication of institutional policies to students	3.19	0.73
Commuting to and from campus as convenient as possible	2.53	0.93
Course registration as a straightforward process	3.08	0.82
Drop-in child-care services	0.22	0.41
Eating facilities open during times convenient for commuting students	3.08	0.80
Faculty interest in students	2.96	0.62
Faculty teaching skill of instructional clarity	3.05	0.56
Faculty teaching skill of organization and preparation	3.21	0.58
Faculty use of active learning practices	2.71	0.55
Family feels welcomed on campus	3.10	0.74
First-year student orientation	2.66	0.81
General-use computers with Internet access available throughout the campus	3.42	0.65
Hours employed off campus	4.49	2.96
Hours employed on campus	1.47	1.31

(*continued*)

Table A.8   (continued)

Variable Name	Mean	Std. Dev.
Important information communicated to significant others	2.36	0.87
Offering classes at times convenient to students	2.97	0.75
Offices that serve students open at times convenient for students who work	2.83	0.82
On-campus employment opportunities for students	0.79	0.40
Parking convenient to the classes of students	2.36	1.03
Participation in a learning community	0.62	0.49
Peer mentoring program	0.32	0.47
Physical facilities for students to study, type papers, and make copies of course materials	0.89	0.31
Physical space open on weekends	0.57	0.49
Principles of good practice: cooperation among students	2.49	0.75
Principles of good practice: encouragement of faculty-student contact	2.14	0.95
Principles of good practice: prompt feedback	2.90	0.81
Principles of good practice: setting of high standards for students	3.01	0.66
Reliable transportation to and from campus	3.54	0.68
Reports of good teaching by faculty	2.35	0.89
Significant others encouraged to attend new student orientation	2.97	0.74
Significant others welcomed at on-campus events	2.93	0.73
Technology to communicate information to students	3.26	0.72
Website for significant others	0.63	0.48

Note: All composite variables are computed as the mean of the items included in the composite.

Appendix B

Technical Appendix for Statistical Procedures

Section 8.1

We conducted three separate regression analyses: one for social integration (propositions 1 to 6), one for subsequent institutional commitment (proposition 7), and one for student persistence (proposition 8) as the dependent variables. For each these three analyses, we used fixed effects for each of the eight colleges and universities included in the data sources used. We used fixed institutional effects to hold constant the unique effects of each specific institution on the focal dependent variables. Specifically, we regressed social integration first on the fixed institutional effects followed by each of the five student entry characteristics, on-campus residence, ability to pay, initial institutional commitment, institutional commitment to the welfare of students, communal potential, institutional integrity, proactive social adjustment, and psychosocial engagement. We regressed subsequent institutional commitment on the same array of variables plus social integration. Moreover, we regressed student persistence on the same array of variables as subsequent institutional commitment, but added subsequent institutional commitment to the analysis. The dichotomous and highly skewed properties of our measure of student persistence required that we also conduct a logistical regression which corroborated the results of the hierarchical regression analyses with student persistence as the dependent variable. We used the 0.05 level of significance to identify those propositions receiving statistically significant support. For each of these three regression analyses, high multicollinearity was not a problem because tolerance and V.I.F. (Variance Inflation

Factor) indices were within acceptable boundaries as recommended by Ethington, Thomas, and Pike (2002).

Section 8.2

We conducted one regression analysis with psychosocial engagement as the dependent variable with fixed effects for each of the eight colleges and universities included in the data sources used for these analyses. We used fixed institutional effects to hold constant the unique effects of each specific institution on the focal dependent variable. Specifically, we regressed psychosocial engagement first on the fixed institutional effects followed by each of the five student entry characteristics (gender, race/ethnicity, parental educational level, parental income, and average grades earned in high school), ability to pay, initial level of institutional commitment, cultural capital, first-year orientation as adequate preparation for the institution's social environment, positive reinterpretation and growth, communal potential, and identity, solidarity, and interaction dimensions of community in residence halls. Such an analysis treats each of these possible forces as competing sources of influence on psychosocial engagement. Because of our focus on dimensions of community in residence halls, we omitted the variable living on campus from this regression. We used the 0.05 level of significance to identify those sources of influence receiving statistically significant affirmation. For this regression analysis, high multicollinearity was not a problem as tolerance and V.I.F. indices were within acceptable boundaries as recommended by Ethington, Thomas, and Pike (2002).

Section 8.3

We performed one regression analysis with communal potential as the dependent variable with fixed effects for the eight colleges and universities included in the data sources used for these analyses. We used fixed institutional effects to hold constant the unique effects of each specific institution on communal potential. More specifically, we regressed communal potential first on the fixed institutional effects followed by each of the five student entry characteristics (gender, race/ethnicity, parental educational level, parental income, and average grades earned in high school), ability to pay, initial level of institutional commitment, cultural capital, first-year orientation as adequate preparation for the institution's social environment, positive reinterpretation and growth, and each of the three dimensions of a sense of community in residence halls: identity, solidarity, and interaction. We used the 0.05 level of significance to identify those sources of influence receiving statistically significant affirmation. For this regression analysis, high multicollinearity was not a problem as tolerance and V.I.F. indices were within acceptable boundaries as recommended by Ethington, Thomas, and Pike (2002). This regression analysis resulted in a statistically significant overall regression equation that accounts for 35 percent of the explained variance in communal potential.

Section 8.4

We performed one regression analysis with commitment of the institution to student welfare as the dependent variable with fixed effects for each of the eight colleges and universities included in the data sources used for these analyses. We used fixed institutional effects to hold constant the unique effects of each specific institution on the focal dependent variable. We regressed commitment of the institution to student welfare first on the fixed institutional effects followed by each of the five student entry characteristics (gender, race/ethnicity, parental educational level, parental income, and average grades earned in high school), initial level of institutional commitment, living on campus, academic advising, fall first-year student orientation, communication, fairness, participation in decision making, student perceptions of prejudice and racial discrimination, faculty interest in students, good faculty teaching, faculty use of active learning practices, faculty violations of the norms of condescending negativism, moral turpitude, particularistic grading, and personal disregard. This simultaneous test views each of these possible forces as competing sources of influence on commitment of the institution to student welfare. We applied the 0.05 level of significance to identify those sources of influence receiving statistically significant confirmation For this regression analysis, high multicollinearity was not a problem as tolerance and V.I.F. indices were within acceptable boundaries as recommended by Ethington, Thomas, and Pike (2002).

Section 8.5

We carried out one regression analysis with institutional integrity as the dependent variable. We also used fixed institutional effects to hold constant the unique effects of each of the eight residential colleges and universities on institutional integrity. We regressed institutional integrity first on the fixed institutional effects followed by each of the five student entry characteristics (gender, race/ethnicity, parental educational level, parental income, and average grades earned in high school) initial level of institutional commitment, living on campus, faculty interest in students, student reports of good teaching, the fulfillment of academic and social expectations for college, and student perceptions of prejudice and racial discrimination. We used the 0.05 level of significance to identify those sources of influence on institutional integrity receiving statistically significant corroboration. For this regression analysis, high multicollinearity does not present a problem as tolerance and V.I.F. indices were within acceptable boundaries as recommended by Ethington, Thomas, and Pike (2002).

Section 9.1

We conducted three separate regression analyses: one for academic and intellectual development (propositions 6 and 7), one for subsequent institutional commitment (propositions 8, 9, and 10), and one for student persistence (propositions 1 to 5, and proposition 11) as the dependent variables. For each these three analyses, we used fixed effects for each of the five colleges and universities included in the data sources used for these analyses. We used fixed institutional effects to hold constant the unique effects of each specific institution on the focal dependent variables. Specifically, we regressed academic and intellectual development first on the fixed institutional effects followed by gender, race/ethnicity, parental educational level, average high school grades, full- or part-time status, costs of college attendance, need for social affiliation, motivation to graduate from college, support from significant others, institutional integrity, and institutional commitment to the welfare of students. We regressed subsequent institutional commitment on the same array of variables plus academic and intellectual development. In addition, we regressed student persistence on the same array of variables as subsequent institutional commitment, but added subsequent institutional commitment to the analysis. We used the 0.05 level of significance to identify those propositions receiving statistically significant support. For each of these three regression analyses, high multicollinearity was not a problem as tolerance and V.I.F. indices were within acceptable boundaries as recommended by Ethington, Thomas, and Pike (2002).

Section 9.2

To execute this regression, we regressed academic and intellectual development first on the fixed institutional effects followed by each of the four student entry characteristics (gender, race/ethnicity, parental educational level, and average grades earned in high school), full-time attendance, participation in a learning community, faculty use of active learning practices, faculty use of principles of good practice including encouragement of faculty-student contact, cooperation among students, prompt feedback, setting of high standards for students, setting expectations, faculty teaching skill of organization and preparation, faculty teaching with instructional clarity, academic advising, first-year student orientation, faculty interest in students, and reports of good teaching by faculty. This simultaneous test regards each of these possible forces as competing sources of influence on perceptions of their academic and intellectual development held by students at commuter colleges and universities. We applied the 0.05 level of significance to identify those sources of influence receiving statistically significant support. For this regression analysis, high multicollinearity was not a problem given that tolerance and V.I.F. indices were within acceptable boundaries as recommended by Ethington, Thomas, and Pike (2002).

Section 9.3

We used ordinary least squares multiple regression to simultaneously test the influence of each of the 25 possible forces, which are delineated in Chapter 9, on student perceptions of the commitment of the institution to student welfare at commuter colleges and universities above and beyond the fixed effects for the five commuter colleges represented in this analysis, four student entry characteristics (gender, race/ethnicity, parental educational level, and average high school grades), and full-time attendance status. We used fixed institutional effects to hold constant the unique effects of each specific institution on the focal dependent variable. Specifically, we regressed commitment of the institution to student welfare first on the fixed effects for each of the five commuter colleges and universities included in the data sources for these analyses followed by each of the four student entry characteristics (gender, race/ethnicity, parental educational level, and average grades earned in high school), full-time attendance, and each of the 25 possible forces described in Chapter 9. We regard each of these 25 possible forces as competing sources of influence on student perceptions of the commitment of their college or university to student welfare. We set the level of statistical significance at the 0.05 level. For this regression analysis, high multicollinearity does not present a problem given that tolerance and V.I.F. indices were within acceptable boundaries as recommended by Ethington, Thomas, and Pike (2002).

Section 9.4

We used ordinary least squares multiple regression to simultaneously test the influence of each of the 16 possible forces identified in Chapter 9 on student perceptions of the institutional integrity at their commuter college or university above and beyond the fixed effects for the five commuter colleges represented in this analysis, four student entry characteristics (gender, race/ethnicity, parental educational level, and average high school grades), and full-time attendance status. We used fixed institutional effects to hold constant the unique effects of each specific institution on the focal dependent variable. More specifically, we regressed institutional integrity first on the fixed effects for each of the five commuter colleges and universities followed by each of the four student entry characteristics (gender, race/ethnicity, parental educational level, and average grades earned in high school), full-time attendance, and each of the 16 possible forces described in Chapter 9. We regard each of these 16 possible forces as competing sources of influence on student perceptions of the institutional integrity of their college or university. We used the 0.05 level of statistical significance to identify statistically significant sources of influence on student perceptions of institutional integrity. For this regression analysis, high multicollinearity does not present a problem given that tolerance and V.I.F. indices were within acceptable boundaries as recommended by Ethington, Thomas, and Pike (2002).

Section 9.5

We used ordinary least squares multiple regression to simultaneously test the influence of each of the 17 possible forces, which are designated in Chapter 9, on support of significant others for college attendance at commuter colleges and universities above and beyond the fixed effects for the five commuter colleges represented in this analysis, four student entry characteristics (gender, race/ethnicity, parental educational level, and average high school grades), and full-time attendance status. We used fixed institutional effects to hold constant the unique effects of each specific institution on the focal dependent variable. More specifically, we regressed support of significant others first on the fixed effects for each of the five commuter colleges and universities included in the data sources for these analyses followed by each of the four student entry characteristics (gender, race/ethnicity, parental educational level, and average grades earned in high school), full-time attendance, and each of the 17 possible forces described above. These 17 possible forces function as competing sources of influence on the support of significant others. We applied the 0.05 level of statistical significance to identify statistically significant forces of influence on support from significant others. Moreover, high multicollinearity does not present a problem for this regression analysis given that tolerance and V.I.F. indices were within acceptable boundaries as recommended by Ethington, Thomas, and Pike (2002).

Section 9.6

Using fixed effects for the five institutions, we executed on one multiple regression analysis with significant others feeling welcomed on campus as the dependent variable. More specifically, we regressed this student perception on each of the following five forces: having "drop-in" child-care services, the college or university having a website that contains information for significant others, encouragement by the university for significant others to attend the orientation for new students, the impression that significant others feel welcomed at university events, and the frequent communication of important information to significant others. We used the 0.05 level of statistical significance to delineate statistically significant relationships. High multicollinearity does not present a problem for each of these five regression analysis since the tolerance and V.I.F. indices were within acceptable boundaries as recommended by Ethington, Thomas, and Pike (2002). This regression analysis produced a statistically significant equation that explains 26.2 percent of the variance in significant others feeling welcomed on campus.

Appendix C

Multivariate Analyses Results Tables

This appendix includes tables that report the results of the execution of our multivariate statistical procedures that we used to derive the findings we present in Chapters 8 and 9. These tables exhibit the variables included in a given regression analysis, the regression coefficients for these variables, and the probability values for those variables designated as statistically significant. Appendix C includes nine tables—Tables C.1 to C.9. Tables C.1 to C.4 concern the findings reported in Chapter 8, whereas Tables C.5 to C.9 relate to the findings reported in Chapter 9.

Table C.1   Results of the Regression Analyses to Test the Revised Theory of Student Persistence in Residential Colleges and Universities

Standardized Regression Coefficients

Variables	DV: Social Integration	DV: Subsequent Institutional Commitment	DV: Student Persistence
Gender	.030 (.029)	−.012 (−.019)	−.019 (−.012)
Race	.109 (.132)*	.089 (.169)	.036 (.028)
Parental education	.003 (.000)	−.086 (−.019)	.100 (.009)
Parental income	.017 (.003)	−037 (−.009)	−.057 (−.006)
HS grades	.016 (.004)	−.022 (−.009)	.044 (.008)
Live on campus	.145 (.210)**	.058 (.131)	−.199 (−.185)**
Initial institutional commitment	.049 (.029)	.102 (.095)*	.138 (.053)**
Ability to pay for college	.004 (.003)	.029 (.033)	−.002 (−.001)
Institutional commitment to student welfare	.276 (.276)***	.277 (.435)***	.005 (.003)
Communal potential	.001 (.002)	.045 (.082)	.021 (.016)
Institutional integrity	.243 (.220)***	.046 (.066)	−.006 (−.004)
Proactive social adjustment	.010 (.008)	−.009 (−.012)	−.048 (−.025)
Psychosocial engagement	.268 (.271)***	−.034 (−.053)	−.052 (−.034)
Social integration	–	.121 (.189)*	.093 (.059)
Subsequent institutional commitment	–	–	.104 (.043)*
Institutional 1	.019 (.029)	.061 (.143)	−.148 (−.145)
Institutional 2	.084 (.082)	−.151 (−.232)	−.026 (−.016)
Institutional 3	.013 (.020)	−.019 (−.049)	−.264 (−.275)
Institutional 4	.047 (.079)	−.035 (−.091)	−.081 (−.087)
Institutional 5	−.052 (−.106)	−.021 (−.067)	−.237 (−.311)
Institutional 6	−.003 (−.004)	−.260 (−.528)	−.193 (−.161)
Institutional 7	−.032 (−.060)	−.032 (−.093)	−.205 (−.243)
Constant	N.A. (.293)	N.A. (.763)	N.A. (.678)***
Adjusted R–Squared	.411 ***	.190 ***	.133 ***
N	408	408	408

$p<0.05$, **$p<0.01$, ***$p<0.001$

Note: Unstandardized regression coefficients in parentheses.

Note: Institution 8 is the omitted variable.

Table C.2   Results of the Regression Analysis to Identify Factors that Influence the Psychosocial Engagement of Students in Residential Colleges and Universities

	Standardized Regression Coefficients
Variables	DV: Psychosocial Engagement
Institutional 1	0.260 (0.346)**
Institutional 2	0.383 (0.348)**
Institutional 3	0.067 (0.155)
Institutional 4	0.133 (0.200)
Institutional 5	0.135 (0.277)*
Institutional 6	0.100 (0.116)
Institutional 7	0.189 (0.322)**
Gender (1 = female)	0.017 (0.015)
Race/ethnicity	–0.069 (–0.078)
Parental education	–0.044 (–0.006)
Parental income	0.145 (0.022)**
High school grades	–0.122 (–0.031)*
Ability to pay	0.009 (0.006)
Cultural capital	0.210 (0.151)***
Initial institutional commitment	–0.025 (–0.014)
First-year orientation—social success	0.049 (0.025)
Proactive social adjustment	0.072 (0.055)
Communal potential	0.198 (0.299)***
Identity: residence halls	0.153 (0.120)*
Solidarity: residence halls	0.056 (0.044)
Interaction: residence halls	0.119 (0.097)*
Constant	N.A. (0.635)*
Adjusted R–squared	0.344***
N	347

*$p<0.05$, **$p<0.01$, ***$p<0.001$

Note: Unstandardized regression coefficients in parentheses.

Note: Institution 8 is the omitted variable.

Table C.3   Results of the Regression Analysis to Identify Significant Influences on Commitment of the Institution to Student Welfare in Residential Colleges and Universities

Standardized Regression Coefficients	
Variables	DV: Institutional Commitment to Student Welfare
Institutional 1	−0.077 (−0.116)
Institutional 2	−0.076 (−0.074)
Institutional 3	−0.078 (−0.126)
Institutional 4	−0.094 (−0.154)
Institutional 5	−0.096 (−0.192)
Institutional 6	0.024 (0.031)
Institutional 7	0.001 (0.003)
Gender (1 = female)	0.014 (0.013)
Race/ethnicity	−0.067 (−0.080)
Parental education	0.083 (0.012)*
Parental income	0.073 (0.012)
High school grades	0.003 (0.001)
Initial institutional commitment	−0.005 (−0.003)
On-campus residence	−0.052 (−0.075)
First-year orientation—academic success	0.057 (0.031)
Academic advising	0.023 (0.015)
Communication	0.000 (8.813E−5)
Fairness	0.117 (0.082)*
Participation in decision making	0.026 (0.015)
Racial discrimination and prejudice	−0.171 (−0.129)***
Faculty interest in students	0.571 (0.446)***
Good faculty teaching	0.081 (0.043)*
Active learning	−0.022 (−0.018)
Faculty violation of the norm of particularistic grading	−0.047 (−0.033)
Faculty violation of the norm of condescending negativism	−0.113 (−0.086)*
Faculty violation of the norm of moral turpitude	0.069 (0.062)
Faculty violation of the norm of personal disregard	0.024 (0.020)
Constant	N.A. (1.430)***
Adjusted R–squared	0.565***
N	397

*$p<0.05$, **$p<0.01$, ***$p<0.001$
Note: Unstandardized regression coefficients in parentheses.
Note: Institution 8 is the omitted variable.

Table C.4   Results of the Regression Analysis to Identify Significant Forces of Influence on Institutional Integrity in Residential Colleges and Universities

	Standardized Regression Coefficients
Variables	DV: Institutional Integrity
Institutional 1	–0.018 (–0.030)
Institutional 2	–0.141 (–0.153)
Institutional 3	–0.121 (–0.211)
Institutional 4	–0.044 (–0.081)
Institutional 5	–0.041 (–0.092)
Institutional 6	–0.013 (–0.018)
Institutional 7	0.035 (0.073)
Gender (1 = female)	–0.001 (–0.001)
Race/ethnicity	–0.005 (–0.007)
Parental education	–0.031 (–0.005)
Parental income	–0.069 (–0.012)
High school grades	–0.004 (–0.001)
Initial institutional commitment	0.014 (0.009)
On-campus residence	–0.100 (–0.155)
Faculty interest in students	0.343 (0.298)***
Good faculty teaching	0.043 (0.026)
Fulfillment of expectations: academic	0.130 (0.089)*
Fulfillment of expectations: social	0.087 (0.055)
Racial discrimination and prejudice	–0.133 (–0.112)**
Constant	N.A. (1.965)***
Adjusted R–squared	0.254***
N	406

*$p<0.05$, **$p<0.01$, ***$p<0.001$

Note: Unstandardized regression coefficients in parentheses.

Note: Institution 8 is the omitted variable.

Table C.5   Results of the Regression Analyses to Test the Theory of Student Persistence in Commuter Colleges and Universities

Variables	Standardized Regression Coefficients		
	DV: Academic and Intellectual Development	DV: Subsequent Institutional Commitment	DV: Student Persistence
Gender	–0.073 (–0.080)*	0.059 (0.079)	0.071 (0.062)
Race	0.051 (0.075)	–0.098 (–0.176)**	0.036 (0.042)
Parental education	–0.026 (–0.005)	–0.097 (–0.021)**	–0.027 (–0.004)
High school grades	–0.049 (–0.013)	–0.078 (–0.025)*	0.050 (0.010)
Full-time status	–0.099 (–0.152)**	0.107 (0.200)**	0.155 (0.190)***
Cost for college	0.058 (0.032)	0.076 (0.052)*	–0.060 (–0.026)
Affiliation need	–0.014 (–0.013)	–0.005 (–0.006)	–0.001 (–0.001)
Motivation	0.044 (0.045)	0.027 (0.034)	0.074 (0.061)
Support from significant others	0.068 (0.070)	0.144 (0.182)***	0.021 (0.017)
Commitment of the institution to student welfare	0.297 (0.353)***	0.092 (0.134)	0.003 (0.003)
Institutional integrity	0.223 (0.250)***	0.152 (0.209)**	0.051 (0.046)
Academic and intellectual development	—	0.106 (0.129)**	0.011 (0.009)
Subsequent institutional commitment	—	—	0.089 (0.058)*
Institutional 1	0.040 (0.078)	0.033 (0.079)	0.082 (0.126)
Institutional 2	0.025 (0.028)	–0.031 (–0.043)	0.049 (0.044)
Institutional 3	0.057 (0.074)	–0.112 (–0.178)	0.063 (0.065)
Institutional 4	0.047 (–0.059)	–0.102 (–0.155)	–0.161 (–0.160)
Constant	N.A. (1.104)	N.A. (1.024)	N.A. (–0.086)
Adjusted R–squared	0.251***	0.201***	0.142***
N	669	669	669

*p<0.05, **p<0.01, ***p<0.001

Note: Unstandardized regression coefficients in parentheses.

Note: Institution 5 is the omitted variable.

Table C.6   Results of the Regression Analysis to Identify Factors That Influence the Academic and Intellectual Development of Students in Commuter Colleges and Universities

	Standardized Regression Coefficients
Variables	DV: Academic and Intellectual Development
Institutional 1	–0.015 (–0.029)
Institutional 2	–0.068 (–0.075)
Institutional 3	–0.013 (–0.016)
Institutional 4	–0.115 (–0.140)
Gender (1 = female)	–0.042 (–0.046)
Race/ethnicity	0.032 (0.046)
Parental education	–0.017 (–0.003)
High school grades	–0.038 (–0.010)
Full-time status	–0.108 (–0.158)**
Academic advising	0.146 (0.099)***
First-year student orientation	0.215 (0.142)***
Faculty interest in students	0.203 (0.182)***
Good faculty teaching	–0.019 (–0.011)
Teaching skill of organization and preparation	0.106 (0.101)*
Teaching skill of instructional clarity	0.156 (0.154)**
Faculty use of active learning	0.089 (0.088)*
Encouragement of faculty-student contact	–0.013 (–0.007)
Prompt feedback	–0.043 (–0.028)
Faculty encouragement of cooperation among students	–0.025 (–0.018)
Faculty communication of high expectations	0.032 (0.026)
Participation in a learning community	0.076 (0.086)*
Constant	N.A. (1.239)***
Adjusted R–squared	0.361***
N	663

$*p<0.05, **p<0.01, ***p<0.001$

Note: Unstandardized regression coefficients in parentheses.

Note: Institution 5 is the omitted variable.

Table C.7   Results of the Regression Analysis to Identify Factors That Influence the Commitment of the Institution to Student Welfare in Commuter Colleges and Universities

	Standardized Regression Coefficients
Variables	DV: Commitment of the Institution to Student Welfare
Institutional 1	0.034 (0.054)
Institutional 2	0.010 (0.010)
Institutional 3	0.009 (0.010)
Institutional 4	0.110 (0.113)
Gender (1 = female)	0.020 (0.018)
Race/ethnicity	−0.015 (−0.018)
Parental education	−0.006 (−0.001)
High school grades	0.029 (0.006)
Full-time status	−0.009 (−0.012)
Academic advising	0.136 (0.076)***
First-year student orientation	0.029 (0.016)
Faculty interest in students	0.204 (0.154)***
Good faculty teaching	0.032 (0.016)
Teaching skill of organization and preparation	0.122 (0.097)**
Teaching skill of instructional clarity	0.149 (0.122)**
Faculty use of active learning	0.003 (0.003)
Encouragement of faculty-student contact	0.021 (0.010)
Prompt feedback	0.048 (0.027)
Faculty encouragement of cooperation among students	0.002 (0.001)
Faculty communication of high expectations	−0.018 (−0.013)
Participation in a learning community	−0.015 (−0.014)
Provision of peer mentoring programs	−0.005 (−0.004)
Provision of on-campus work opportunities	0.011 (0.014)
Provision of drop-in child-care services	0.008 (0.009)
Provision of student work space	0.005 (0.008)
Provision of weekend work space	−0.031 (−0.028)
Provision of weekend library service	−0.033 (−0.030)
Ample on-campus parking	0.100 (0.045)**
Parking convenient to classrooms	0.051 (0.022)
Convenient commuting to and from campus	−0.003 (−0.002)
Offering classes at convenient times	0.064 (0.038)
Provision of student services	0.124 (0.069)***
Clear communication of campus policies	0.057 (0.035)
Clear communication of campus activities	0.057 (0.031)

Table C.7   (continued)

Variables	Standardized Regression Coefficients
	DV: Commitment of the Institution to Student Welfare
Use of technology for student communication	–0.025 (–0.016)
Straightforward registration process	0.013 (0.007)
Eating facilities open during convenient times for commuting students	0.032 (0.018)
General-use computers and Internet access available on campus	0.077 (0.054)*
Constant	N.A. (0.587)**
Adjusted R–squared	0.50***
N	610

*p<0.05, **p<0.01, ***p<0.001
Note: Unstandardized regression coefficients in parentheses.
Note: Institution 5 is the omitted variable.

Table C.8   Results of the Regression Analysis to Identify Factors That Influence Institutional Integrity in Commuter Colleges and Universities

Variables	Standardized Regression Coefficients
	DV: Institutional Integrity
Institutional 1	–0.088 (–0.151)
Institutional 2	–0.126 (–0.124)
Institutional 3	–0.127 (–0.147)
Institutional 4	–0.015 (–0.016)
Gender (1 = female)	0.086 (0.084)**
Race/ethnicity	0.080 (0.104)*
Parental education	0.026 (0.004)
High school grades	–0.041 (–0.009)
Full-time status	0.033 (0.045)
Academic advising	0.154 (0.092)***
First-year student orientation	0.196 (0.115)***
Faculty interest in students	0.083 (0.067)*
Good faculty teaching	0.003 (0.002)
Teaching skill of organization and preparation	0.100 (0.085)*
Teaching skill of instructional clarity	0.142 (0.125)**
Offering classes at convenient times	0.107 (0.068)**

(continued)

Table C.8   (continued)

Standardized Regression Coefficients	
Variables	DV: Institutional Integrity
Provision of student services	0.075 (0.045)*
Provision of drop-in child-care services	–0.014 (–0.015)
Provision of student work space	0.047 (0.083)
Provision of weekend work space	–0.048 (–0.047)
Provision of weekend library service	0.053 (0.052)
Ample on-campus parking	0.106 (0.052)**
Parking convenient to classrooms	–0.042 (–0.020)
Convenient commuting to and from campus	0.025 (0.013)
Eating facilities open during convenient times for commuting students	0.055 (0.034)
Straightforward registration process	0.044 (0.026)
General-use computers and Internet access available on campus	0.036 (0.027)
Constant	N.A. (0.697)***
Adjusted R–squared	0.425***
N	612

*p<0.05, **p<0.01, ***p<0.001
Note: Unstandardized regression coefficients in parentheses.
Note: Institution 5 is the omitted variable.

Table C.9   Results of the Regression Analysis to Identify Factors That Influence Support from Significant Others in Commuter Colleges and Universities

Standardized Regression Coefficients	
Variables	DV: Support from Significant Others
Institutional 1	–0.170 (–0.309)*
Institutional 2	–0.297 (–0.314)*
Institutional 3	–0.225 (–0.282)
Institutional 4	–0.327 (–0.386)**
Gender (1 = female)	0.080 (0.083)*
Race/ethnicity	–0.018 (–0.025)

Table C.9   (continued)

	Standardized Regression Coefficients
Variables	DV: Support from Significant Others
Parental education	0.026 (0.005)
High school grades	–0.005 (–0.001)
Full-time status	0.117 (0.167)**
Costs of college attendance (financial support)	0.036 (0.019)
Hours worked on-campus	0.018 (0.007)
Hours worked off-campus	0.019 (0.003)
Provision of website with information for significant others	–0.045 (–0.050)
Provision of drop-in child-care services	–0.014 (–0.017)
Provision of on-campus work opportunities	0.006 (0.008)
Significant others encouraged to attend new student orientation	0.036 (0.025)
Significant others welcomed at campus events	0.088 (0.064)
Frequent communication of important information to significant others	–0.097 (–0.059)*
Convenient commuting to and from campus	–0.006 (–0.003)
Offering classes at convenient times	0.110 (0.076)*
Provision of student services	–0.054 (–0.034)
Reliable transport to and from campus	0.284 (0.218)***
Family welcomed on campus	0.166 (0.116)***
Academic advising	–0.035 (–0.023)
Faculty interest in students	0.088 (0.077)*
Good faculty teaching	0.049 (0.028)
Constant	N.A. (2.088)***
Adjusted R–squared	0.232***
N	587

*$p<0.05$, **$p<0.01$, ***$p<0.001$

Note: Unstandardized regression coefficients in parentheses.

Note: Institution 5 is the omitted variable.

References

Adelman, C. (1999). Answers in the Tool Box: Academic Intensity, Attendance Patterns, and Bachelor's Degree Attainment. Technical report, United States Department of Education, National Center for Education Statistics, Washington, D.C.

Adelman, C. (2006). The Toolbox Revisited: Paths to Degree Completion from High School Through College. Technical report, United States Department of Education, Washington, D.C.

Alexander, K. L., Riordan, C., Fennessey, J., & Pallas, A. M. (1982). Social Background, Academic Resources, and College Graduation: Recent Evidence from the National Longitudinal Survey. *American Journal of Education, 90*(4), 315–333.

Allen, D. F., & Nelson, J. M. (1989). Tinto's Model of College Withdrawal Applied to Women in Two Institutions. *Journal of Research and Development in Education, 22*(3), 1–22.

American College Testing Program. (2012). National Collegiate Retention and Persistence to Degree Rates. Iowa City, IA. Retrieved from http://act.org /research/policymakers/pdf/retain_2012.pdf.

Anderson, J. A., & Adams, M. (1992). Acknowledging the Learning Styles of Diverse Student Populations: Implications for Instructional Design. *New Directions for Teaching and Learning, 49*, 19–31.

Astin, A. W. (1977). *Four Critical Years: Effects of College on Beliefs, Attitudes, and Knowledge.* San Francisco: Jossey-Bass.

Astin, A. W. (1984). Student Involvement: A Developmental Theory for Higher Education. *Journal of College Student Personnel*, 25, 297–308.

Baird, L. L. (2000). College Climate and the Tinto Model. In J. M. Braxton (Ed.), *Reworking the Student Departure Puzzle* (pp. 62–80). Nashville: Vanderbilt University Press.

Barrileaux, C. J., & Miller, M. E. (1988). The Political Economy of State Medicaid Policy. *American Political Science Review*, 82(4), 1089–1107.

Bean, J. P. (1980). Dropouts and Turnover: The Synthesis of a Causal Model of Student Attrition. *Research in Higher Education*, 12(2), 155–187.

Bean, J. P. (1983). The Application of a Model of Turnover in Work Organizations to the Student Attrition Process. *Review of Higher Education*, 6(2), 129–148.

Bean, J. P., & Metzner, B. S. (1985). A Conceptual Model of Nontraditional Student Attrition. *Review of Educational Research*, 55, 485–540.

Berger, J. B. (1997). Students' Sense of Community in Residence Halls: Social Integration, and First-Year Persistence. *Journal of College Student Development*, 38(5), 441–452.

Berger, J. B. (2000). Optimizing Capital, Social Reproduction, and Undergraduate Persistence: A Sociological Perspective. In J. M. Braxton (Ed.), *Reworking the Student Departure Puzzle* (pp. 95–124). Nashville, TN: Vanderbilt University Press.

Berger, J. B. (2001–2002). Understanding the Organizational Nature of Student Persistence: Empirically-based Recommendations for Practice. *Journal of College Student Retention: Research, Theory & Practice*, 3(1), 3–22.

Berger, J. B., & Braxton, J. M. (1998). Revising Tinto's Interactionalist Theory of Student Departure Through Theory Elaboration: Examining the Role of Organizational Attributes in the Persistence Process. *Research in Higher Education*, 39(2), 103–119.

Berger, J. B., & Milem, J. F. (1999). The Role of Student Involvement and Perceptions of Integration in a Causal Model of Student Persistence. *Research in Higher Education*, 40, 641–664.

Bers, T. H. (1985). Student Major Choices and Community College Persistence. *Research in Higher Education*, 29(2), 161–173.

Bettinger, E., & Long, B. T. (2004). Do College Instructors Matter? The Effects of Adjuncts and Graduate Assistants on Students' Interests and Success. Working Paper 10370. Cambridge, MA: National Bureau of Economic Research.

Bettinger, E. P., & Long, B. T. (2009). Addressing the Needs of Under-Prepared Students in Higher Education: Does College Remediation Work? *Journal of Human Resources*, 44(3), 736–771.

Bloom, B. S. (Ed.). (1956). *Taxonomy of Educational Objectives, Volume 1: Cognitive Domain*. New York: McKay.

Bonwell, C., & Eison, J. (1991). Active Learning: Creating Excitement in the Classroom. AAHE-ERIC Higher Education Report No. 1. Washington, D.C.: The George Washington University School of Education and Human Development.

Bourdieu, P. (1973). Cultural Reproduction and Social Reproduction. In R. Brown (Ed.), *Knowledge, Education and Cultural Change: Papers in the Sociology of Education* (pp. 487–510). London: Tavistock.

Bourdieu, P. (1977). *Outline of a Theory of Practice*. (R. Nice, Trans.). Cambridge, U.K.: Cambridge University Press.

Bourdieu, P. (1986). The Three Forms of Capital. In J. G. Richardson (Ed.), *Handbook of Theory and Research for the Sociology of Education* (pp. 241–258). New York: Greenwood Press.

Bourdieu, P. (1990). Artistic Taste and Cultural Capital. In J. Alexander & S. Seidman (Eds.), *Culture and Society: Contemporary Debates* (pp. 205–215). Cambridge, U.K.: Cambridge University Press.

Bourdieu, P. (1992). *The Logic of Practice*. Cambridge, U.K.: Polity Press.

Bourdieu, P. (1994). Structures, Habitus, Power: Basis for a Theory of Symbolic Power. In N. Dirks, G. Eley, & S. Ortner (Eds.), *Culture/Power/History: A Reader in Contemporary Social Theory* (pp. 155–199). Princeton, NJ: Princeton University Press.

Bourdieu, P., & Boltanski, L. (1981). The Education System and the Economy: Titles and Jobs. In C. C. Lemert (Ed.), *French Sociology: Rupture and Renewal Since 1968* (pp. 141–145). New York: Columbia University Press.

Boyer, E. L. (1990). *Scholarship Reconsidered: Priorities of the Professoriate.* Stanford, CA, Carnegie Foundation for the Advancement of Teaching. San Francisco: Jossey-Bass.

Boylan, H. R., & Goudas, A. (2012). Knee-Jerk Reforms on Remediation. *Inside Higher Ed.* Retrieved from http://www.insidehighered.com/views/2012/06/19 /essay-flawed-interpretations-research-remedial-education.

Braxton, J. M. (2000). Reinvigorating Theory and Research on the Departure Puzzle. In J. M. Braxton (Ed.), *Reworking the Student Departure Puzzle* (pp. 257–274). Nashville, TN: Vanderbilt University Press.

Braxton, J. M. (2003). Persistence as an Essential Gateway to Student Success. In S. Komives & D. Woodard, Jr., and Associates (Eds.), *Student Services: A Handbook for the Profession* (4th Edition) (pp. 317–335). San Francisco: Jossey-Bass.

Braxton, J. M. (2008). Toward a Theory of Faculty Professional Choices in Teaching That Foster College Student Success. In J. C. Smart (Ed.), *Higher Education: A Handbook of Theory and Research*, Volume 23 (pp.181–207). The Netherlands: Springer.

Braxton, J. M. (2009–2010). Catalysts and Constraints to College Student Persistence. *Journal of College Student Retention: Research, Theory, & Practice,* 11(1), 1–5.

Braxton, J. M., & Bayer, A. E. (1999). *Faculty Misconduct in Collegiate Teaching.*Baltimore: The Johns Hopkins University Press.

Braxton, J. M., Bray, N., & Berger, J. (2000). Faculty Teaching Skills, and Their Influences on the College Student Departure Process. *Journal of College Student Development,* 41(2), 215–227.

Braxton, J. M., & Brier, E. M. (1989). Melding Organizational and Interactional Theories of Student Attrition: A Path Analytic Study. *Review of Higher Education,* 13(1), 47–61.

Braxton, J. M., & Hirschy, A. S. (2004). Reconceptualizing Antecedents of Social Integration in Student Departure. In M. Yorke & B. Longden (Eds.), *Retention and Success in Higher Education* (pp. 89–102). Buckingham, U.K.: Open University Press.

Braxton, J. M., & Hirschy, A. S. (2005). Theoretical Developments in College Student Departure. In A. Seidman (Ed.), *College Student Retention: Formula for Student Success* (pp. 61–87). Westport, CT: Praeger Publishers.

Braxton, J. M., Hirschy, A. S., & McClendon, S. A. (2004). Understanding and Reducing College Student Departure. In *ASHE-ERIC Higher Education Report*, *30*(3). San Francisco: Jossey-Bass.

Braxton, J. M., Jones, W. A., Hirschy, A. S., & Hartley, H. V. (2008). The Role of Active Learning in College Student Persistence. *New Directions for Teaching and Learning*, *115*, 71–83.

Braxton, J. M., & Lee, S. D. (2005). Toward Reliable Knowledge About College Student Departure. In A. Seidman (Ed.), *College Student Retention: Formula for Student Success* (pp. 107–127). Westport, CT: Praeger Publishers.

Braxton, J. P., & Lien, L. A. (2000). The Viability of Academic Integration as a Central Construct in Tinto's Interactionalist Theory of Student Departure. In J. M. Braxton (Ed.), *Reworking the Student Departure Puzzle*.Nashville, TN: Vanderbilt University Press.

Braxton, J. M., & McClendon, S. A. (2001–2002). The Fostering of Social Integration and Retention Through Institutional Practice. *Journal of College Student Retention: Research, Theory, & Practice*, *3*(1), 57–72.

Braxton, J. M., Milem, J. F., & Sullivan, A. S. (2000). The Influence of Active Learning on the College Student Departure Process. *Journal of Higher Education*, *71*(5), 569–590.

Braxton, J. M., & Mundy, M. E. (2002). Powerful Institutional Levers to Reduce College Student Departure. *Journal of College Student Retention: Research, Theory, & Practice*, *3*(1), 91–118.

Braxton, J. M., Sullivan, A. S., & Johnson, R. M. (1997). Appraising Tinto's Theory of College Student Departure. In J. C. Smart (Ed.) *Higher Education: Handbook of Theory and Research, Volume 12* (pp. 107–164). New York: Agathon Press.

Bray, N. J., Braxton, J. M., & Sullivan, A. S. (1999). The Influence of Stress-Related Coping Strategies on College Student Departure Decisions. *Journal of College Student Development, 40*(6), 645–657.

Brier, E. M. (1999). Strategic Initiatives. Unpublished paper presented at the Southern Graduate Student Association Meeting, New Orleans.

Brier, E. M., Hirschy, A. S., & Braxton, J. M. (2008). The Strategic Retention Initiative: Theory-Based Practice to Reduce College Student Departure. *About Campus, 13*(4), 18–20.

Burke, J. C. (2002). *Funding Public Colleges and Universities for Performance: Popularity, Problems, and Prospects.* Ithaca, NY: State University of New York Press.

Burke, J. C. (2005). *Achieving Accountability in Higher Education: Balancing Public, Academic, and Market Demands.* San Francisco: Jossey-Bass.

Cabrera, A., Castaneda, M. B., Nora, A., & Hengstler, D. (1992). The Convergence Between Two Theories of College Persistence. *Journal of Higher Education, 63*(2), 143–164.

Cabrera, A. F., & Nora, A. (1994). College Students' Perceptions of Prejudice and Discrimination and Their Feelings of Alienation. *Review of Education, Pedagogy, and Cultural Studies, 16,* 387–409.

Cabrera, A. F., Nora, A., & Castaneda, M. B. (1993). College Persistence: Structural Equation Modeling Test of an Integrated Model of Student Retention. *Journal of Higher Education, 64,* 123–139.

Cabrera, A., Nora, A., Pascarella, E. T., Terenzini, P. T., & Hagedorn, L. S. (1999). Campus Racial Climate and the Adjustment of Students to College: A Comparison Between White Students and African-American Students. *Journal of Higher Education, 70*(2), 134–160.

Cabrera, A., Stampen, J. O., & Hansen, W. (1990). Exploring the Effects of Ability to Pay on Persistence in College. *Review of Higher Education, 13*(3), 303–336.

Callan, P. M., Finney, J. E., Kirst, M. W., Usdan, M. D., & Venezia, A. (2006). Claiming Common Ground: State Policymaking for Improving College Readiness and Success. National Center Report #06–1. San Jose, CA: National Center for Public Policy and Higher Education.

Callan, P. M., Kirst, M. W., Spence, D. S., & Usdan, M. D. (2009). States, Schools, and Colleges: Policies to Improve Student Readiness for College and Strengthen Coordination Between Schools and Colleges. National Center Report #09–2. San Jose, CA: National Center for Public Policy and Higher Education.

Carmines, E. G., & Zeller, R. A. (1979). *Reliability and Validity Assessment.* Thousand Oaks, CA: Sage Publications.

Carnegie Foundation for the Advancement of Teaching. (2003). Retrieved from http://www.carnegiefoundation.org/.

Carnegie Foundation for the Advancement for Teaching. (2010). The Carnegie Classification of Institutions of Higher Education. Retrieved from http://classifications.carnegiefoundation.org/.

Carver, C. S., Scheier, M. F., & Weintraub, J. K. (1989). Assessing Coping Strategies: A Theoretically Based Approach. *Journal of Personality and Social Psychology, 56*(2), 267–283.

Chafetz, J. S. (1978). *A Primer on the Construction and Testing of Theories in Sociology.* Itasca, IL: F. E. Peacock Publishers.

Chickering, A. W. (1974). *Commuting Versus Resident Students: Overcoming the Educational Inequities of Living Off Campus.* San Francisco: Jossey-Bass.

Chickering, A. W., & Gamson, Z. F. (1987). Seven Principles for Good Practice in Undergraduate Education. *AAHE Bulletin, 39*(7), 3–7.

Christie, N. G., & Dinham, S. M. (1991). Institutional and External Influences on Social Integration in the Freshman Year. *Journal of Higher Education, 62,* 412–436.

Clark, B. R. (1972). The Organizational Saga in Higher Education. *Administrative Science Quarterly, 17*(2), 178–184.

Clark, B., Heist, P., McConnell, T., Trow, M., & Yonge, G. (1972). *Students and Colleges: Interaction and Change.* Berkeley, CA: Center for Research and Development in Higher Education.

Complete College America. (2012). Remediation: Higher Education's Bridge to Nowhere. Retrieved from http://completecollege.org/docs/CCA-Remediation-final.pdf.

Cook, R. W., & Zallocco, R. L. (1983). Predicting University Preference and Attendance: Applied Marketing in Higher Education Administration. *Research in Higher Education, 19*(2), 197–211.

DeJong, A. J. (1992). Making Sense of Church-Related Higher Education. *New Directions for Higher Education, 79*, 19–27.

Delaney, J. A., and Doyle, W. R. (2011). State Spending on Higher Education: Testing the Balance Wheel over Time. *Journal of Education Finance, 36*(4), 343–368.

Dougherty, K. J., Natow, R. S., & Vega, B. E. (2012). Popular But Unstable: Explaining Why State Performance Funding Systems in the United States Often Do Not Persist. *Teachers College Record, 114*(3), 1–41.

Dougherty, K. J., & Reddy, V. T. (2011). *The Impacts of State Performance Funding Systems on Higher Education Institutions: Research Literature Review and Policy Recommendations.* New York: Community College Research Center.

Doyle, W. R. (2010). Open-Access Colleges Responsible for Greatest Gains in Graduation Rates. San Jose, CA: National Center for Public Policy and Higher Education.

Doyle, W. R., Braxton, J. M., & Jones, W. A. (2008). Making the Connection Between State and Institutional Policies for Completion. Presented at the American Educational Research Association Annual Meeting, New York.

Doyle, W. R., & Gorbunov, A. V. (2011). The Growth of Community Colleges in the American States: An Application of Count Models to Institutional Growth. *Teachers College Record, 113*(8), 1794–1826.

Doyle, W. R., McLendon, M. K., & Hearn, J. C. (2010). The Adoption of Prepaid Tuition and Savings Plans in the American States: An Event History Analysis. *Research in Higher Education, 51*(7), 659–686.

Dungy, G. J. (2003). Organization and Functions of Student Affairs. In S. S. Komives & D. Woodard, Jr., and Associates (Eds.), *Student Services: A Handbook for the Profession* (4th Edition) (pp. 339–357). San Francisco: Jossey-Bass.

Dunphy, L., Miller, T. E., Woodruff, T., & Nelson, J. E. (1987). Exemplary Retention Strategies for the Freshman Year. *New Directions for Higher Education*, 60, 39–60.

Durkheim, E. (1951). *Suicide: A Study in Sociology*. (J. A. Spaulding & G. Simpson, Trans.) Glencoe, IL: The Free Press. (Original work published 1897).

Eagan, M. K., & Jaeger, A. J. (2008). Closing the Gate: Part-Time Faculty Instruction in Gatekeeper Courses and First-Year Persistence. In J. M. Braxton (Ed.), *The Role of the Classroom in College Student Persistence: New Directions for Teaching and Learning*. San Francisco: Jossey-Bass.

Eaton, S. B., & Bean, J. P. (1995). An Approach/Avoidance Behavioral Model of College Student Attrition. *Research in Higher Education*, 36, 617–645.

Eckland, B. K. (1964). College Dropouts Who Came Back. *Harvard Educational Review*, 34(3), 402–420.

Ehrenberg, R. G., & Zhang, L. (2005a). Do Tenured and Tenure-Track Faculty Matter? *Journal of Human Resources*, 40(3), 647–659.

Ehrenberg, R. G., & Zhang, L. (2005b). The Changing Nature of Faculty Employment. In R. L. Clark & J. Ma (Eds.), *Recruitment, Retention, and Retirement in Higher Education: Building and Managing the Faculty of the Future* (pp. 32–54). Northhampton, MA: Edward Elgar Publishing.

Elazar, D. (1966). *American Federalism: A View from the States*.New York: Harper and Row.

Erikson, R. S., Wright, G. C., & McIver, J. P. (1993). *Statehouse Democracy: Public Opinion and Policy in the American States*.Cambridge, U.K.: Cambridge University Press.

Ethington, C. A., Thomas, S. L., & Pike, G. R. (2002). Back to the Basics: Regression as It Should Be. In J. C. Smart (Ed.), *Higher Education: Handbook of Theory and Research, Volume 17* (pp. 263–293). New York: Agathon.

Fidler, P. P., & Hunter, M. S. (1989). How Seminars Enhance Student Success. In M. L. Upcraft, J. N. Gardner, & Associates (Eds.), *The Freshman Year*

Experience: Helping Students Survive and Succeed in College (pp. 216–237). San Francisco: Jossey-Bass.

Fryer, R. G. (2010). Financial Incentives and Student Achievement: Evidence from Randomized Trials. National Bureau of Economic Research Working Paper Series, No. 15898.

Goldrick-Rab, S., & Roksa, J. (2008). *A Federal Agenda for Promoting Student Success and Degree Completion.* Washington, D.C.: Center for American Progress. Retrieved from http://www.americanprogress.org/issues/2008/08/pdf/highered2.pdf.

Grites, T. J. (1979). *Academic Advising: Getting Us Through the Eighties.* AAHE-ERIC Higher Education Research Report No. 7. Washington, D.C.: American Association of Higher Education.

Grogan, C. M. (1994). Political-Economic Factors Influencing State Medicaid Policy. *Political Research Quarterly, 47*(3), 589.

Habley, W. R., Bloom, J. L., & Robbins, S. (2012). *Increasing Persistence: Research-Based Strategies for Student Success.* San Francisco: Jossey-Bass.

Hagedorn, L. S. (2005). How to Define Retention: A New Look at an Old Problem. In A. Seidman (Ed.), *College Student Retention: Formula for Student Success* (pp. 89–105). Westport, CT: Praeger Publishers.

Hagedorn, L. S., Maxwell, W., & Hampton, P. (2001–2002). Correlates of Retention for African-American Males in Community Colleges. *Journal of College Student Retention: Research, Theory & Practice, 3*(3), 243–263.

Halpin, R. L. (1990). An Application of the Tinto Model to the Analysis of Freshman Persistence in a Community College. *Community College Review, 17*(4), 22–32.

Harris, D. N., & Goldrick-Rab, S. (2010). *The (Un)Productivity of American Higher Education: From Cost Disease to Cost-Effectiveness.* Working Paper. Retrieved from http://www.lafollette.wisc.edu/publications/workingpapers/harris2010-023.pdf.

Hartley, H. V., Jr., Hirschy, A. S., & Braxton, J. M. (2006). The Role of Cultural Capital in Social Integration and College Student Persistence. Unpublished paper presented at American Educational Research Association Annual Meeting, San Francisco.

Heath, D. H. (1980). Wanted: A Comprehensive Model of Healthy Development. *Journal of Personnel and Guidance*, 58, 391–399.

Helland, P., Stallings, H., & Braxton, J. M. (2001–2002). The Fulfillment of Expectations for College and Student Departure Decisions. *Journal of College Student Retention: Research, Theory & Practice*, 3(4), 381–396.

Hermanowicz, J. C. (2003). *College Attrition at American Research Universities: Comparative Case Studies*. New York: Agathon.

Hoffmann, F., & Oreopoulos, P. (2009). Professor Qualities and Student Achievement. *Review of Economics and Statistics*, 91(1), 83–92.

Holland, J. L. (1997). *Making Vocational Choices: A Theory of Vocational Personalities and Work Environments* (3rd Edition). Odessa, FL: Psychological Assessment Resources.

Horn, L., & Nevill, S. (2006). Profile of Undergraduates in U.S. Postsecondary Education Institutions: 2003–04, with a Special Analysis of Community College Students. Retrieved from http://nces.ed.gov/pubsearch/pubsinfo .asp?pubid=2006184.

Hossler, D., & Bean, J. P. (1990). Principles and Objectives. In D. Hossler, J. P. Bean, & Associates (Eds.), *The Strategic Management of College Enrollments* (pp. 1–20). San Francisco: Jossey-Bass.

Hossler, D., Schmit, J., & Vesper, N. (1999). *Going to College: How Social, Economic, and Educational Factors Influence the Decisions Students Make*. Baltimore: Johns Hopkins University Press.

Hovey, H. A. (1999). State Spending for Higher Education in the Next Decade: The Battle to Sustain Current Support. San Jose, CA: Technical report, National Center for Public Policy and Higher Education.

Howell, J. S., Kurlaender, M., and Grodsky, E. (2010). Postsecondary Preparation and Remediation: Examining the Effect of the Early Assessment Program at California State University. *Journal of Policy Analysis and Management, 29*(4), 726–748.

Immerwahr, J. (1999). Doing Comparatively Well: Why the Public Loves Higher Education and Criticizes K–12. In Perspectives in Public Policy: Connecting Higher Education and the Public Schools. Technical report, Public Agenda Foundation.

Immerwahr, J., & Foleno, T. (2000). Great Expectations: How the Public and Parents—White, African American, and Hispanic—View Higher Education. San Jose, CA: Technical report, National Center for Public Policy and Higher Education.

Immerwahr, J., & Johnson, J. (2007). Squeeze Play: How Parents and the Public Look at Higher Education Today. San Jose, CA: Technical report, National Center for Public Policy and Higher Education.

Immerwahr, J., & Johnson, J. (2009). Squeeze Play 2009: The Public's Views on College Costs Today. San Jose, CA: Technical report, National Center for Public Policy and Higher Education.

Immerwahr, J., & Johnson, J. (2010). Squeeze Play 2010: Continued Public Anxiety on Cost, Harsher Judgments on How Colleges Are Run. San Jose, CA: Technical report, National Center for Public Policy and Higher Education.

Johnson, D. W., Johnson, R. T., & Smith, K. A. (1991). Cooperative Learning Returns to College: What Evidence Is There That It Works? *Change: The Magazine of Higher Learning, 30*(4), 26–35.

Jones, W. A., & Braxton, J. M. (2009). Cataloging and Comparing Institutional Efforts to Increase Student Retention Rates. *Journal of College Student Retention: Research, Theory & Practice, 11*(1), 123–139.

Kamens, D. H. (1977). Legitimating Myths and Educational Organization: The Relationship Between Organizational Ideology and Formal Structure. *American Sociological Review, 42*(2), 208–219.

Karabel, J. (1972). Community Colleges and Social Stratification. *Harvard Educational Review, 42*(4), 521–562.

Kelly, P. J. (2009). The Dreaded "P" Word: An Examination of Productivity in Public Postsecondary Education. Delta Cost Project, Washington, D.C. Retrieved from http://www.deltacostproject.org/resources/pdf/Kelly07–09 _WP.pdf.

Kelly, P. J., & Jones, D. P. (2005). A New Look at the Institutional Component of Higher Education Finance: A Guide for Evaluating Performance Relative to Financial Resources. Technical report, National Center for Higher Education Management Systems.

Kezar, A., & Kinzie, J. (2006). Examining the Ways Institutions Create Student Engagement: The Role of Principles Mission. *Journal of College Student Development*, 42(2), 149–172.

Kirst, M. W., & Venezia, A. (2004). *From High School to College: Improving Opportunities for Success in Postsecondary Education*. San Francisco: Jossey-Bass.

Kitchener, K. (1986). The Reflective Judgment Model: Characteristics, Evidence, and Measurement. In R. Mines & K. Kitchener (Eds.), *Adult Cognitive Development: Methods and Models* (pp. 76–91). New York: Praeger Publishers.

Kuh, G. D., Gonyea, R. M., & Palmer, M. (2001). The Disengaged Commuter Student: Fact or Fiction? *Commuter Perspectives*, 27(1), 2–5.

Kuhn, T. S. (1962). *The Structure of Scientific Revolutions*. Chicago: University of Chicago Press.

Kuhn, T. S. (1970). *The Structure of Scientific Revolutions* (2nd Edition). Chicago: University of Chicago Press.

Majone, G. (1989). *Evidence, Argument, and Persuasion in the Policy Process*. New Haven, CT: Yale University Press.

Marshall, C., Mitchell, D. E., & Wirt, F. (1985). Assumptive Worlds of State Policymakers. *Peabody Journal of Education*, 62(4), 90–115.

Marshall, C., Mitchell, D. E., & Wirt, F. M. (1989). *Culture and Education Policy in the American States*. London: Falmer.

McKeachie, W. J., Pintrich, P. R., Yi Guang, L., & Smith, D.A.F. (1986). *Teaching and Learning in the College Classroom: A Review of the Research Literature.* Ann Arbor, MI: University of Michigan.

McLendon, M. K., Hearn, J. C., & Deaton, R. (2006). Called to Account: Analyzing the Origins and Spread of State Performance-Accountability Policies for Higher Education. *Educational Evaluation and Policy Analysis, 28*(1), 1.

McLendon, M. K., Tuchmayer, J. B., & Park, T. J. (2009). State Policy Climates for College Student Success: An Analysis of State Policy Documents Pertaining to College Persistence and Completion. *Journal of College Student Retention: Research, Theory & Practice, 11*(1), 33–56.

Merton, R. K. (1968). *Social Theory and Social Structure.* New York: The Free Press.

Merton, R. K. (1973). *The Sociology of Science: Theoretical and Empirical Investigations.* Chicago: University of Chicago Press.

Milem, J. F., & Berger, J. B. (1997). A Modified Model of College Student Persistence: Exploring the Relationship Between Astin's Theory of Involvement and Tinto's Theory of Student Departure. *Journal of College Student Development, 38,* 387–400.

Miller, G. D. (1994). Predicting Freshmen Persistence and Voluntary Withdrawal from Heath's Model of Maturing. Unpublished dissertation, Syracuse University, Syracuse, NY.

Mitchell, D., Marshall, C., & Wirt, F. (1991). Building a Taxonomy of State Education Policies. *Peabody Journal of Education, 62*(4), 7–47.

Mortenson, T. G. (2005). The Measurement of Persistence. In A. Seidman (Ed.), *College Student Retention: Formula for Student Success* (pp. 31–60). Westport, CT: American Council on Education and Praeger Publishers.

Mutter, P. (1992). Tinto's Theory of Departure and Community College Student Persistence. *Journal of College Student Development, 33*(4), 310–318.

National Center for Public Policy and Higher Education. (2000). *Measuring Up 2000: The State-by-State Report Card for Higher Education.* San Jose, CA: National Center for Public Policy and Higher Education.

National Center for Public Policy and Higher Education. (2006). *Measuring Up 2006: The State-by-State Report Card for Higher Education*. San Jose, CA: National Center for Public Policy and Higher Education.

National Governors Association and National Association of State Budget Officers. (2012). *The Fiscal Survey of States*. Washington, D.C.

Newcomb, T. M. (1966). The general nature of peer group influence. In T. M. Newcomb & E. K. Wilson (Eds.), *College Peer Groups: Problems and Prospects for Research* (pp. 2–16). Chicago: Aldine.

Nora, A., Attinasi, L., & Matonak, A. (1990). Testing Qualitative Indicators of Precollege Factors in Tinto's Attrition Model: A Community College Population. *Review of Higher Education, 13*(3), 337–356.

Okun, M. A., Benin, M., & Brandt-Williams, A. (1996). Staying in College: Moderators of the Relation Between Intention and Institutional Departure. *Journal of Higher Education, 67*(5), 577–596.

Palmer, J. (Ed.). (2012). *Grapevine: An Annual Compilation of Data on State Fiscal Support for Higher Education*. Normal, IL: Center for the Study of Education Policy.

Parsons, T., & Platt, G. (1973). *The American University*. Cambridge, MA: Harvard University Press.

Pascarella, E. T. (1986). A Program of Research and Policy Development in Student Persistence at the Institutional Level. *Journal of College Student Personnel, 27*(2), 100–107.

Pascarella, E. T., & Chapman, D. W. (1983). A Multi-institutional, Path Analytic Validation of Tinto's Model of College Withdrawal. *American Educational Research Journal, 20*(1), 87–102.

Pascarella, E. T., Duby, P., & Iverson, B. (1983). A Test and Reconceptualization of a Theoretical Model of College Withdrawal in a Commuter Institution Setting. *Sociology of Education, 56*(2), 88–100.

Pascarella, E. T., & Terenzini, P. T. (1980). Predicting Freshmen Persistence and Voluntary Dropout Decisions from a Theoretical Model. *Journal of Higher Education, 51*(1), 60–75.

Pascarella, E. T., & Terenzini, P. T. (1983). Predicting Voluntary Freshman Year Persistence/Withdrawal Behavior in a Residential University: A Path Analytic Validation of Tinto's Model. *Journal of Educational Psychology, 75*(2), 215–226.

Pascarella, E. T., & Terenzini, P. T. (1991). *How College Affects Students: Findings and Insights from Twenty Years of Research.* San Francisco: Jossey-Bass.

Pascarella, E. T., & Terenzini, P. T. (2005). *How College Affects Students, Volume 2: A Third Decade of Research.* San Francisco: Jossey-Bass.

Pascarella, E. T., Terenzini, P. T., & Wolfe, L. M. (1986). Orientation to College and Freshman Year Persistence/Withdrawal Decisions. *Journal of Higher Education, 57*(2), 155–175.

Pavel, D. M. (1991). Assessing Tinto's Model of Institutional Departure Using American Indian and Alaskan Native Longitudinal Data. Paper presented at the Association for the Study of Higher Education, Boston.

Pike, G. R., Schroeder, C. C., & Berry, T. R. (1997). Enhancing the Educational Impact of Residence Halls: The Relationship Between Residential Learning Communities and First-Year College Experiences and Persistence. *Journal of College Student Development, 38*(6), 609–621.

Reason, R. D. (2009). An Examination of Persistence Research Through the Lens of a Comprehensive Conceptual Framework. *Journal of College Student Development, 50*(6), 659–682.

Richardson, R., Bracco, K. R., Callan, P., & Finney, J. (1999). *Designing State Higher Education Systems for a New Century.* Phoenix, AZ: ACE/Oryx Press.

Richardson, R., Jr., & Martinez, M. (2009). *Policy and Performance in American Higher Education: An Examination of Cases Across State Systems.* Baltimore: Johns Hopkins University Press.

Schuster, J. H. (2011). The Professoriate's Perilous Path. In J. C. Hermanowicz (Ed.), *The American Academic Profession: Transformation in Contemporary Higher Education* (pp. 1–17). Baltimore: Johns Hopkins University Press.

Schwartz, S. A. (1990). Application of a Conceptual Model of College Withdrawal to Technical College Students. Unpublished paper presented at American Educational Research Association Annual Meeting, Boston.

Shulman, L. S. (1995). The Pedagogical Colloquium: Three Models. *AAHE Bulletin, 41*(10), 6–9.

Sorcinelli, M. D. (1991). Research Findings on the Seven Principles. *New Directions for Teaching and Learning, 47*, 13–25.

Springer, M. G., Ballou, D., Hamilton, L., Vi-Nhuan, L., Lockwood, J. R., McCaffrey, D. F., Pepper, M., & Stecher, B. M. (2011). Teacher Pay for Performance: Experimental Evidence from the Project on Incentives in Teaching (POINT). Nashville, TN: Technical report, National Center for Performance Incentives.

St. John, E. P. (1994). Prices, Productivity, and Investment: Assessing Financial Strategies in Higher Education. In *ASHE-ERIC Higher Education Report* No. 3. Washington, D.C.: George Washington University.

St. John, E. P., Cabrera, A. F., Nora, A., & Asker, E. H. (2000). Economic Influences on Persistence Reconsidered: How Can Finance Research Inform the Reconceptualization of Persistence Models? In J. M. Braxton (Ed.), *Reworking the Student Departure Puzzle* (pp. 29–47). Nashville: Vanderbilt University Press.

St. John, E. P., Paulson, M. B., & Starkey, J. B. (1996). The Nexus Between College and Persistence. *Research in Higher Education, 37*, 175–220.

St. John, E. P., & Starkey, J. B. (1995). An Alternative to Net Price: Assessing the Influence of Prices and Subsidies on Within-Year Persistence. *Journal of Higher Education, 66*(2), 156–186.

Stampen, J. O., & Cabrera, A. F. (1988). The Targeting and Packaging of Student Aid and Its Effect on Attrition. *Economics of Education Review, 7*(1), 29–46.

State Higher Education Executive Officers Association. (2012). State Higher Education Finance FY 2011. Boulder, CO. Accessed at http://www.sheeo.org /sites/default/files/publications/SHEF_FY11.pdf.

Stern, G. (1970). *People in Context: Measuring Person-environment Congruence in Education and Industry.* New York: Wiley-Interscience.

Stewart, S. S., & Rue, P. (1983). Commuter students: Definition and distribution. *New Directions for Student Services, 24*, 3–8.

Strauss, L. C., & Volkwein, J. F. (2004). Predictors of Student Commitment at Two-Year and Four-Year Institutions. *Journal of Higher Education, 75*(2), 203–227.

Svinicki, M. D. (1994). Ethics in College Teaching. In W. J. McKeachie (Ed.), *Teaching Tips: Strategies, Research, and Theory for College and University Teachers* (pp. 269–277). Lexington, MA: D.C. Heath.

Tennessee Higher Education Commission. (2011). Tennessee Higher Education Commission Outcomes Based Formula Explanation. Nashville, TN. Accessed at http://www.tn.gov/thec/complete_college_tn/ccta_files/outcomes_based_ff /Outcomes_Based_Formula_Explanation.pdf.

Terenzini, P. T., Pascarella, E. T., Theophilides, C., & Lorang, W. G. (1985). A Replication of a Path Analytic Validation of Tinto's Theory of College Student Attrition. *Review of Higher Education, 8*(4), 319–340.

Tierney, W. G. (1988). Organizational Culture in Higher Education: Defining the Essentials. *Journal of Higher Education, 59*(1), 2–21.

Tinto, V. (1975). Dropout from Higher Education: A Theoretical Synthesis of Recent Research. *Review of Educational Research, 45*(1), 89–125.

Tinto, V. (1982). Limits of Theory and Practice in Student Attrition. *Journal of Higher Education, 53*(6), 687–700.

Tinto, V. (1986).Theories of Student Departure Revisited. In J. C. Smart (Ed.), *Higher Education: Handbook of Theory and Research, Volume 2* (pp. 359–384). New York: Agathon Press.

Tinto, V. (1993). *Leaving College: Rethinking the Causes and Cures of Student Attrition* (2nd Edition). Chicago: University of Chicago Press.

Tinto, V. (1997). Classrooms as Communities: Exploring the Educational Character of Student Persistence. *Journal of Higher Education, 68*(6), 599–623.

Tinto, V. (1998). Colleges as Communities: Taking Research on Student Persistence Seriously. *Review of Higher Education, 21*(2), 167–177.

Tinto, V. (2000). Linking Learning and Leaving: Exploring the Role of the College Classroom in Student Departure. In. J. M. Braxton (Ed.), *Reworking the Student Departure Puzzle* (pp. 81–94). Nashville, TN: Vanderbilt University Press.

Tinto, V. (2006–2007). Research and Practice of Student Retention: What Next? *Journal of College Student Retention: Research, Theory & Practice*, 8(1), 1–19.

Tinto, V. (2011). From Theory to Action: Exploring the Institutional Conditions for Student Retention. In J. C. Smart (Ed.), *Higher Education: A Handbook of Theory and Research* (pp. 51–89). The Netherlands: Springer.

Tinto, V. (2012). *Completing College: Rethinking Institutional Action*. Chicago: University of Chicago Press.

Turner, S. (2004). Going to College and Finishing College. Explaining Different Educational Outcomes. In C. M. Hoxby (Ed.), *College Choices: The Economics of Where to Go, When to Go, and How to Pay for It* (pp. 13–62). Chicago: University of Chicago Press.

Umbach, P. D., & Wawrzynski, M. R. (2005). Faculty Do Matter: The Role of College Faculty in Student Learning and Engagement. *Research in Higher Education*, 46(2), 153–184.

Voorhees, R. A. (1990). A Survey of Academic Advising as an Area of Inquiry. In J. C. Smart (Ed.), *Higher Education: Handbook of Theory and Research, Volume 6* (pp. 291–335). New York: Agathon Press.

Wallace, L. W. (1971). *The Logic of Science in Sociology*. Chicago: Aldine-Atherton.

Webb, M. W., II. (1990). Development and Testing of a Theoretical Model for Predicting Student Degree Persistence at Four-Year Commuter Colleges. Unpublished paper presented at American Educational Research Association Annual Meeting, Boston.

Wood, P. (1983). Inquiring Systems and Problem Structure: Implications for Cognitive Development. *Human Development*, 26(5), 249–265.

Zhang, R., & RiCharde, R. S. (1998). Prediction and Analysis of Freshmen Retention. Unpublished paper presented at the Annual Forum of the Association for Institutional Research, Minneapolis.

Index

If you enjoyed this book, you may also like these:

Increasing Persistence,
by Wesley R. Habley,
Jennifer L. Bloom,
Steve Robbins
ISBN: 9780470888438

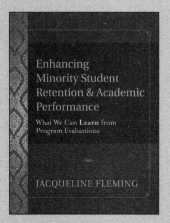

Enhancing Minority Student
Retention & Academic
Performance,
by Jacqueline Fleming
ISBN: 9780787957131

Student Success in College,
by George D. Kuh,
Jillian Kinzie, John H. Schuh,
Elizabeth J. Whitt and
Associates
ISBN: 9780470599099

Motivating and Retaining
Online Students,
by Rosemary M. Lehman,
Simone C. O. Conceição
ISBN: 9781118531709

WILEY